As Mirrors Are Lonely

As Mirrors Are Lonely:
A Lacanian Reading on the Modern Irish Novel

By

Peter Guy

CAMBRIDGE SCHOLARS
PUBLISHING

As Mirrors Are Lonely: A Lacanian Reading on the Modern Irish Novel,
by Peter Guy

This book first published 2014

Cambridge Scholars Publishing

12 Back Chapman Street, Newcastle upon Tyne, NE6 2XX, UK

British Library Cataloguing in Publication Data
A catalogue record for this book is available from the British Library

ISBN (10): 1-4438-6527-3, ISBN (13): 978-1-4438-6527-2

Dedicated to my parents for their lasting support and in memory of my late grandparents, Pierce & Celia Guy and Patrick & Ellen King.

CONTENTS

CHAPTER ONE

INTRODUCTION

Background

The central conceit of any concept is, by nature, problematic. As Mary McCarthy once wrote: 'There are no new truths, but only truths that have not been recognized by those who have perceived them without noticing.'[1] That is the nature of academic scholarship: to present a truth as something that everybody can be shown to know or to challenge yourself and create a new truth of your own. For this book, I would propose two separate 'truths' of my own, firstly what I term the reinvention of the modern Irish novel, which I would argue took place in the late nineteen fifties, to be superseded by more speculative trends in the late eighties; and secondly the importance of Lacanian analysis in the context of this timeframe, where the focus is upon uncertainty, alienation, sexual relations and the deconstruction of such totalizing forms as patriarchy, identitarian ideologies and primacy of the religious orders.

To enter into an epistemological debate on the Irish novel, to attempt to place it into set patterns of linearity, would be foolhardy indeed. That is not my concern. What I term the 'modern Irish novel' may be construed as something of a misinterpretation to begin with. Should we not, logically, begin with James Joyce? Naturally this would seem to be the case, but my concern rather is on the resurgence (renaissance is too loaded a word) of the Irish novel in the late fifties when the post-colonial experiment was deemed a failure, when the totemic influence of Joyce had overshadowed his subsequent successors and the novel form could be dismissed by a writer such as O'Faoláin as unsuitable in the face of a shattered world where the short story (In Ireland, at least) was in the ascendancy.[2]

By 1982 however, the novelist and critic Thomas Kilroy could write:

---

[1] Mary McCarthy, *On The Contrary*, p.47.

[2] Sean O'Faoláin, 'Fifty Years of Irish Writing', pp. 102-103.

> There is the widely accepted view nowadays among the historians that contemporary Ireland derives from the late fifties, that from that period one can trace the economic, social and cultural changes by which the country.... moved from being essentially rural-based, tradition-bound society to something resembling a modern, urbanized, technological state.... Something important appears to happen in the arts, too, in that decade. [3]

This is a field that has invited much contemporary research but not, perhaps, as a unified whole. I view this period, from the mid-late fifties to the early nineties within set boundaries that can be delineated by a number of key events: in the religious sphere, the furore over the Mother & Child scheme in 1951 proved to be the apex of Catholic Church's supremacy. In the timeframe I propose, we see a gradual decline, from Vatican II through to the acrimonious debates on contraception and divorce right up to the resignation and disgrace of the Bishop of Galway, Eamon Casey, in 1990. In the political sphere, we witness the resignation of Eamon De Valera and Richard Mulcahy, bastions of civil war politics, and the accession of Lemass' brand of *Realpolitik* in 1959. In the intervening years, Irish politics went through a period of upheaval culminating in the election of Mary Robinson as our first female President in 1990.

To further develop this argument, and to quantify Kilroy's observations I wish to first turn to the Russian theorist Mikhail Bakhtin and his work on language and the national epic.[4] Bakhtin is of particular interest as his observations segue in rather suggestive ways with those of Lacan, particularly in terms of the notion that all transcription systems are inadequate to the multiplicity of the meaning they seek to convey. For Bakhtin, there is no such thing as a general example of language, a language spoken by a general voice divorced from a specific meaning. Language, when it means anything at all, is simply somebody talking to somebody else. Lacan would argue that there is no stable one-to-one correspondence between signified and signifier, an inherent ambiguity which is at the heart of all discourse and indeed, in the formation of the unconscious. In Lacan's words: 'Language is as much there to found us in the Other as to drastically prevent us from understanding him.'[5]

---

[3] Thomas Kilroy, 'The Irish Writer – Self & Society', in Peter Connolly (ed.), *Literature and the Changing Ireland*, p. 171.

[4] For this section, I am indebted to the work of Gerry Smyth and his seminal text, The Novel; & the Nation.

[5] Jacques Lacan, *The Seminar Book II,* p. 244.

At the heart of Bakhtin's work is the duality between the centrifugal forces which aim to keep things apart and the centripetal forces that strive to make things cohere – the result of these forces at work can be found in the development of the human language and the best transcription of language can be found in the novel. The two contending tendencies are not of equal force – the centrifugal draw is, in Bakhtin's theory, the reality of actual articulation whereas the centripetal force is something akin to what anthropologists regard as the activity of culture in modelling a complete different order called nature. What results from this conflict is in part the inherent fragility of language complicated by a more durable resistance where language, stratified into wider nets of meaning penetrates into deeper levels of actuality, eventually becoming an almost living breathing organism. It is alive and forever developing, forever in process of *becoming.* As Bakhtin states:

> Alongside the centripetal forces, the centrifugal forces of language carry on their uninterrupted work; alongside verbal-ideological centralization and unification, the uninterrupted processes of decentralization and disunification go forward.[6]

Bakhtin uses the word *raznorečie* – heteroglossia – to describe the fundamental manner of all communicational and some of the fundamental ambiguities within the theory of language. While transcription must be a more or less fixed system, one must also bear in mind that the power of any particular utterance is in the power of the particular context in which the utterance is made and the context of any given situation can add or subtract from the amount of meaning the utterance may be said to have. Expanding his theories onto a national level, Bakhtin claimed all western societies experienced a struggle between two contradictory politico-cultural tendencies. All such societies will tend towards monoglossia – one language – to centralise the verbalideological word to the point where language and meaning merge into an almost organic unit. Irish society in particular demonstrated such a tendency, for the success of any anti-colonial movement depends upon monoglossia: the subjects of the state speaking the one language, the same questions and eventually coming up with the same answers. The key medium for expressing the drive towards centralising national discourse is the epic, which encapsulates an imagined

---

[6] M.M. Bakhtin, *The Dialogic Imagination: Four Essays*, p.272.

community partaking in a single straightforward narrative, in Bakhtin's words: 'creative consciousness…realised in closed pure languages.'[7]

But the cultural nationalists would search in vain for a true Irish epic which would serve to demonstrate the unity and coherence of the nation at a formal and generic level for such early and pre-modern texts that existed merely showed a nation bedevilled by a fragmented conception of nationhood. An alternative had to be sought. The nationalists duly experimented with other forms but the novel would remain tainted by its association with British cultural history. The didactic novel also threatened to contradict the fictional representation of our new national reality, where the emphasis on nation-building was paramount. For Bakhtin, the basic characteristics of the novel as a genre have been:

> Powerfully affected by a very specific rupture in the history of European civilisation: its emergence from a socially isolated and culturally deaf semipatriarchal society, and its entrance into international and interlingual contacts and relationships. A multitude of different languages, cultures and times became available to Europe, and this became a decisive factor in its life and thought.[8]

In contrast to other forms of transcription, the novel 'can be defined as a diversity of social speech types (sometimes even diversity of languages) and a diversity of individual voices, artistically organized.'[9] In other words, the novel tends to exploit the social stratification of language while, in Bakhtin's theory, also emphasising the inherent fragmentation at the heart of the medium, for 'there is no unitary language or style in the novel… the author as creator cannot be found at one of the novel's language levels.'[10]

However, Bakhtin discerned a counter-movement to monoglossia – the aforementioned heteroglossia – which acted as a foil to the centralising ideology. Any national language which is stratified into all manner of social languages and language, in Bakhtin's theory, depends upon the context in which it is spoken. It is therefore dialogic, always in the process of becoming rather than acting as some pre-ordained code. It is perhaps significant to note here that Lacan also posited the difference between a code/indice and that of language/signifier as the fixed bi-univocal

[7] M.M. Bakhtin, *The Dialogic Imagination: Four Essays*, p.12.
[8] Ibid., p.11.
[9] Ibid., pp. 261-262.
[10] Ibid., p. 48.

relationship between an index and its referent in contrast to the lack of any such relationship existing between a signifier and a referent. Because of the bi-univocal relation of indices and referents, codes lack what Lacan regards as the fundamental feature of human languages: the potential for ambiguity and equivocation.

For Bakhtin, literary discourse in general, and the novel specifically, developed to introduce heteroglossia into monologic national discourse. After all, a novel quotes from the multitude of languages available within the social formations which it is produced and the author forms these languages into an artistic whole. Here lies the crux of my argument. The traditional society which was consolidated in the early part of the century, began to disintegrate by the 1950s, the monologic discourse collapsing in the face of modernizing trends which undermined the whole symbolic system, forcing it into an abrupt *volte-face*. Why did this happen? There were a number of political and religious changes which altered Irish society forever, complimenting James Whyte's observation that since the 1960s: 'Ireland has moved from being a traditional, predominately agricultural and rural society to being a post-industrial society.'[11] And what was the nature of the catalyst?

The simple answer to that question is that Ireland, prior to the early sixties, was a failed entity. For Brendan O'hEithir: 'The 50's meant repression, emigration, clerical dominance, spurious patriotism and an educational system that seemed to train people to be physically fearless and morally cowardly.'[12] The facts illustrate that O'hEithir was not engaging in hyperbole. Net emigration per annum between 1951 and 1956 was 39,353 or 9.2 per thousand of the population. That figure increased to 42,401 between 1956 and 1961 – in total, about 400,000 emigrated during that decade.[13] Furthermore, the lack of confidence in the economy, 'associated with falling employment and population, created an atmosphere unfavourable to the enterprise required for successful entry into export markets.'[14] Patrick Kavanagh, in his short-lived paper *Kavanagh's Weekly*, spoke in his first editorial about the 'victory of mediocrity' in Ireland. In later editions however, he appeared to rage against the spread of despair, believing that 'something is still possible in

[11] James Whyte, *History, Myth and Ritual*, p.92.
[12] Brendan O'hEithir, *The Begrudger's Guide to Irish Politics*, p.122.
[13] James Meehan, *The Irish Economy Since 1922*, p.204 ff.
[14] Kieran Kennedy, *Economic Growth in Ireland: The Experience Since 1947*, p. 218.

this country', illustrating the mounting frustration that was building up amongst the Diaspora generation:

> We came to the wake that had been going uproariously for at least thirty years and at the moment we are trying to get the family to remove the corpse – the corpse of 1916, the Gaelic language, the inferiority complex – so that the house may be free for the son to bring in a wife. Will they take our advice or will the wake proceed to explosion point…[15]

Bakhtin's theories on movements are invaluable when discussing this period. In the words of Terence Browne, the Irish novel, with its origin in an enclosed oral tradition, was 'a fiction that, delighting in objectivity, was undisturbed by the subjective or psychologically complex, unless they can be embodied in concrete actions.'[16] Prior to the nineteen-sixties, the Irish novel had grown out of an agrarian, pre-modern culture antipathetic to the conventional realist novel with its roots in an industrial, stratified society. The dominant tone of Irish fiction from 1920 to 1950 was one where:

> The oral voice, having survived the shift in the early twentieth century from the tale of countryside and farm, to the story set in shop, convent, school and presbytery, set in short in the petit bourgeois world of post-revolutionary Ireland.[17]

As Bakhtin illustrated, the epic was the key medium through which national discourse could be centralised for it offered an idealised picture of a harmonious world, where the individual is at one both with society and his environment. With the advent of the fifties and sixties and the fragmentation of Irish society – an inevitable trend given the social condition already illustrated – Irish writers were forced to contend with the rupturing of this epic world into heteroglossia.

By 1991, John McGahern could state: 'I see Irish society as healthily fragmented, as no longer cohesive…'[18] The writers that I am covering in this book – Broderick, McGahern and Moore – were thus faced with the task of bridging this gap between pre- and post-modern Ireland, and the extent of their success will be measured over the course of this text. While

---

[15] Patrick Kavanagh, *Patrick Kavanagh, Man and Poet*, p.129.

[16] Terence Brown, 'John McGahern's *Nightlines*: Tone Technique and Symbolism', in Patrick Rafroidi and Terence Brown (eds), *The Irish Short Story*, p. 290.

[17] Ibid., p. 290.

[18] Joe Jackson, 'Tales from the Dark Side', in *Hot Press*, p.20.

each of these authors grappled with modern modes of literary expression, I would argue that there remained a thread of nostalgia throughout their fiction, a hankering after this fallen world where matters were, perhaps, more clear-cut. As David Lloyd states:

> One of the problems of the Irish novel, precisely insofar as it conforms to the symbolic mode of realism, is the sheer volume of inassimilable residue that it can neither properly contain nor entirely exclude.[19]

Such a tone exists in McGahern's last novel, *That They May Face The Rising Sun*, in Broderick's uncompleted trilogy based on the Athlone of his childhood and in Moore's novella *Catholics*. As such, there remains a certain frisson in the work of each author – the clash between experimentation with new literary forms and the traditional monological language possible only in the pre-modern society which produced the epic. What has been the result of this experiment? That is, how successful were each of the authors in ordering the numerous voices in their fiction and what has been excluded as a result? Such questions can be integrated into a Lacanian reading of the text and I will demonstrate the value of such a reading in the next section of this chapter. Suffice to say, Bakhtin is invaluable for demonstrating a much more flexible criticism with the English novel acting as a centripetal force, centralising the disparate voice of which it is composed, with the Irish novel and the emergence of the modernist tradition linked rather to the centrifugal tendencies in Irish fiction. As Bakhtin has perceptively observed, language, especially in its literary incarnation, is a powerful tool in the deconstruction of such centralizing drives, as the 'uninterrupted processes of decentralization and disunification go forward' alongside the language of 'verbal-ideological centralization and unification.'[20] In Ireland, cultural nationalists attempted to appropriate the novel as a medium through which a monologic experiment could be conducted. The failure of such an experiment gave rise to the emergence of what I refer to as the modern Irish novel, capable of articulating and resisting both a colonial mind-set *and* a nationalistic discourse. Bakhtin's theory of metalanguage is extremely complicated but he is invaluable in any investigation discussing Lacan, for as much as Bakhtin referred to the primacy of speech – what he has to say about the novel becomes incomprehensible if the emphasis on utterance is not kept

---

[19] David Lloyd, *Anomalous States: Irish Writing and the Post-Colonial Moment*, pp. 152-153.
[20] M.M. Bakhtin, *The Dialogic Imagination: Four Essays*, p.272.

in mind – Lacan also argued that speech is the only means of access to the truth about desire – 'speech alone is the key to that truth'– and if there is any one concept which can claim to be the very centre of Lacan's thought, it is the concept of desire.[21] The next question that arises is: why this time-frame in particular?

For one, it is during this period that Irish culture morphs into a novel-driven discourse and the other forms of expression, the oral tradition, poetry and the short story form, have either been subsumed into the greater metanarrative or have been made wholly redundant. This may be because the novel, in the words of Bakhtin, is the 'only developing genre and therefore reflects more deeply, more essentially, more sensitively and rapidly, reality itself in the process of its unfolding. Only that which is itself developing can comprehend development as a process.'[22] The Irish nation was one of the first to begin a concerted effort in decolonisation and the novelist, in any decolonising formation, must also be a teacher; their task is to interrogate and expose the received narrative of the dominate culture, and to educate the oppressed population as to the alternatives.

Robert Welch, in his *Changing States: Transformations in Irish Writing*, notes that 'Irish culture, now, and for the last one hundred years, has been preoccupied with the question of continuity, and this at a time when it seems that the idea of continuity and the related one of community are cracking up irremediably.'[23] In a nation, dominated by the colonizers' life and thought, the English novel acted as a dialogic, centripetal (centralising) force to the voices it was silencing and the Irish tradition reacted in an erstwhile centrifugal (decentralising) pattern. These are terms used by Bakhtin, who was describing the bind between the centralising tendencies of colonial power and the decentralising exchange with the colonised nation. Ergo, in order to command a central dialogic voice, it becomes necessary to reach out and silence the disparate voice of which it is itself partly composed, which is in itself, a centripetal action. This bind becomes more complex when we realise that the Irish novelist attempted a similar exchange in the drive towards modernism and helps explain somewhat, the stop-start nature in the development of cultural trends.

Homi Bhabha wrote that 'colonial power produces the colonized as a fixed reality which is at once an 'other' and yet entirely knowable and

---

[21] Jacques Lacan, *Écrits* (1977) p.172.

[22] M.M. Bakhtin, *The Dialogic Imagination Four Essays by M.M. Bakhtin*, p.7.

[23] Robert Welch, *Changing States – Transformations in Modern Irish Writings*, p.37.

visible.'[24] Bhabha opened up 'the possibility of a cultural hybridity that entertains difference without an assumed or imposed hierarchy.'[25] It should allow us to think beyond narratives of originary and initial subjectivities and to focus on those moments or processes that are produced in the articulation of cultural differences. These 'in-between' spaces provide the terrain for elaborating strategies of selfhood – singular or communal – that initiate new signs of identity, and innovative sites of collaboration, and contestation, in the act of defining the idea of society itself.[26] Externally, the Irish were indistinguishable from their colonial masters. Yet the master text of English literature needs an 'other' to construct itself. The cultural nationalists of the nineteenth century looked back with fondness towards the Gaelic bardic tradition as the high water mark of Irish culture. What was inherent in Irish expression soon mirrored the Irish psyche – the carnivalesque, playful society was not conducive to the complexities of the traditional form and hence the emphasis on drama, poetry and short fiction.

The critic Luke Gibbons wrote: 'Celticism…was an attempt by a colonial power to hypostasize an alien, refractory culture in order to define it within its own controlling terms.'[27] In his innovative *Transformations in Irish Culture*, Gibbons further develops this notion. Influenced by Fanon's theory of national movements, Gibbons posited the theory that historians drew on a discourse of race to advance the notion of 'an original native purity' which they could control by blocking out the 'impure' influences of colonial discourse. The past was not part of recorded history, rather it was tied up in the oral tradition, where words were 'not about history but part of history.'[28] The text existed in an open-ended space, where 'reality…becomes dislocated from structures of signification, and takes the form of the random impression.'[29] Because of Ireland's close proximity to England, with Dublin as the centre of a 'metropolitan colony', our culture was far more deeply affected by English literary

---

[24] Homi K. Bhabha, 'Differences, Discrimination and the Discourse of Colonialism', in Houston A. Baker et al, *Black British Cultural Studies: A Reader*, pp. 92-93.

[25] Homi K. Bhabha, *The Location of Culture*, p.4.

[26] Ibid., pp. 1-2.

[27] Luke Gibbons, 'Challenging the Canon: Revisionism and Cultural Criticism', in Seamus Deane (ed.), *The Field Day Anthology of Irish Writing – Volume III*. p. 563.

[28] Luke Gibbons, *Transformations in Irish Culture*, p.135.

[29] Ibid., p. 137.

trends and political traditions. But while the postcolonial stance affirms the value of otherness, radical decolonisation remains 'caught within the very terms that are being disputed.'[30]

This bind lends credence to Gerry Smyth's assertion that:

> The peculiar political formation of post-colonial Ireland… is characterised by insecurity and a constant need for self-identification, conditions which are themselves left over from colonial times: Who am I in relation to the groups and the beliefs and the political affiliations I perceive around me? Who am I in relation to the past from which I believe myself to have emerged and the future towards which I believe myself to be moving?[31]

Post-independence, novelistic discourse was in danger of being overwhelmed by a sort of anthropological discourse in which, as part of a general decolonising programme, Irish writers used their intimate knowledge of the manner and morals of the nation to combat negative and disabling colonial representations. Throughout this early period writers like Sean O'Faoláin would boast that 'we have explored Irish life with an objectivity never hitherto applied to it, and in this Joyce rather than Yeats is our inspiration.'[32] Between the publication of *Ulysses* in 1922 and *Finnegans Wake* in 1939, we witness perhaps the first stage in the evolution of the modern Irish novel post-independence. This is an assertion shared by Maurice Harmon who suggested that 'modern Irish prose fiction may be said to have begun with George Moore and James Joyce and to have developed thereafter in two separate generations, that of the twenties and that of the fifties.'[33] Joyce's influence predominates this period, as Darcy O'Brien affirms: 'To say that portrait has influenced subsequent Irish writing is like saying that *A Preface to Lyrical Ballads* influenced the English romantic movements.'[34]

In order to structure this book, a more manageable timeframe is needed and if I have chosen to overlook this earlier phase it is partially due to those themes which Robert Caswell aptly describes as 'exile and resignation' that predominate this period, with exile personified by

---

[30] Ibid., p.137.

[31] Gerry Smyth, *The Novel and the Nation – Studies in the New Irish Fiction*, p.4.

[32] Quoted in Klaus Lubbers, 'Irish Fiction: A Mirror for Specifics', p.101.

[33] Maurice Harmon, 'Generations Apart: 1925-1975', in Patrick Rafroidi and Terence Brown (eds), *The Irish Novel in our Time*, p.49.

[34] Darcy O'Brien, 'In Ireland After A Portrait', in Thomas F. Stanley & Bernard Benstock (eds.) *Approaches to Joyce's "Portrait": Ten Essays*, p.214.

Stephen Dedalus and resignation embodied in Leopold Bloom.[35] Here, the development of the novel branches off into more torturous passageways overshadowed always by Joyce and later Beckett – it was during this period that the heady expectations of independence were met by a narrow, chauvinistic, self-protective brand of nationalism. As Frantz Fanon illustrated in *The Wretched of the Earth*, anti-colonial nationalism was locked into Western imperialist modes of thought. The intellectuals and social-elite that were responsible in leading the nationalist drive were the ones who, once they came to power, quickly reinstated the systems of hierarchy and privilege that had characterised the colonial policy.[36] The flight from colonial discourse only served to extenuate the divide between the elite and the working class. Those who could master the language of the colonists were the ones who betrayed their own ideal, as Fanon asserts: '[t]he native intellectual is anxiously trying to create a cultural work' and failing 'to realise that he is utilizing techniques and language which are borrowed from the stranger in his country.'[37]

For writers, the harshest result of the new puritanical ethos was the Censorship of Publications Act of 1929, which further alienated the native author, with the result that two separate strands emerged from this period, a quasi-realist strand which aimed to expose these puritanical tendencies and a fabulist strand which sought to escape or satirize them. Thus the resurgence of the Irish novel in the fifties owes as much to the failure of its predecessors to escape from the spectres of nationalism and the disappointment of the emerging state than to any faltering approach to form. For those experimental writers, the case of Joyce's influence is different. The reaction of subsequent Irish writers to his work exemplifies Harold Bloom's notions about 'the anxiety of influence,' with the later writers overshadowed by their great literary father, and in the best Freudian traditions, subsequently seeking to kill him off in a figurative and symbolic sense.[38] Some Irish writers of this period, such as Kate O'Brien, felt compelled to deny, rather unconvincingly, Joyce's influence altogether: 'The Joyce influence, which is or has been everywhere in Europe, is not now very evident in Irish writing. It is as if there is a kind of

---

[35] Robert Caswell, 'The Irish Novel: Exile, Resignation or Acceptance', in *Wascana Review*, p. 7.
[36] Frantz Fanon, *The Wretched of the Earth*, p.12.
[37] Ibid., p.47.
[38] Harold Bloom, *The Western Canon: The Books and School of the Ages*, p. 137.

revolt against his greatness'[39]; while Brinsley Sheridan's 'Novelist' in *The Various Lives of Marcus Igoe* boasted: "'I'll beat Joyce at his own game!'"[40]

Another reason why I aim to focus upon the period 1955 – 1990 is that many cultural nationalists in this earlier period felt that the novel was inadequate to the task of representing the nation, and it therefore retains a more problematic relationship in itself than the one which I am attempting to resolve. Given the distortions of which it was capable, and the kind of readership it seemed to attract, the novel was seen as a debased cultural form wherein it was impossible to address the serious concerns of nation-building. Bakhtin spoke of struggle between two contradictory politico-cultural tendencies as a clear demand towards centralizing the verbalideological world. He claims that this is typical of the way power has traditionally operated within Western societies, and its effects can be discerned in all manner of cultural and political discourses. For Bakhtin, literary discourse in general, and the novel specifically, developed to introduce heteroglossia (many/voices, or those which a nation uses to measure its sense of identity) into the monologic (essential truths in the essential language) national discourse. Thus, in this early period, the novel is too often seen in Jameson's term as an 'allegory', a straightforward statement appropriated by writers to perform monologic ideological tasks for which it was palpably unsuited.[41]

It is only in the period 1955–1990, where we witness an increased eclecticism and internationalism of influences and perspectives. This is one of the keys to the expansion of my argument, which I shall discuss later in this chapter. Some of the more notable examples include Aidan Higgins *Langrishe, Go Down,* which is more clearly influenced by Faulkner's *Go Down, Moses* than by Beckett or Joyce and, like its literary forebear, it offers a multifaceted and highly complex examination of a number of interrelated themes: the relationship of man to nature, the idea of property and ownership, the nature of the family and the nature of inheritance. William Trevor's *Fools of Fortune* similarly shared Faulkner-esque influences, notable in that, as in *The Sound and the Fury*, one of the crucial stream of consciousness narrators in the novel is Imelda, the deranged young offspring of incestuous pairing. There were others in this

[39] Kate O'Brien, 'Imaginative Prose by the Irish, 1820 – 1970', in Joseph Ronsley (ed.), *Myth and Reality in Irish Literature*, p.312.
[40] Brinsley MacNamara, *The Various Lives of Maurice Igoe*, p.195.
[41] Frederic Jameson, *The Political Unconscious: Narrative as a Socially Symbolic Act*, p.141

period that followed a similar trend, most notably the three authors who form the basis of this book, John Broderick, John McGahern and Brian Moore.

The Authors and their Context 1960 – 1990

Following on from Bakhtin's theories on heteroglossia, in an essay written for the first Kate O'Brien weekend, Colin Tóibín would question:

> How… the novel [can] flourish in such a world? The novel explores psychology, sociology, the individual consciousness; the novel finds a form and a language for these explorations. We require an accepted world for the novel to flourish, a shared sense of time and place.[42]

For Tóibín, Irish history was a series of vignettes portraying our romantic, embattled tradition, but it was a history without continuity and no clear legacy. Fragmentation was integral to the Irish experience. By the dawning of the twentieth-first century, as George O'Brien put it:

> The Irish novel – long the poor relation of our literary family, the resort of exiles, eccentrics and other misfits including the not infrequent crawthumper; occasion of the censor's official repression, official and otherwise; by virtue of formal insecurity and thematic ambivalence the very image of the quaking sod – is now the elephant in the room.[43]

Initially, it seemed that an Irish writer had to live somewhere else, like Joyce, Beckett and William Trevor. While they remembered their Irish childhood with affection and wrote about it with great feeling, they lived in exile. This applied also, to a greater or lesser degree, to Elizabeth Bowen, Kate O'Brien, Brian Moore and Edna O'Brien. John McGahern was forced to emigrate, albeit briefly, as a result of the furore over the publication of *The Dark*. Censorship certainly contributed to this exodus, as did the structures of the Irish publishing industry but, as I indicated earlier, there also seemed to be a certain psychological reluctance. Tóibín's argument is certainly of interest and he would argue that the lack of a sophisticated readership in Ireland meant that authors had no other option but to depart and attempt to find an audience elsewhere. Following on from the essay already quoted, Tóibín suggested:

---

[42] Colin Tóibín, 'Martyrs and Metaphors', in Dermot Bolger (ed.), *Letters from the New Island*, p. 45.
[43] George O'Brien, 'The Elephant of Irish Fiction', p. 134.

> There was no audience for such books. It was not just that Ireland did not offer a shelter between history and destiny for the novelists to pitch their tent, thus causing them to write at one remove from what was happening. But there was no-one to read the books, no set of educated, curious, open-minded literate people. It should not be assumed that censorship did not deeply affect what was written and in what style it was written during this period. The result was a tradition of the novel that was clever, inventive and self-obsessed.[44]

It is a contentious argument. John Broderick, a writer whose first novel was banned by the Censorship Board, spoke on how censorship could adversely affect a writer's style. For Broderick:

> [If I had censorship] at the back of my mind… two things then would happen to you. One was that you would write in order to get past the censors; therefore, you would suppress certain truths which you think should have been told. The other one was that you would do something in order to shock them, and both these attitudes upset the artistic balance.[45]

Fiscal considerations would have been a factor. Broderick admitted that if he were a schoolteacher or librarian in Athlone at that time: 'I couldn't possibly have written that [*The Pilgrimage*] book and published it. I would have met the same fate as John McGahern.'[46] The background to the banning of John McGahern's *The Dark* is examined later. It resulted in the writer's sacking from his schoolteacher position for having the audacity to publish a novel which openly dealt with the themes of small town inhibitions and sexual frustration.

Another question which Tóibín poses is whether there was a sophisticated audience for such works. This is again questionable. It is true that there was a pervasive air of anti-intellectualism at play and the Church played a significant part in removing a number of modern classics from the book-shelves. The novelist formed his own moral majority outside the pale of clerical and political influence and was regarded as being something of a subversive force. Did the rolling out of free secondary education, coupled with the decline of Church authority, act as a catalyst? It appears to be an over-simplification but there is little doubt that the

---

[44] Colin Tóibín, 'Martyrs and Metaphors', p. 46.

[45] Quoted in Julia Carlson, *Banned in Ireland – Censorship and the Irish Writer*, p.40.

[46] Ibid., pp.42-43.

changing narratives of Irish life have contributed in helping the novelist transcend the inhibitions that had restricted them since then.

John Broderick, Brian Moore and John McGahern were in the 'first wave' of artists who chose the novel as their preferred medium of expression. Curiously, each chose a female character to act as the central protagonist in their first novel – the result was a virtual renaissance in Irish fiction and the publication of *The Lonely Passion of Judith Hearne* (1955), *The Pilgrimage* (1961) and *The Barracks* (1963) appeared to herald something of a new departure. Each of these three novels, in part, concentrated on desire and sexuality, clerical ignorance or repression and the claustrophobic atmosphere of the small towns and villages in Ireland.

Whether Irish society was ready for this form of catharsis is another matter. The censorship board acted with archetypical heavy-handedness and banned both *Judith Hearne* and *The Pilgrimage. The Barracks* was spared as there was no overt display of sexuality in the novel but ironically, of the three, it is perhaps the most subversive. What occurred afterwards was a gradual malaise borne out of frustration on the author's part rather than that of his audience. Moore abandoned Ireland as a theme in his fiction and became better known as a Canadian author. As he said in an interview with Julia Carlson: 'The fact that Irish writers didn't look upon me as a native son is counterbalanced in my mind by the fact that the English have never treated me as a purely Irish writer.'[47] Broderick wrote four novels in rapid succession which represent his best work. But by the late sixties he had retreated into alcoholism and wrote nothing for a period of eight years. McGahern was forced to emigrate after the banning of *The Dark* and he too stopped writing for a number of years afterwards.

A second wave of Irish novelists emerged in the mid to late seventies. Drawn mostly from the disaffected urban communities and seeking a more coherent form of expression, high profile examples includes John Banville, Colm Tóibín, Roddy Doyle Dermot Bolger, Patrick McCabe and Eoin McNamee. As Ray Ryan explains, these novelists drew attention to a world:

> [n]either country not city – these streets possessed no place in the school books and poems we learnt at our wooden desks... This aspect of Irish life, despite being an everyday reality for an increasingly large percentage of the population, was almost totally absent from Irish writing until recently... it is only in the post-1968 generation that the confidence to

[47] Quoted in Julia Carlson, *Banned in Ireland*, p. 118.

> remain true to ordinary modern experience around them finally begins to be displayed.[48]

However, as Joe Cleary has pointed out, the style, subject and setting of Irish literature can be modernized without disturbing established narrative codes.[49] Tóibín's first novel *The South* (1987), concerns a woman who leaves her husband and child behind her to become an artist in Spain. Set partly in mid-fifties provincial Ireland, partly in Franco's Spain, the novel charts Katherine Proctor's gradual and painful process of development as a person and artist. While many of the themes in the novel are divorced from the traditional schema, the established codes evident in the work of McGahern and Broderick are evident also in *The South*: Irish antipathies, memories and repressions are set against a portrait of rural Catalonia and Tóibín duly pays homage to both the 'Big House' genre and to McGahern's studies in isolation, repression and the traumatic effects of war on an individual or community. Dermot Bolger has also consciously set himself the task of redefining the connections between the present crisis and the imagined past. John Banville began by parodying the Big House memoirs of the early twentieth century in *Birchwood* (1973) before embarking on a tetralogy of sorts which plumbs the biographies of great scientists and questions the methods and parameters of scientific inquiry. Roddy Doyle alternates his tragic-comic depictions of inner-city 'Barrytown' with novels about Irish history. Anne Enright's second novel is based on the life of the nineteenth-century Irish adventuress Eliza Lynch – like McGahern, her forte remains the secret sexual histories encoded in families.

It is evident then that the burden of history plays an important part in the development of the modern novel, unsurprising perhaps in a society where the textbooks were replete with the hagiography of Republican martyrs, tales of doomed romantics and perfidious Albion. The triumphantism of Fianna Fáil and the old slogans of spiritual obedience and frugal comforts sufficed for an earlier generation but were wholly redundant for those forced to endure inner-city poverty and deprivation. Curiously, neither McGahern nor Broderick chose to develop this theme in their fiction – their vision is firmly set against the backdrop of the small rural communities they knew best. Indeed, it is one of the reasons why I

---

[48] Ray Ryan, 'The Republic and Ireland: Pluralism, Politics and Narrative Form', in Ray Ryan, *Writing in the Irish Republic*, p.84.

[49] Joe Cleary, 'Modernization and Aesthetic Ideology in Contemporary Irish Culture', in Ray Ryan, *Writing in the Irish Republic*, p.105-129.

chose these three authors for this book. Their oeuvre is built on the repressive nature of the community and the Church, on family trauma and the deconstruction of empty nationalist rhetoric. These are themes that I will develop and examine over the course of the book. I chose the six specific texts as they tie in with each other, offering far better scope for a unified examination on repression, desire, feminine sexuality and the claustrophobic nature of Irish society.

So Broderick's *The Fugitives* can be compared to McGahern's *Amongst Women* or Moore's *Cold Heaven* as an examination of female resistance to patriarchal dominance. The respective protagonists – Lily Fallon, Shelia Moran and Marie Davenport – draw a number of similarities to each other; they are free-spirited, libidinous, they operate successfully within the confines of a male-dominated order and undermine the stereotype of the Irish womanhood as confined to hearth and home. There are a number of similarities between *The Waking of Willie Ryan* and *The Dark*, notably as an examination of secret (and incestuous) sexual codes of Irish families. Judith Hearne's recurrent dilemma on how one may be both a sexual being and a practicing Catholic is shared by young Mahoney in *The Dark*. The claustrophobic nature of a closed society ready to expel any form of sexual transgression is shared by all. As I examine each of these novels, further connections will become equally apparent. Both of Broderick's novels, as well as *Judith Hearne* and *The Dark* collectively offer an image of the social tumult affecting Irish society in the sixties. Moore's *Cold Heaven*, although set in the America, offers an excellent comparative to some of the changes (or lack of them) affecting Ireland during the seventies and eighties. Lastly, McGahern's *Amongst Women* is a fascinating examination of Irish historicity – his view on this period is a contentious though authoritative one.

Ireland – Society 1960 – 1990

Declan Kiberd, in his *Inventing Ireland – The Literature of the Modern Nation*, dedicates a chapter to 'The Writer and Society 1960 – 1990', detailing how the posture of 'inherited dissent' was dismantled in the early sixties to make way for what Augustine Martin called the 'forces of affirmation.'[50] If censorship, ostracism and exile were the lot of the previous generation of Irish writers, this period proved a turning point.

[50] Declan Kiberd, *Inventing Ireland – The Literature of the Modern Nation*, pp. 580 – 613, p. 581.

The banning of John McGahern's *The Dark* was significant in that the preceding murmurs of dissent suddenly became a national outcry. A new mood was fermenting and the Church, once unquestioned bastion of moral probity, soon found themselves on the defensive. By the mid-sixties Episcopal decrees were being questioned in a way that was unheard of before; indeed a number were held up to ridicule.[51] The departure of De Valera in 1959 could be seen as a signpost for change and his successor, Sean Lemass, though of De Valera's generation, was a man more in tune with economic and social realities. He oversaw the implementation of T.K. Whitaker's ground-breaking five year plan for economic recovery – a marked development in that the emphasis suddenly shifted from protectionism to free trade, to the encouragement of foreign investment and greater emphasis on industry rather that export-orientated agriculture. Through favourable international circumstances, G.P.A. increased from a one per cent average between 1950 and 1958 to a four per cent average between 1959 and 1973.[52]

With economic expansion came significant social change. A reversal in emigration and a rise of about fifty per cent in material living standards helped towards a rise in the population from 2.82 million in 1961 to 2.98 million in 1971. The number of marriages rose from a trough of 14,700 in 1957 to 22,000 in 1971.[53] The changes, while not spectacular in absolute terms, assumed a historical significance in that they reversed the trend of more than a century. With growth came the increased realisation of the importance of education. An OECD report, titled *Investment in Education,* was published in 1965 highlighting the particularly serious situation which existed at second level.[54] The balance of power between the traditional hegemonic Church and the state began to shift and by 1967, the then

---

[51] An example of which was 'The Bishop and the Nightie Affair' as detailed in John Cooney's *John Charles McQuaid – Ruler of Catholic Ireland*, pp. 304-305. See also J.H. Whyte's *Church & State in Modern Ireland*, pp. 331-362.

[52] B.M. Walsh, 'Economic Growth & Development, 1945-1970', in J.J. Lee, *Ireland 1945 – 1970*, p.33.

[53] J.J. Lee, *Ireland 1912 – 1985*, p. 360. During the 1960s immigration, perhaps the best barometer of Irish society, fell from 43,000 per annum between 1956 and 1961 to 11,000 between 1966 and 1971.

[54] John Coolahan, *Irish Education: Its History and Structure*, pp.165-166. The OEDC report highlighted a 'test year' which analysed a cohort of 55,000 pupils, of which 17,500 left full-time education at primary level and 13,500 left at Inter-Cert level. Of the 10,000 who sat the Leaving Certificate Examination, only 2,000 entered University.

Minister of Education Donogh O'Malley was confident enough to announce free education at second level without having consulted the cabinet, who were swept along on the tide of public enthusiasm. Between 1966 and 1969 the number of secondary school pupils rose from 104,000 to 144,000, or as much in the previous ten years.[55]

During this period, the Catholic Church in Ireland was distracted by more pressing concerns. Its conservative hierarchy found itself at odds with the *aggiornamento* policies of the Second Vatican Council, and while many Bishops responded by relaxing their older, more autocratic styles of address, there were others who retreated further into more indentured orthodoxy. This set the trend for the next thirty years, with most religious debates internal to the Catholic Church though the hierarchy remained vociferously opposed to the staple concerns of contraception, divorce and abortion. However, this was set against Irish sexual behaviour, both within and outside marriage, which became markedly more liberal; many rights denied to women – such as the right to work in the civil service after marriage – were restored.[56] The right of married couples to use contraceptives as an aspect of family planning had been upheld by the Supreme Court in 1973, but in the teeth of conservative opinion the sale of contraceptives became farcical – they could only be purchased by a married couple on prescription from their GP. 'An Irish solution to an Irish problem', as the then Health minister wryly opined.[57]

In 1983, a bitterly acrimonious debate on abortion was held in which the conservatives won something of a Pyrrhic victory and three years later, a similarly divisive referendum on rescinding the ban on divorce was defeated, illustrating that the dominancy of the Catholic Church remained battered but ultimately resolute. But the economic climate had changed in the intervening years. By the late eighties, a clear majority of the people

[55] Richard Breen, *Understanding Contemporary Ireland – State, Class and Development in the Republic of Ireland,* p. 132.

[56] Eunice McCarthy, 'Women and Work in Ireland', in Margaret Mac Curtain and Donncha Ó Corráin (eds), *Women in Irish Society – The Historical Dimension*, pp. 104-117. In 1971, working women in Ireland represented only 27.3 per cent (287,867) of the total Irish workforce of 1.1 million - progress during the 1970s was slow but consistent. The Council for the Status of Women was set up in 1973. The Anti-Discrimination (Pay) Act of 1974 was a major advance. The Employment Equality Act was passed in 1977 and the Employment Equality Agency was set up in the same year.

[57] Dermot Keogh, *Twentieth Century Ireland – Nation and State*, pp.335-337.

were better educated, housed and cared for than ever before.[58] Yet there were nearly three hundred thousand people unemployed and one in three lived below the official poverty line.[59] The sixties revival was checked in the mid-seventies by international recession, fluctuating oil prices and increased competition through our involvement with the EEC. Borrowing to make up the shortfall led the Irish economy into a morass, exacerbated by political upheaval and the spectre of the Northern troubles. Poverty and want had been tolerated before under the cloak of spurious patriotism or through the Church's emphasis on spiritual rather than material comforts, but by now this was no longer an acceptable coda to an increasingly disenfranchised population. The lack of employment, high taxation and a burgeoning debt crisis induced many young people to leave the country and emigration soon began to reach chronic proportions. It seemed clear that new political, social and cultural changes were needed to give voice to the transformation which occurred during the intervening thirty years.

In 1990, Mary Robinson, a feminist and civil rights lawyer, defeated two male candidates in the Presidential Election on a platform that focused on attempting to bring fresh perspectives to bear on traditional concerns. Her victory, as Carol Coulter explains: 'was widely welcomed as a triumph for those who supported a modernising, liberal agenda for Ireland, and as a defeat for those associated with nationalism and Catholic traditionalism.'[60] Shortly after her ascendancy to the Presidency, the Catholic Bishop of Galway resigned in disgrace after it was discovered both that he had fathered a child with an American divorcee and that he had embezzled diocesan funds to pay for her silence.[61] The Bishop Casey scandal, like Robinson's election as President, was a watershed in Irish life. The Church soon found itself facing a barrage of allegations

---

[58] Ray MacSharry, *The Making of the Celtic Tiger – The Inside Story of Ireland's Boom Economy,* p.26ff.: 'In 1964, just one in four of seventeen-year-olds were still in secondary education; by 1994 that figure had risen to 83 per cent.'

[59] Ibid., p.38: 'Unemployment rose steadily from 1970 to 1976, where it peaked for the decade with 9 per cent – 105,000 out of work. However the subsequent decline to 7.1 per cent was short lived. And by 1986, a record 226,000 – some 17 per cent of the labour force – were jobless.'

[60] Carol Coulter, *The Hidden Tradition: Feminism, Women and Nationalism in Ireland*, p.1.

[61] Gene Kerrigan, *This Great Little Nation*, p.44: 'In July 1990 Casey agreed to Murphy's terms: $100,000 for her, $25,000 for her lawyer. Casey financed this with £70,669 from a diocesan account. He made up the balance of $8,000 out of his own funds.'

concerning abuses perpetuated by the hierarchy and the religious orders, lurching from one scandal to another throughout the nineties.[62] By the decade's close, the Catholic Church's standing had effectively collapsed, as much a victim of its own conceited excesses as of its sheer immutability. Fianna Fáil, which at one point equalled the Church in its ubiquitous position in Irish society, was rocked by a series of scandals, mostly notably through the sacking of Minister for Defence Brian Lenihan for lying about the contents of an interview he conducted with a young UCD post-graduate. It was something of a tragic-comic fiasco and effectively cost Lenihan the Presidency. The psychic effects of this cannot be underestimated – the Presidency had been traditionally both a male *and* Fianna Fáil preserve. It would be interesting, perhaps, to draw a comparison between Fianna Fáil and the Catholic Church in this period – both were seen as monolithic institutions, but hopelessly outdated (or perhaps no longer fashionable) and by the early nineties open to increasing ridicule and dissent. Fianna Fáil's status as the ideologically pure 'legion of the rearguard' was destroyed by the revelation of corruption and embezzlement perpetuated by then Taoiseach Charles Haughey and his fellow Ministers. Curiously, while the Church continued to collapse throughout the nineties, Fianna Fail staged a revival of sorts and have since returned and remained in power since 1997. Some sins are more forgivable than others it seems.

In this period, the Irish novel adapted according to the mood of the times. While upper-class and Catholic novelists continued to emerge, the bourgeoning middle-class was much more prominent in both authorship and the readership of the Irish novel. In general, Irish readership today resembles the English readership of a century ago more than the Ascendancy-dominated readership of the nineteenth century. Yet it is striking how many of the earlier subgenres have gained prominence in the novel, say for example the Big House form which has been borrowed by writers such as Aidan Higgins, John Banville and Jennifer Johnson. The *Bildungsroman* has become a common fictional testing ground but the rise in Irish novels by women during this period is certainly noteworthy, expanding beyond the traditional Ascendancy background to incorporate writers such as Edna O'Brien, Janet McNeill, Julia O'Faoláin and Eilis Dillon.

---

[62] Ref. esp. Patrick Touher, *Fear of the Collar: Artane Industrial School*, and Chris Moore, *Betrayal of Trust: The Father Brendan Smyth Affair and the Catholic Church.*

Certainly, one can trace a sort of remorseless privatisation of experience during this period, an art which located its interest in the pathology of the alienated individual. Something fundamentally different has overtaken novelistic discourse since the early nineties, combining a willingness to confront the formal and conceptual legacies of a received literary tradition to reflect Ireland's post-modern circumstances. So I would argue that the period I am investigating is the period when modernism moved from opposition to accepted form and the Irish novelist explored the way in which cultural narratives mediated the indelible changes which occurred during the years 1960 – 1990.

Belfast and Society

The passage of the Government of Ireland Act on the 23 December 1920 provided the legal basis for the setting up of devolved state of Northern Ireland. Comprising the six north-eastern counties, it constituted 17 per cent of the land area of the whole island. From the beginning, it served as a sort of middle-space between nationalist aims of unity and loyalist intransigence. When Home Rule appeared inevitable, northern Protestants' settled for partition, self-government and a permanent majority that copper-fastened their supremacy by gerrymandering constituencies and extending additional voting privileges to the property classes – the largest of whom were, inevitably, Protestant. Discrimination in the allocation of jobs and homes kept Catholics in the position of second-class citizens. As Kiberd states:

> Life for northern nationalists was hard. Some of their elected leaders boycotted the Stormont parliament in Belfast; and those who took part in it were never embraced. In all the years of Stormont's existence until it was prorogued in 1972, the Unionist party voted in only one amendment proposed by nationalists and that was to a wildlife bill![63]

Pre-war, depression in the staple industries, linen and shipbuilding, kept unemployment at disproportionately high level – having reached 25 per cent of the insured workforce in 1932, it climbed to 28 per cent in 1938.[64] The war economy brought relative prosperity to Ulster and subsequently the expansion of the British welfare state, together with measures adopted

---

[63] Declan Kiberd, *Inventing Ireland – The Literature of the Modern Nation*, p. 415.

[64] Patrick Buckland, *The Factory of Grievances: Devolved Government in Northern Ireland, 1921 – 1939*, p. 52.

by the government such as extending the provisions of the Industrial Development Act of 1945, brought around a marked refinement in the quality of life. However, unemployment remained high, particularly for Catholics and as late as 1971, male unemployment among Catholics was 17.3 per cent compared with 6.6 per cent among Protestants.[65]

This sense of economic and cultural malaise is immediately palpable in Brian Moore's *The Lonely Passion of Judith Hearne*:

> Mrs Hearne started at the houses opposite and thought of her aunt's day when there were only private families in this street, at least one maid to every house, and dinner was at night, not at noon. All gone now, all those people dead and all the houses partitioned off into flats… she turned from the window to the photograph on the mantelpiece. All changed, she told it, all changed since your day. And I'm the one who has to put up with it. (*LPJH*, 7)

Moore's view of Belfast is strikingly similar to that of John Broderick's Athlone:

> The drawing-room door was open and she went over and looked in. It was a huge room, embalmed in Lily's memory for the frightening dead things that it had always been in her childhood... it was a monument to the prosperous days before Lily was born, when her grand-parents had furnished the room in the style of the 1880's. No-one had ever sat in it, made love, quarrelled or hated in it. It was the dead end of a dead end. (*TF*, 12)

Censorship, by no means as pervasive in Ulster as it was in the South, nonetheless existed even when such draconian measures were absent from the statue books. When Judith visits the O'Neill's for the second time, she makes a remark to Professor O'Neill about George Sand to which he replies: '"Well, I haven't read her books… [s]he's on the index I believe"' (*LPJH*, 124). In an interview with Julia Carlson, Moore remarked:

> There was a feeling in my mind, a feeling that's always been there, that Ireland was a small repressive country as far as literature was concerned and that to make it in Ireland wasn't enough. There was something wrong with you if you were a "darling" writer. In my childhood I knew that the

65 John Simpson, 'Economic Development: Cause or Effect in the Northern Ireland Conflict', in John Darby (ed.), *Northern Ireland: The Background to the Conflict*, p.82 .

> most popular sort of writers, like Maurice Walsh and Kate O'Brien, were all thrashmongers – third rate.[66]

The Lonely Passion of Judith Hearne is set in a dismal season and the city is perpetually bleak and uninviting: 'The rain began to patter again on the windows, growing heavier, soft, persistent Irish rain coming up Belfast Lough, caught in the shadow of Cave Hill' (*LPJH*, 29). Although Moore had departed from Belfast more than a decade prior to the publication of the novel, as Patricia Craig states:

> *Judith Hearne* and *The Feast of Lupercal* were written during the nineteen fifties and each has a contemporary setting; it wasn't necessary for Brian Moore to revisit the past in order to make Miss Hearne's tribulations, since the atmosphere prevailing in the 'thirties went on prevailing for another couple of decades. Belfast – World War Two notwithstanding – was in a monotonous phase of its history… [f]or Caroline Blackwood, writing about the same period, "boredom… seemed to be hanging over Northern Ireland like the grey mists that linger over her loughs": a monumental boredom, the implication is, that finally generated its own antidote.[67]

For John Wilson Foster:

> Judith's Belfast is a mere enlargement of the villages and towns we meet in the rural fiction, an inquisitive, scandal-hunting, puritanical, passionless place characterised by the burger mentality of its Presbyterian rulers and the apathy of a vestigial Catholic peasantry. It is a world dominated by ceremony and rite: Judith Hearne reflects this not only in its use of Catholic liturgy but also in the painful human relationship it skilfully dissects.[68]

But like Broderick's Athlone or McGahern's postage-stamp community in Leitrim, Moore's Belfast was about to undergo a number of seismic changes. Northern Ireland had been a 'closed shop' almost since its inception. It was not recognized by the Southern Government and the outside world held little attraction to those who remained. When Mrs Henry Rice remarks, '"Jim would sit here boring the life out of you with his talk about New York,"' Madden retorts: '"This lady is interested in what goes on in the world. Not like you and Bernie"' (*LPJH*, 24). Judith,

---

[66] Julia Carlson, *Banned in Ireland*, p.117.

[67] Patricia Craig, 'Moore's Maladies: Belfast in the Mid-Twentieth Century', in the *Irish University Review* (1988), p.16.

[68] John Wilson Foster, *Forces and Themes in Ulster Fiction*, p.151.

conscious of her ignorance of the outside world, goes in search of some literature on America. In the library, she finds only 'a picture book of New York and two books on America in general' (*LPJH*, 26).

The next day, we witness a farcical scene at the breakfast table, with both Bernard Rice and Mr Lenehan displaying their ignorance and prejudice: '"America sells refrigerators for culture,"' Bernard said '"They come to Europe when they need ideas"' (*LPJH*, 32). To this, Madden replies: '"Why nobody in New York or anywhere else, gives a good ghaddam – pardon me ladies – what happens to the Six Counties"' (*LPJH*, 34). Lenehan then states: '"Well, I'll have you know, my fine Yank, that there's more famous men ever came out of Ireland than ever came out of America"' (*LPJH*, 34). Later, when Madden retreats to a public house, he reflects on how he was cajoled into buying rounds for fellow emigrants in New York: 'And when he had stopped buying, they began to talk about corn and crops, and pigs and the fair day' (*LPJH*, 41).

Thus, the concerns of this 'enlarged village' as Foster phrases it, do not extend beyond their own border, and their world view is rudimentary and clichéd at best, such as when Mrs Henry Rice suggests that communists are: '"no worse than the Protestants and Freemasons that are running this city… Hitler was no worse than the British"' (*LPJH*, 32).

All this would change over the next decade and *The Lonely Passion of Judith Hearne* offers us an intriguing snapshot of an insular community on the precipice of what I would term the new symbolic order. Northern Ireland was changing in tandem with the wider world as J.J. Lee attests:

> With an Irish Catholic in the White House… with a Taoiseach in Dublin apparently seeking conciliation, with a Pope in the Vatican acknowledging the humanity of communists, much less Protestants, problems further compounded when Harold McMillan resigned in October 1963, raising the spectre of an imminent Labour government in Britain, any Northern Premier would have had to take increasing cognisance of life beyond Ulster, however he chose to interpret it.[69]

In March of 1963, the ailing premier, Basil Brookeborough, was replaced by Terence O'Neill, a moderate who sought to integrate Catholics into the Northern State and modernize the economy whilst engaging in far reaching social planning. His economic reforms, which like Southern Ireland included opening up the borders for foreign investment and manufacturing, did not quell the rising resentment of a growing Catholic

[69] J.J. Lee, *Ireland 1912 – 1985: Politics and Society*, p. 414.

middle-class. Like the O'Neills in Moore's novel, those Catholics in white-collar professions were the privileged few. Ironically, because improvement now began to seem a possibility for the first time, Catholics became more conscious of occupational discrimination in general. Simultaneously, O'Neill also began to alienate his own followers who were alarmed by such conciliatory gestures as the first North-South meeting of Prime Ministers in 1965. They saw concessions to the Catholic minority as a diminution of their own impregnable authority. That O'Neill was progressing too quickly with his sweeping reforms was a common complaint from his increasingly recalcitrant Unionist followers – sadly, that he was progressing too *slowly* was the contrary argument from the Catholic community.

In 1967, the new Northern Ireland Civil Rights Association (NICRA) was formed to campaign for Catholic equality: one man, one vote, no gerrymandering of constituency boundaries, fair distribution of local council houses, the repeal of the draconian Special Powers Act (first introduced in 1922 to deal with potential subversion during the Irish civil war, it remained on the Statute Books for the next fifty years), the disbanding of the B Specials (the RUC reserve force, noted for their rabid sectarianism) and a formal complaints procedure against local authorities.[70] O'Neill could move only as quickly as his followers allowed and while he appealed for moderate support, matters were lurching beyond his control. In January 1969, a NICRA march from Belfast to Derry was brutally assaulted by members of the Protestant community, aided in part by individual policemen. It sparked off serious rioting in Derry. With ebbing support and with Unionist extremists now in the ascendancy, a series of explosions caused by Unionist paramilitaries at electricity and water installations in March and April forced O'Neill's hand. He resigned on April 28 and his cousin, James Chichester Clarke, immediately emerged as a candidate for succession. Clarke inherited a virtually hopeless situation. Once the Orange marching season, with its ritual invocation of triumphant tribalism, opened in earnest in July, the resources of the RUC were stretched beyond breaking point.

In August, riots broke out in Belfast which quickly threatened to plunge Northern Ireland into a state of civil war. Law and order collapsed, 7 people were killed and about 3,500 Catholics were driven out of their homes in one of the largest forced evacuations in Europe since the Second World War. Chichester-Clarke was forced to turn to Westminster for

[70] David Harkness, *Northern Ireland Since 1920*, p. 145.

assistance and on the 15th of August, some 10,000 British troops were dispatched to the North. The British presence has remained ever since. The IRA split after the August riots, one side blaming the other for the failure to protect the nationalist ghettoes. This heralded the birth of the Provisional IRA and a renewal of their campaign against both the Unionist state and the British presence in Northern Ireland. For the years covered by this investigation, that war would be fought in earnest until a temporary ceasefire was called in 1994.The old order had indeed been swept away and a new symbolic order emerged which catapulted Northern Ireland onto the world stage.

CHAPTER TWO

LACAN AND THE DEVELOPMENT OF THE IRISH NOVEL

Lacan and Reading the Modern Irish Novel

To begin with, my primary interpretative focus will be on the fiction of Broderick, McGahern and Moore and not on Lacan's theory. Throughout this book, I aim to offer my own readings of Lacan's ideas but I shall refrain from exploring the frequent contradictions which emerged in his theory over the course of several decades. I will define most of the Lacanian terms in the next section but my central application of Lacanian theory lies in a close textual reading of the individual authors, focusing in particular on the cultural and ideological constructs of gender, religion, family, sexual desire and politics. Similarly, a feminist re-reading of the text can be particularly rewarding given the primacy of strong, self-assured female protagonists in the work of McGahern, Moore and Broderick and the way in which the masculine subject is shown to be in constant danger of dissolution.

Lacan defines the phallus as a sort of transcendent signifier that bestows a mastery of the symbolic order on the masculine subject. The phallic function is the function that institutes lack, the alienating function of language and is one of the three elements in the triangle that constitutes the preoedipal phase, the others being the mother and the child. The mother desires the object and the child seeks to satisfy this desire by identifying with the phallus. In the Oedipus phase, the father enters as a fourth element, breaking the triangle and 'castrating' the child, making it impossible for the child to identify with the imaginary phallus – the child is then forced to choose between accepting his castration or rejecting it. Lacan would argue that both sexes must assume this sense of castration – that is, each child must reject acting the possibility of acting as the phallus for the mother. There is a complication in that man can only lay claim to the symbolic phallus after accepting his initial castration while woman's lack is also seen as, a kind of possession. As Dylan Evan's states: 'Thus even the woman, who lacks the symbolic phallus in one way, can also be said to possess it, since not having it the symbolic is itself a form of having.'[1]

For Lacan, sexual relations consist of two interrelated myths – the myth of psychic unity which is designated as the masculine subject, and the myth of the feminine as 'other' that guarantees the unity of the masculine subject. There is some confusion in Lacanian theory over the role of the 'real' phallus, that is, the penis located with the 'real' father, the imaginary phallus which may be detached from the body by castration and the symbolic phallus which is where the question of sexual difference comes into play. The phallus has no corresponding female signifier and unlike the imaginary phallus, the symbolic phallus cannot be negated. Thus even woman, who lack the symbolic phallus, can also be said to possess it since not having the symbolic is itself a form of having.

The woman, then, becomes crucial to the myth of masculinity because her lack serves as veil in front of the phallus protecting the masculine subject from the knowledge that the signifier that signifies him does not exist. Lacan's most radical attempt to construct a distinctive and irreducible 'feminine sexuality' comes in the twentieth volume of his seminar, in a chapter titled 'God and Woman's *jouissance* '. According to Lacan 'woman' is an endless sequence of projections and fabrications. There is no signifier for woman as such because woman's position in our culture is either automatically defined by her husband or is defined only with great difficulty. This by no means implies that women have no sexual identity of their own.

For Lacan, sexual identity is constituted on at least two different levels: (1) the successive identifications that constitute the ego, accounting for an imaginary level of sexual identity, and (2) any given subject, masculine or feminine, able to situate itself on the different sides of Lacan's formulas of sexuality. These two levels represent the ego and the subject, where at one time, woman may identify with her father as much as identifying with her level of desire, where she may be characterised by her feminine structure. True, once a woman forms a relationship with a man she is likely to be viewed as an object but by the adopting of a position in respect to *jouissance,* it involves and implies subjectivity. In short, feminine structure means feminine subjectivity.

---

[1] Dylan Evans, *A Introductory Dictionary of Lacanian Psychoanalysis*, p.143. See also Jacques Lacan, *Seminar IV*, p.153, for a further development of this theory.

I devote a great deal of this book to exposing gender as a social construct, detailing the self-subverting dimension of the phallic order, which necessitates the patriarchal order to repress the Other's gaze in order to protect the myth of patriarchal authority. The undermining of the set patriarchal system is reflected in the way in which the three writers at the centre of this study have gone about investigating and critiquing the role that patriarchal cultural discourses have played in delimiting Irish gendered identities. John McGahern has, for example, concentrated on what Judith Butler has called the 'promising ambivalence' of violent and patriarchal speech. This ambiguity accounts for the possibility that speech can sometimes fail to act, or act in ways that counter the intention of the speaker.[2] Butler argues that all cultural discourses, including those which validate patriarchy, share an unstable relationship with the intentions that accompany their deployment, and that it is this instability which can provide the impetus for their subversion.

Take for example McGahern's novel *Amongst Women.* There are a number of subtle ways in which the patriarchal structure is undermined in this novel – for one, the reliance on the family as a sphere of power is itself a concession of power. The patriarch, Moran, is a domestic tyrant who threatens and cajoles his family into obsequious obedience. In order to bolster his authority in the home, Moran has to embark on the offensive, the aim of which is to remind his audience that while the home relies on the cooperation of an idealized mother figure, the real source of authority lies with him.

While Moran accepts that the domestic authority of the Irish mother figure is an old story which has powerful citational force, he is also forced to use it for his own benefit – notably when he remarries because he believes that it is only through the presence of a mother figure that will keep his family together:

> He saw each individual member gradually slipping away out of his reach. Yes, they would eventually all go. He would be alone. That he could not stand. He saw with bitter lucidity that he would marry Rose Brady now. (*AM*, 22)

Secondly, while he harnesses the Rosary as a tool of promoting some form of patrifocal myth, the reality is that the Rosary is clearly invoked to construct and repair that authority, rather than confirm it automatically. This can be seen in his daughter Maggie's return from London, where she

---

[2] Judith Butler, *Excitable Speech: A Politics of Performance*, p.91.

becomes the centre of attention – 'She was the centre of the table' – displacing Moran from his self-assumed role. He attempts to displace her by starting the Rosary earlier than usual, but the formulaic manner in which it is recited breaks down and rather than confirming his familial role as head of the family, it positively discourages it:

> This night Moran enunciated each repetitious word with slow clarity and force as if the very dwelling on suffering, death and human supplication would scatter all flimsy vanities of a great world; and the muted responses giving back their acceptance of human servitude did not improve his humour. (*AM*, 79)

Once he loses the physical strength which has helped him regulate the patriarchal power structure in the family, the words of the Rosary no longer contribute to or endorse his claims. The family home, the new fragility of which helped to challenge the stability of Moran's power, now comes to signify the authority of benevolent mothers rather than that of powerful patriarchs.

Karen Lawrence, in an essay on Joyce's *Ulysses*, made an observation which is equally relevant, not just to McGahern's novel but my argument as a whole:

> Joyce presents the incertitude of paternity even as he presents its power… the maternal silently undermines patriarchal power and the cultural and linguistic structures it underwrites… Maternity… is a different kind of 'fiction' than paternity, a fiction of a source before law and identity.[3]

The view of the mother as an engulfing force which threatens to devour the child is a common motif in Lacanian theory. For Jung:

> On the negative side, the mother archetype may connote anything secret, hidden, dark; the abyss, the world of the dead, anything that devours, seduces and poisons, that is terrible and inescapable like fate.[4]

In his pre-war writings, Lacan alludes several times to Melanie Klein's work, and describes the cannibalistic fantasies of devouring, and being devoured, by the mother. To begin with, it is important to differentiate between the real, symbolic and imaginary mother. The mother manifests

---

[3] Karen Lawrence, 'Paternity, The Legal Fiction', in Robert. D. Newman (ed.), *Joyce's Ulysses: The Larger Perspective*, p.95.

[4] Jung, C.G. 'Psychological Aspects of the Mother Archetype', in *Four Archetypes: Mother, Rebirth, Spirit, Trickster,* p.16.

herself in the real by acting as the primary caregiver of the infant, for the infant is helpless and relies upon the mother to care for him. These objects take on a symbolic function, symbolic tokens of a mother's love. As it is, the mother's presence which testifies to her love, her absence is explained a traumatic rejection. The child attempts to cope with this loss by symbolizing the mother's presence and absence in games and language. Lacan thus regards thus primary symbolism as the child's first steps into the symbolic order. The mother is manifested in the imaginary order by a number of images – one of which I have already mentioned – the devouring mother which is at the root of anxiety. Other maternal images consist of the phallic mother, the mother imagined as possessing the imaginary phallus. Ultimately, Lacan argues that the child must detach himself from the imaginary relation with the mother in order to enter the social world – the failure to do so results in various abnormalities, from phobia to perversion.

It is because of their perceived innate maternal power that women are often the object of fear, even hate, in McGahern's fiction. Women exist within enclosed spaces – a barracks, a house, a kitchen, a sickbed, and so forth – and it is within this context that the mother archetype in McGahern's fiction often assumes connotations of claustrophobia, imprisonment, secrecy and death. In *The Pornographer*, fear of the female approaches misogyny in the case of the protagonist and his uncle. To the former, Josephine is a threatening figure – he is terrified by her desire to 'eat and drink him' while in *The Leavetaking* Lightfoot states that his mother, '"devoured her wretch of a husband my father and all my brothers."'[5]

There are several other reasons why applying Lacanian criticism to the modern Irish novel constitutes a rewarding interplay of theory and fiction. Lacan treats a text similarly to the way he treats a patient – he views the symptom as palimpsest and tries to understand the 'hole' created by a signifier into which signification disappears. As such, language can provide the key to the structure of the unconscious, a structure which helps provide some of the most fundamental codes of society. For Lacan:

> The literary work fails or succeeds, but this failure is not due to the limiting of the effects of structure. The work only exists in that curvature which is of the structure itself… the curvature mentioned here is no more a metaphor for the structure than the structure is a metaphor for the reality of

[5] John McGahern, *The Leavetaking*, p.31.

> the unconscious. It is real, and, in this sense, the work imitates nothing. It is, as fiction, a truthful structure.[6]

It is a theory which invites the reader to experience language not just as an essential means of communication, but as an active medium that enables critical thought whilst permitting psychoanalysis to function as a talking cure. As such, one could argue that Lacanian analysis invites the subject to see the 'moi' as a fictional construct that performs a masquerade of truth. For Lacan, the ego is a construction which is formed by identification with the specular image in the mirror stage. It is the place where the subject becomes alienated from himself, transforming himself into the counterpart. The ego (*moi*) is thus an imaginary function in opposition to the subject (*je*), which is part of the symbolic order. The 'je' is controlled because the 'moi' exerts pressure on the 'je' to complete the 'moi's' self-sufficient autonomy.

Beyond this split in the subject is the Real subject of the unconscious that cannot be signified in language. The subject is therefore reliant on others in Real situations in order to recognize its unity so as to enable the moi to reconstitute itself as conscious of reality. The subject itself is very much aware of individual myths of reality, but actual Truth orbits around this representation in the real and can only be glimpsed in those moments where the 'je' experiences the fact that the 'moi' is fiction. For Lacan, the ego is incurable and he was totally opposed to the idea that the aim of the psychoanalyst is to strengthen the ego – rather, by undermining the fixity of the ego, psychoanalytical treatment should aim to restore the dialectic of desire and reinitiate the coming-into-being of the subject. The ego merely papers over a lack-in-being that can be exposed but never satiated and this identity crisis is evident, for example, in Moore's *Cold Heaven* – every time Marie thinks that she has found the answer to the questions she asks of herself, the answer serves only as the backdrop to a further crisis. Her best attempts to establish herself as a secular, independent woman are repeatedly neutralised in order to inscribe her within Catholic iconography because it makes her a Magdalene figure whose unexpected redemption helps to confirm God's benevolence.

I have chosen to focus my study solely upon two novels from each of the three authors. I have chosen to give each novel a clearly demarcated section of its own as an over-emphasis on interrelation between the texts can blur the subversive quality by maintaining that what is inexplicable in one story can be explained by reference to another. The range of Lacan's

---

[6] Jacques Lacan, 'C'est à la lecture de Freud…', in Robert Georgin, *Lacan*, p.16.

literary readings was not immense but his theory plays an essential role in a discourse that attempts to mine the opacity of the unconscious. Though his theories were often convoluted, they do force the reader to be more curious, to be aware of the productive role of equivocation, grammatical dislocation and homophonic punning. It should invite the reader to experience language not just as an instrumental means of communication but as a site for new critical thought.

The three authors are connected, not just by a time-frame or a particular set of socio-economic or cultural circumstances, but also by an attempt to raise the status of the novel into an art form. From our reading of Bakhtin, we perceive that the novel was the poor relation of Irish literature up to the 1960s – the prejudices that each of these authors faced, both through censorship and the deep-seated partiality towards the novel in general, was formidable indeed, but they were pivotal in emergence of the novel as the pre-eminent Irish cultural form. The key to this book is built around analysing these authors in a simultaneous reading and applying a theory which will help explain some of the reasons behind the novel's pre-eminent standing of today. To quote David Lloyd:

> We are only just beginning to forge the theoretical terms in which the atypicality of the Irish novel can be analysed but… it may be that we are approaching a less coherent but in many ways more interesting theory of the novel.[7]

From a Lacanian perspective, most of the protagonists in these novels search for substitute objects that will complete them and return them to the mirror stage where they first imagined their unity. The search for unity or completeness often takes the form of the family unit, but like the cracked plate on the dresser in McGahern's *Amongst Women* or the mock family triumvirate in Broderick's *The Fugitives*, the realisation that the objects of desire are once again a substitute often seems to serve as the epiphany of the story. For Lacan, castration refers to the fact that people are permanently incomplete and however much they try to complete themselves with signifiers, they are only dealing with substitute objects of desire that merely stand in for the unity they imagined in the mirror phase. The castration complex affects both sexes because its appearance is closely linked with the phallic phase, a moment of psychosexual development when the child knows only one sexual organ – the male one. The fear of castration can be understood as fear of falling out of the world

[7] David Lloyd, *Anomalous States*, p. 155.

of words into the void of the real. In analysing a story, readers impose their own discourse on the text and therefore occupy the place of the Real relative to what they see as the author's fictional creations. The key protagonists in these texts expose ideology as just another meaning system designed to deny castration and compensate for a structural lack of being. The novels at hand therefore help expose reality as a fictional construct that permits the split-subject to misrecognize the actual indifferent and subversive power of the unrepresentable Real as the imagined benevolent gaze of the Other.

The use of Lacanian theory therefore offers us, in Lloyd's words, a less cohesive but more interesting theory of the Irish novel. It centres in particular on gender relations but spans a number of other complex themes and departs from more archetypical readings of modern Irish fiction in its analysis and offers instead a template in which we may assess the fragmentary nature of Irish society as a whole. The rise of feminist and queer theory is of particular importance – one should not forget that sexual identities are produced by unconscious performative agencies and it is only a determination by the unconscious that can make sense of sexual identities. I shall return back to the theme later but for the moment, I aim to further discuss some of the concepts that will emerge throughout this book.

Theoretical Framework – The Symbolic Order

During the 1950s, Lacan developed his own triadic style of thinking – the symbolic, the imaginary and the real. The imaginary is the order of the mirror-phase, identification and reciprocation. By way of the imaginary, the original identification procedures which the ego into being are repeated and reinforced by the individual in his relationship with the external world. The imaginary is thus the order of surface appearances which are, above all, deceptive, observable phenomena which hide the/any underlying structure. It is also the order of a dyadic and ideal relationship where the reflection becomes an idealised object as well as misrecognition of the self.

In the prelinguistic 'mirror phase', the child, from within the imaginary state of being, starts to project a certain unity into the fragmented self-image in the mirror; he or she produces a fictional ideal. The imaginary tendency continues even after the formation of ego, because the myth of unified selfhood depends upon this ability to identify with objects in the world as 'others'. According to Darian Leader: '[t]he ego ideal is the symbolic point which gives you a place and supplies the point from which you are looked at.'[8] Nevertheless, the child must also learn to differentiate itself from others if it is to become a subject in its own right. With the father's prohibition the child is thrown into the 'symbolic' world of differences. The symbolic order is, in the words of Malcolm Bowie:

> [...] Spoken of admiringly. It is the realm of movement rather than fixity, and of heterogeneity rather than similarity. It is the realm of language, the unconscious and an otherness that remains other. This is the order in which the subject as distinct from the ego comes into being, and into a matter of being that is always disjointed and intermittent.[9]

According to Lacan: '[n]othing exists except on an assumed foundation of absence. Nothing exists except in so far as it does not exist.' [10] The symbolic order is also the realm of the Other, of culture in opposition to the imaginary order of nature and perhaps most importantly of all, it is the realm of absence, lack and death. It is important to note the difference between 'the little other' which is not really an other at all but a projection of the ego, and the 'big Other', a term that is broadly co-terminous with the symbolic order – the law, society, etc. The real is that which lies outside the symbolic process and it is to be found in the mental as well as the material world: it comes close to meaning the ineffable and is ascribed with an even greater regard than the symbolic.

Together, the three orders comprise a complex topological space in which the human mind can be read and this space is fluid and ever-changing. Lacan has symbolised this interaction in the shape of the Borromean Knot – *see. Figure 1*. The effects of the real and imaginary on the symbolic order of communication are significant in terms of the close readings offered by this thesis.

The intersection of the Real-Symbolic-Imaginary constitutes a unified whole and 'together they cover the whole field of psychoanalysis.'[11] Each of the orders corresponds roughly to the stages in the development of the infant human as it approaches maturity. As Bowie states: 'The symbolic, the imaginary and the real are not mental forces, personifiable on the model-builder's inner stage, but orders each of which serves to position the individual within a force-field that traverses him.'[12] The Real-

[8] Darian Leader, *Introducing Lacan,* p. 48.
[9] Malcolm Bowie, *Lacan*, p.92.
[10] Jacques Lacan, *Écrits* (1977), p.392
[11] Dylan Evans, *An Introductory Dictionary of Lacanian Psychoanalysis*, p.132.
[12] Malcolm Bowie, *Lacan*, p.91.

Symbolic-Imaginary is a force that traverses the individual and together they comprise a structure, a structure that is far from static. Rather, the various orders contained in the Real-Symbolic-Imaginary configuration constantly act on each other, defining each other in contradistinction to one another: 'The symbolic, the imaginary and the real pressurize each other continuously and have their short-term truces, but they do not allow any embracing programme for synthesis to emerge inside or outside the analytic encounter. The three orders together comprise a complex topological space in which the characteristic disorderly motions of the human mind can be plotted.'[13]

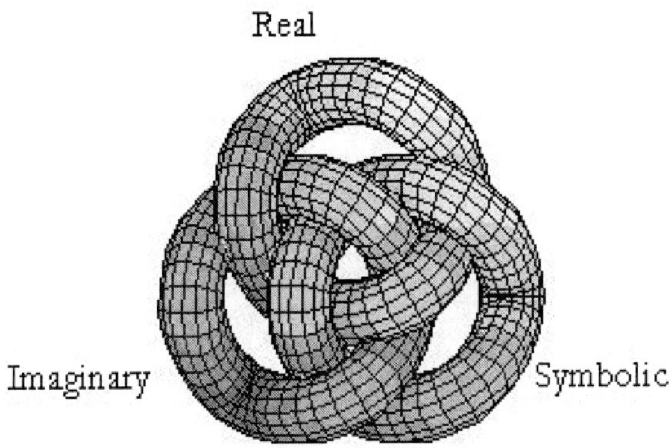

Figure 1- The Borromean Knot

Lacan's symbolic father (*Nom-du-Père*) is regarded as the fundamental signifier which permits signification to proceed normally. As Lacan states: 'It is in the name of the father that we must recognize the support of the symbolic function which, from the dawn of history, has identified his person with the figure of the law.'[14] The 'Name-of-the-Father' is the paternal metaphor, a symbol of authority at once legislative and punitive. It represents that which makes the symbolic possible and is the inaugurating agent of Law, but also represents the interconnectedness of the signifying chain. Without it, we are left with a hole in the symbolic universe. Lastly, it is the metaphorical realm through which the constructions

[13] Ibid., pp.98-99.
[14] Jacques Lacan *Écrits (*1977), p.67.

of masculinity are constructed and this will be of particular significance to us throughout the book.

However, Lacan does not simply equate the symbolic order with language, as language involves both real and imaginary dimensions. The symbolic dimension of language is that of the 'signifier', a term Lacan borrows from Ferdinand de Saussure. For Saussure, words are not symbols which correspond to referents but a 'sign' which is made up of two units – a conceptual element which is called the signified and a phonological unit called the signifier. In this instance, say the signifier is the colour 'red' and the signified 'stop'. The relationship here is arbitrary: there is no natural bond between the colour red and stop no matter how natural it may feel. Each colour in the traffic system signifies not by asserting a positive univocal meaning but by marking a difference, a distinction within a system of opposites and contrasts: traffic-light 'red' is precisely 'not-green'; 'green' is 'not-red'. But while Saussure argued that the signifier and the signified are independent of one another, Lacan argued that the signifier is primary and thus produces the signified.

Lacan considers that human subjects enter into a pre-existing system of signifiers which take on a meaning only within a language system. The entry in language enables us to find a subject position within a relational system (male/female, father/mother/daughter). In Lacan's version of the sign, the signified 'slides' beneath a signifier which 'floats' – as such, the unconscious hides meaning in symbolic images which need to be interpreted. Of particular interest for this book are the ways in which performative creativity works upon both the micro and macro in Irish society, building a bridge between the personal and the political. For Lacan, the question of phallocentrism is inseparable from the structure of the sign. The signifier, the phallus, holds out the promise of full presence and power, which, because it is unobtainable, threatens both sexes with the castration complex. Social and cultural factors, such as gender stereotypes, will accentuate or diminish the impact of this unconscious lack but the phallus, being a signifier of full presence and not a physical organ, remains a universal source of the castration complex. The father's role in society as lawgiver is not based upon a superior procreative function but merely as part of the linguistic system. The female recognizes the speech of the father because she has access to the signifier of the paternal function which regulates desire in a civilized manner. Only by accepting the necessity of sexual difference and regulated desire can a child become socialized. Thus changes in the structuration of the little and big Other make for changes in the symbolic order – by 1990, the president of

Ireland, always a phallocentric presence, has now become a woman with concomitant effects on the symbolic order of Irish society

However, although the authors that I aim to examine maintain a concern with the effects of words on gendered identities, none of them simply endorse the belief that patriarchal language always 'acts' automatically and with violent effect. Instead they tend to focus upon what Judith Butler calls the 'promising ambivalence' of violent and patriarchal speech.[15] Butler argues that all cultural discourses, including those which validate patriarchy, share an unstable relationship with the intentions that accompany their deployment, and that it is this instability which can provide the impetus for their subversion, 'that the utterance can be turned, untethered from its origin, is one way to shift the locus of authority in relation to the utterance.'[16] Disruption can go beyond the merely literary to the social level. Literature and philosophy greatly influenced Lacan and they supported his perspective on language but poetical language can also show how dominant social discourses can be undermined by the creation of new subject positions. Thus, far from being a mere blank which awaits its social and sexual role, the subject is in process and is capable of being other than it is.

Let us take the period of time being discussed, Ireland 1960 – 1990. The nexus of colonialism and gender had left a deep impression on the Irish cultural psyche, and so, uncritically adopting the gender division imposed by colonialism, Irish decolonisation attempted to deny its representation as an essential feminine race by reconfiguring the national division of the sexes along patently unequal lines. Thus the Irish male was constructed as active, a fighter and earner occupying the political and public realm outside the home. Irish women were, by contrast, seen as passive, as nurturers and as bastions of the homestead. This symbolic order was all-encompassing and once the symbolic order in general has arisen, it creates the sense that it always has been there, since, 'we find it absolutely impossible to speculate on what preceded it other than by symbols.'[17] The name-of-the-father was the inaugurating agent of Law but as I shall demonstrate in the chapters ahead, such a law was less totalising than we may first assume. For Lacan, desire is both the heart of human existence and the central concern of psychoanalysis. However, there is a limit to how far desire can be articulated in speech because of a

[15] Judith Butler, *Excitable Speech: A Politics of the Performance*, p.91.
[16] Ibid., p.93.
[17] Jacques Lacan, *Seminar. Book II*, p.5.

fundamental incompatibility between desire and speech – it is this incompatibility which explains the irreducibility of the unconscious. However, desire is not merely a private affair but is constituted in a dialectic relationship with the perceived desires of other subjects – it is, in essence, a social product.

The period of 1960–1990, as a symbolic order, witnessed the diminution of the patrifocal discourse, and witnessed rather a process by which prior memories (desires) expelled or censored from the public consciousness returned in a distorted form. The key question thus revolves the uncovering and investigation of the thematic codas inherent in the novels of this period and how they ultimately impacted upon the unflinching moral (symbolic) order. To further develop this point I aim to explain the Lacanian terms of reference in the next chapter and then apply them to the novels in question. So before we further develop our hypothesis, let us first look at how Lacanian theory can assist us in our reading of the modern Irish novel.

The Imaginary Order and the Phallus

The mirror stage was the subject of Lacan's first official contribution to psychoanalytic theory and became a constant point of reference throughout his later work. The mirror stage describes the formation of the Ego via the process of identification, the Ego being the result of identifying with one's own specular image. At six months, the baby still lacks coordination; however, he can recognize himself in the mirror before attaining control over his bodily movements. He sees his image as a whole, and the synthesis of this image produces a sense of contrast with the un-coordination of the body, which is perceived as a fragmented body. This contrast is first felt by the infant as a rivalry with his own image, because the wholeness of the image threatens him with fragmentation, and thus the mirror stage gives rise to an aggressive tension between the subject and the image. To resolve this aggressive tension, the subject identifies with the image: this primary identification with the counterpart is what forms the Ego. The moment of identification is to Lacan a moment of jubilation since it leads to an imaginary sense of mastery. As Dylan Evans explains:

> However, the jubilation may also be accompanied by a depressive reaction, when the infant compares his own precarious sense of mastery

> with the omnipotence of the mother. This identification also involves the ideal ego which functions as a promise of future wholeness sustaining the Ego in anticipation.[18]

Thus the ego is a sort of ghost and identification belongs to the modality that Lacan has defined as the 'imaginary.' In Malcolm Bowie's words:

> The imaginary is the scene of a desperate delusion attempt to be and to remain 'what one is' by gathering to oneself ever more instances of sameness, resemblance and self-replication…Lacan's 'Imaginary' thus creates a bridge between inner-directed and outer-directed mental acts, and belongs as much to the objects of perception as to those internal objects for which the word is usually reserved in ordinary speech.[19]

The reason that the infant resorts to identification is to deny its separation from the mother by incorporating her persona in its ego. For this reason Lacan regards the imaginary as a maternal realm, and he argues that this duel universe of mother and child has to be disrupted by a third term – the father. According to Bruce Fink:

> If we hypothesize an initial child-mother unity, the father… typically acts in such a way as to disrupt this unity, intervening therein as a third term – often perceived as foreign or undesirable.[20]

The father's function is to introduce the law against incest into the oedipal drama of the home. By forbidding incest, the father instates the symbolic order which distinguishes parent from child, mother from father, sister from brother. Of course, this theory does seem to suppose that every child has a loving mother and jealous father, but Lacan insists that these are both symbolic roles transcending the individuals performing them.

The father is not a simple concept and Lacan distinguishes between the imaginary, symbolic and real father. The symbolic father is also referred to as the Name-of-the-Father and his function is to impose the Law – that is, the fundamental principles which underlie all social relations. For Lacan: 'the true function of the father… is fundamentally to unite (and not set in opposition) a desire and the Law.'[21] He intervenes in the imaginary relationship between mother and child, introducing the necessary symbolic

---

[18] Dylan Evans, *Dictionary of Lacanian Psychoanalysis*, pp. 115-116.
[19] Malcolm Bowie, *Lacan*, p.92.
[20] Bruce Fink, *The Lacanian Subject – Between Language and Jouissance*, p.55.
[21] Jacques Lacan, *Écrits (*1977), p.321.

distance between them and thus becomes the fundamental element in the symbolic order.

The imaginary father is an imago, a composite of the various fantasies built up by the subject around the figure of the father. The imaginary father can be seen as either the ideal father or the opposite – that is the bad father. In both guises, where as an ideal father or cruel agent of privation, the imaginary father is omnipotent. As to the real father, Lacan states that he is the agent of castration, the one who performs the operation of symbolic castration. By promoting the name over the person of the father, Lacan is taking up a hint of Freud's that paternal power is linguistic rather than corporeal. Thus, the real father is an effect of language, so the real here is the real of language rather than the real of biology. The name of the father is an epitaph, destined to outlive the dissolution of the flesh and Lacan insists that death inheres in language as a whole, where every vocable enfolds a void. Languages originate in absence and due to the fear of castration all pleasures are substitutive, for sexuality consists of the pursuit of metaphorical alternatives to lost felicities.

In the opening chapter of this book, I made reference to Lacan's debt to Ferdinand de Saussure, whose theory implied that words and meanings are forever shifting under the semantic contagion of their neighbours. However, for Lacan it was the phallus which provided a form of anchorage in language. Lacan, in Seminar XX, argues that the signifier and signified are separated by a bar, which he calls "the phallus."[22] The signifiers can slide over the top of this bar, with the signified elements beneath. This means that there is never an easy correlation between signifier and signified and, as a result, all language and communication is actually produced by the failure to fully communicate, like for example in the misrecognition of the mirror stage. The asymmetrical relationship between signifier and signified is further complicated by the fact that the bar between them (in other words, the phallus) cannot itself be signified. For this reason, there is a distinct difference between the phallus as an image of the male penis, and the Lacanian phallus.

According to Lacan, seen from a child's perspective the imaginary phallus represents the object of the mother desire. Thus, a pre-oedipal triangle of mother, phallus and infant arises. At first the infant tries to be the phallus for the mother until the moment of a crucial transformation when the child, after identifying the phallus as a static image of completeness and sufficiency, sees it as representing the mother's desire,

---

[22] Bruce Fink, *Lacan to the Letter – Reading Écrits Closely*, p. 159.

and thus her lack. The prestige accorded to the phallus has led to a division amongst feminists, with some arguing that this prestige derives from the privileges of the penis in reality. According to Elizabeth Grosz:

> In spite of Lacan's claims, the phallus is not a 'neutral' term functioning equally for both sexes, positioning them both in the symbolic order. As the word suggests, it is a term privileging masculinity, or rather, the penis… its position as a threshold signifier is symptomatic of the assumed patriarchal context in Freud's and Lacan's work.[23]

Lacan's counter argument to such accusations is rather opaque, but it appears that he would argue that desire, founded in loss, never closes on a final signified but presses on from sign to sign in pursuit of impossible satiety. Thus, the signifying chain consists of 'rings of a necklace that is a ring in another necklace made of rings.'[24] Within the non-elitist chain, the phallus merely functions as an 'exchange value' – Lacan illustrates this point in his reading of Poe's 'The Purloined Letter' in which the letter of the title circulates between Queen, Minister and the detective Dupin, who eventually restores it back to its original position.[25] And while Lacan never identifies the letter with the phallus, we are invited to make the inference. Thus the letter/phallus ends up back into the possession of the Queen which suggests that the mother, rather than the father, is the rightful owner.

The Real, Desire and *Jouissance*

As Sean Homer states:

> The difficulty of understanding the real is partly due to the fact that it is not a 'thing'; it is not a material object in the world or the human body or even 'reality'. For Lacan, our reality consists of symbols and the process of signification…the real is the unknown that exists at the limit of this socio-symbolic universe and is in constant tension with it.[26]

The paradox of the real lies in this 'tension' – it supports our social reality while at all times undermining said reality:

---

[23] Elizabeth Grosz, *Jacques Lacan: A Feminist Introduction,* p.122.
[24] Jacques Lacan, *Écrits (*1977), p.153.
[25] Jacques Lacan, *Écrits* (2006), pp. 6 – 51.
[26] Sean Homer, *Jacques Lacan*, p.81.

> The Real is that which lies outside the symbolic process and it is to be found in the mental as well as in the material world: a trauma, for example, is as intractable and unsymbolizable as objects in their materiality…the Real, that is to say, is the endlessly daunting power which supersedes the already very considerable power that Lacan ascribes to the Symbolic.[27]

Unlike the symbolic however, the Real is monolithic and without any absence or opposition. It is, ultimately, impossible because it is impossible to imagine or attain. Take for example the infant who feels hungry. This hunger can be temporarily satisfied by breast or bottle-feeding but these are merely objects of hunger and in Lacan's theory wholly imaginary as they can never satisfy an infant's demand. The real is thus a place from which that need originates and is pre-symbolic in the sense that we have no way of symbolizing it. We know that it is real because we experience it, it enters into our discourse as a sign but the place from which it originates is outside of symbolization. As Alan Sheridan states in his 1989 translation of *Écrits*:

> The term 'real', which was at first of only minor importance… has gradually been developed. It began by presenting… a function of constancy: 'the real is that which always returns to the same place'. It then became that before which the imaginary faltered… hence the formula: 'the real is the impossible'. It is in this sense that the term begins to appear regularly… to describe that which is lacking in the symbolic order, the inclinable residue of all articulation, the foreclosed element, which may be approached, but never grasped: the umbilical cord of the symbolic.[28]

Paradoxically, the real also has connotations of matter, implying a material substance underlying the imaginary and symbolic. There is also a connection between the Real and the realm of biology – the body in actuality – and throughout his work, Lacan uses the Real to shed light on a number of clinical phenomena including trauma (not medical trauma but the way in which Real becomes the object of anxiety) and hallucination. Succinctly, no matter how we try to put our pain and suffering into language, to symbolize it, there is always something left over, a residue that cannot be transformed into language. This excess is the real and the real is thus associated with the death drive and *jouissance* as the ultimate, unspeakable limit of human existence. As Lacan states:

---

[27] Malcolm Bowie, *Lacan*, pp. 94-95.
[28] Jacques Lacan, *Écrits – A Selection* (1977), p.ix.

> Here we might return to the passage from Bataille quoted earlier: 'Dead matter, the pure idea, and God in fact answer a question in the same way … a question that can only be posed by philosophers, the question of the essence of things, precisely of the *idea* by which things become intelligible.' Psychoanalysis understands the symbiotic relation between matter and idea, object *qua* nominal essence as well as nominal essence *qua* object, it can dismiss neither science nor metaphysics, nor align itself wholly with either.[29]

Desire moves itself from one signifier to another trying to satisfy itself. For Lacan, 'what's important is to teach the subject to name, to articulate, to bring this desire into existence' but there is a limit to how far desire can be articulated in speech.[30]

Although the truth about desire is present in all speech, speech can never articulate the whole truth about desire. Desire is then the surplus produced by the articulation of need in demand and it can never be satisfied. According to Lacan:

> Desire is produced in the beyond (*l'au-delà*) of demand, in that, in articulating the life of the subject according to its condition, demand cuts off the need from that life. But desire is also hollowed on its near side (*son en-deçà*) in that, as an unconditional demand of presence and absence, demand evokes the want-to-be under the three figures of the nothing that constitutes the basis of the demand for love, of the hate that even denies the other's being, and of the unspeakable element in that which is unknown in its request.[31]

For Lacan, all our human drives are the manifestation of a single force called desire and there is only one object of desire – *object petit a*. The *object a* signifies the Other's lack – not in the sense of a specific object that is lacking but lack itself – the lack around which the symbolic order is structured. It ultimately represents an object of anxiety and the final reserve of the libido.

Contrary to desire which moves from one signifier to another in an attempt to justify itself, *jouissance* is absolute. Dylan Evans defines *jouissance* thus:

---

29 Jacques Lacan and Joan Copjec, *Television: A Challenge to the Psychoanalytic Experiment*, p.149.
30 Jacques Lacan, *The Seminar. Book II,* p. 275.
31 Jacques Lacan, *Écrits (*1977), p.265.

> The pleasure principal functions as a limit to enjoyment; it's a law which commands the subject to 'enjoy as little as possible.' At the same time, the subject constantly attempts to transgress the prohibitions imposed on his freedom, to go 'beyond the pleasure principal'. However, the result of transgressing the pleasure principal is not more pleasure, but pain, since there is only a certain amount of pleasure that the subject can bear. Beyond this limit, pleasure becomes pain, and this 'painful pleasure' is what Lacan calls *jouissance* .[32]

The belief in excessive *jouissance* is sustained through fantasy, one of the key ways through which we reconcile ourselves to dissatisfaction with our *jouissance.* This ultimate limit which we cannot overcome is always related to the death drive which Lacan's situates in the symbolic. Lacan affirmed Freud's theory that the death drive is associated with repetition but argued that we are not driven towards death but *by* death. According to Tim Dean:

> It bears repeating that the death drive is not an essentialist or organicist concept, since it derives from an inference about the effect of language on bodily matter; it as cultural subjects that humans are afflicted with the death drive. There is no essential, inborn death drive; rather, the dysfunctional, antinaturalistic way in which partial drives fail to conduce towards life lends every drive an uncanny, death like quality.[33]

If *jouissance* is Lacan's version of 'Beyond the Pleasure Principle' it is important to remember that this concept remains crucial in his approach to literature. It is a complex term, especially fruitful in the handling of clinical cases but literature provides another privileged field of investigation. In his reading of Joyce and Poe, Lacan identifies the structural function of a letter that never betrays its contents but gives shape to the libidinal object by which the subject is determined. His seminar on Poe's 'Purloined Letter' is an example of this and its importance is reflected by Lacan giving it the place of honour in *Écrits*.

---

[32] Dylan Evans, *Dictionary of Lacanian Psychoanalysis*, pp. 91-92.

[33] Tim Dean, 'Lacan and Queer Theory', in Jean-Michel Rabaté (ed.), *The Cambridge Companion to Lacan*, p.247.

CHAPTER THREE

JOHN BRODERICK

JOHN BRODERICK (1924 – 1989) was born in Athlone in 1924 where his family owned a prosperous bakery. His childhood was marked by two seminal events – the death of his father in 1927 and his mother's subsequent remarriage to the bakery manager. Growing up in a provincial midlands town during the nineteen-thirties he was, in his own words, 'ill-at-ease with people outside my own family circle' and it was this painful diffidence, compounded by his mother's *nouveau-riche* sensibilities, which demarcated the early life of the author.[1] He first attracted attention as an accomplished broadcaster and book reviewer and it was through this medium he expounded his Francophilia, his pre-modernist tastes and staunchly orthodox concerns. Post-Vatican II, his sympathies would have probably been with Archbishop Lefèbvre – in Broderick's words, 'this attitude of forging change and a particular brand of liberalism on the laity was really the same old Curial method put behind a different policy.'[2] His attitude towards the clergy reflects his frustration at the direction the Church was taking: 'The average priest, intoxicated…drunk with the power of the charismatic idea, loses no opportunity to express his ego, which is usually an inflated one.'[3]

Hence the priest in his fiction is something of an aberration, either dourly apathetic or too consumed with pop trends and fads. This remained the case until more sympathetic portrayals began to emerge in his later fiction. His first novel, *The Pilgrimage*, was banned by the Irish Censorship Board in 1961. His early output was prolific – he published four novels in less than five years – but his later career was blighted by

---

[1] Gearoid O'Brien, 'John Broderick: A Life Vindicated', in *The Westmeath Examiner*, 1999, p. 17.

[2] John Broderick, 'A Man for all Seasons – Pope John XXIII', in Madeline Kingston (ed), *Stimulus of Sin: Selected Writing of John Broderick*, p.135.

[3] John Broderick, 'A Curate's Egg at Easter', in *The Irish Times*, 14 April 1979, p.7.

alcoholism and a general decline in his writing powers. He moved to Bath in 1981, and suffered a debilitating stroke shortly after the airing of a RTÉ interview in 1987 in which his sexuality was the main focus. If he was a homosexual, he never openly admitted to being one, but it would seem that his religious beliefs were ever in conflict with his personal desires. He died on the 28 May, 1989.

Broderick based the majority of his novels in his hometown of Athlone, leading certain critics to describe him, perhaps fancifully, as 'a kind of minor Balzac of the Irish midlands.'[4] There were twelve novels in total, his last, *The Irish Magdalen*, published posthumously in 1991. In this chapter, I aim to focus upon two of the early novels – *The Fugitives* (1962) and *The Waking of Willie Ryan* (1964) - with contrasting reference to some of his other novels. Despite a somewhat erratic authorial career, there are many reasons why Broderick is a suitable candidate in the framework of this book. In the context of Lacanian criticism there is much scope for interpretation in his work which I will later illustrate. As Patrick Murray states in an article from *Eiré-Ireland*:

> A critic with a taste for the psychoanalytical interpretation of authors and their work would certainly be tempted to read Broderick in Freudian terms. His father died at the age of forty-two when John was three years old. His mother, whose dominant influence on his life was evident to everyone who knew him, remarried. This was a step which did not enjoy her son's unqualified approval. The Hamlet-Oedipus parallel, whether justified or not, is inescapable.[5]

Secondly, in reference to what I termed the 'internationalisation of influence' in the development of the Irish novel, Eamon Maher's description of Broderick as an 'Irish novelist in the European tradition' is apposite.[6] On a very basic level, his work may draw a correlation with other lace-curtain melodramas such as Brinsley McNamara's *The Valley of the Squinting Windows*, but Broderick transcends this adumbrated précis through repeated allusion to the French Catholic school of authors and Mauriac in particular – 'the only literary influence of which he was aware.'[7] Mauriac, scrutinizer of the *coeurs inquiets* and foremost practitioner of a complex religious plerophory that defies any simple elucidation,

---

[4] Anon, 'Obituaries – John Broderick', in *The Daily Telegraph*, p.16.

[5] Patrick Murray, 'Athlone's John Broderick', in *Eire-Ireland*, p.29.

[6] Eamon Maher, *Crosscurrents and Confluences – Echoes of Religion in Twentieth Century Fiction*, pp. 110-121.

[7] Anon, 'Obituaries – John Broderick', in *The Irish Times*, 1 June 1989.

stands behind much of Broderick's earlier work. For example, I have little doubt that Broderick used Mauriac's early novel *La Baiser au Lépreux* as the basis for *The Pilgrimage.*

Balzac, not surprisingly, was another influence as they share the same preoccupation with human emotions, with provincial life and mundane routine, with physical and material captivation, with psychology and introspection — particularly in regards to the feminine subconscious – and a preoccupation with the possibility of salvation, even with spirituality.[8] As Maher attests: 'In my view he owes more to a European, and more specifically French, tradition of challenge and protest than he does to any Irish influence. He did not hesitate to expose the foibles inherent in the Ireland of his time.'[9] This act of defiance came at a cost, for his first novel, *The Pilgrimage* (with a foreword by Julien Green), was promptly banned in Ireland and he earned a reputation as a purveyor of 'dirty books.' Notably, he shares this dubious distinction with both McGahern (*The Dark*) and Moore (*Judith Hearne*).

Another reason why I chose Broderick is that he has been largely overlooked in academic criticism, while those few critical treatments of him have been, in the main, negative. However, this does not tell the whole story. In the words of John Kenny, Broderick was 'One of the important Irish "middle" writers from whom much about the sociology and history, if not its high aesthetics, can be learned.'[10] If such a thing as Irish Catholic school of writing emerges it will owe a debt to Broderick, a writer more in tune with European literary trends than any other of his generation, as will those who reflect upon the verve and pathos of his early work. In short, I feel he is an author worthy of re-examination, and I would hope this chapter goes some way towards justifying that assertion. Another reason would be that he shares a number of similar traits with John McGahern and Brian Moore – both literary and sociological comparisons abound. All three grew up in somewhat hermeneutical societies – Broderick's Athlone, McGahern's Leitrim borderlands and

---

[8] A number of reviewers have made a comparison between Broderick and Balzac. See Hugh Leonard, 'Overkill of the money-grubbers', Review of *An Apology for Roses*, in *The Irish Independent*, 27 January 1973; Benedict Kiely, 'A Black hymn to Mannon', Review of *An Apology for Roses*, in *Hibernia*, 2 February 1973; Douglas Sealy, 'In the darkest Midlands', Review of *The Pride of Summer*, in *The Irish Times*, 10 July 1976 and John Jordan, 'Misanthropy in the Midlands', Review of *The Pride of Summer*, in *The Irish Independent*, 10 July 1976.

[9] Eamon Maher, *Crosscurrents and Confluences,* p. 121.

[10] John Kenny, 'John Broderick', in *The Irish Times*, Saturday 29 May 1999.

Moore's Belfast Catholic enclave. All three suffered the effects of censorship early on in their career and all three chose to emigrate, albeit briefly in McGahern's case. Feminine psychology plays an integral part in the novels of all three authors as does the preoccupation with sin, salvation, causality and redemption. While they had a difficult relationship with the Catholic Church, Christian themes and motifs proliferate in their work.

The Fugitives

First published by Weidenfeld and Nicolson in 1962, *The Fugitives* concerns a young IRA gunman, Paddy Fallon, on the run after a political assassination, returning to his home town (a thinly veiled Athlone) in search of sanctuary. With him comes his minder, Hugh Ward. A triumvirate is created with the introduction of Paddy's sister, Lilly, home from London in search of her brother. Lily quickly falls under the Svengali-like influence of Ward. Her relationship with Paddy is problematic at best, while Paddy regresses into puerile abstractions in which his sexual attraction to his sister is reawakened. The other significant players are Lily and Paddy's stepmother, Hetty, her friend Mrs Langan and the bedridden Aunt Kate.

As the novel progresses, Lily seems to fall in love with Ward who happily leads her on, for through such partial relationships does he retain his power. As the net around Paddy tightens, he becomes increasingly agitated. Ward removes him to a safe house on the bog and after a short interval, Lily joins them there. It isn't long before the police uncover their whereabouts and on a chaotic night, as the police are about to capture Paddy, Lily exposes Ward's homosexual attraction for her brother. In the ensuing melee, Lily accidentally shoots and kills her brother. The novel closes in a conversation between Mrs Langan and Hetty, where it transpires that Ward has been imprisoned and Lily given a suspended sentence. She returns to England though her life as a 'kept woman' has been exposed.

One thread which works its way through *The Fugitives* recurs in both *The Leavetaking* and *Cold Heaven* – the death drive. By situating the death drive firmly in the symbolic, Lacan articulates it with culture rather than nature. As Lacan states: 'The death instinct is only the mask of the symbolic order.'[11] Accordingly, it is only through death that we can be

[11] Jacques Lacan, *The Seminars. Book II,* p. 326.

truly free from the symbolic order – that is, if every drive is virtually a death drive, then every drive is an attempt to go beyond the pleasure principle, to the realm of excess '*jouissance*' where enjoyment is experienced as suffering. Ergo, compounded experience is essentially nihilistic. This strand of nihilism is evident throughout *The Fugitives* as we shall see, but also in the rejection of moral and religious principals in both the aforementioned novels.

This is essentially why I chose to critique *The Fugitives* as a representative text of Broderick's – it represents a waiting game in much the same way Patrick Moran in *The Leavetaking* awaits the disclosure from the school authorities that he has been living in sin, a situation that is counterpoised with his vigil at the bedside of his dying mother, and Marie who also waits by the bedside of an ailing husband in *Cold Heaven*. They all wait for a sign, the next link in the path through the network of signifiers which constitute the symbolic world of the subject. Each drive bears the mark of impossibility – each is desire seeking and failing to find its point of satiation. Failing to find this point, it pursues its own extinction: 'every drive is virtually a death drive.'[12] Lacan, in his later writings, would simplify Freud's *Todestrieb* by deeming that its action is merely immanent to the signifying chain; that is, the subject comes into being barred by the signifier and thereby injected with a sense of death. The protagonists' desire for death in *The Fugitives* is not something acquired through experience – it has been there from the beginning, a gift from the signifier, and one that cannot be refused. According to Bowie:

> The drive, as it circles round the excavated centre of being, is pulled outwards towards the objects that promise gratification, but inwards too towards the completest form of a loss that it already knows.[13]

In *The Fugitives*, the spectre of death is pervasive. Lily speaks 'in a dead voice' (*TF*, 8). The drawing room in the family home is 'the dead end of a dead end' (*TF*, 12). Aunt Kate and Hetty 'inhabit the big, empty house like strangers, waiting silently for death' (*TF*, 16), while for Hetty, 'only the dead, the dying, the anointed could touch the strong hidden current of life within her' (*TF*, 17).

[12] Jacques Lacan, *Écrits* (2006), p.848.
[13] Malcolm Bowie, *Lacan,* p.163.

Memory

The murder that opens the novel is alluded to in a series of flashbacks. When Lily Fallon returns home from London, the word 'remember' is used six times in the first three pages. In the signifying chain, the past is recorded in the chain itself, determining what is yet to come. Rather than being remembered by the individual in an active way, that is, with some sort of subjective participation, things are remembered for Lily by the signifying chain. Lacan makes it clear that memory is not biological, for memory is the symbolic history of the subject, thus something is memorable only when it is 'registered in the signifying chain.'[14]

The phenomena associated with memory which most interest the analyst are those moments when something goes wrong with the memory, when the subject cannot recall a part of their history. Lily cannot remember the barmaid who greets her at the station. She claims to remember the taxi driver but this is merely an excuse to flee the inquisitiveness of Eileen Foley. Her face is 'the face of a stranger' while 'the station meant nothing to her' (*TF*, 8-9). All these memories increase Lily's sense of isolation in the privacy of her own self so that the boundaries of time and place become limits she is reluctant to accept as real. Hence, when the author refers to Lily, he states: 'Few people ever listen to others when they are trapped in a dream: they seek the verbal echo of their own illusions' (*TF*, 127). As Lacan says in his seminar on 'The Purloined Letter':

> Such is the case of the man who retreats to an island to forget, what? He has forgotten – such is the case of the minister who, by not using the letter, winds up forgetting it…But the letter, no more than the neurotics unconscious, does not forget him.[15]

The unconscious cannot forget in an autonomous way; it preserves in the present what has affected it in the past, eternally holding onto each and every element, remaining forever marked by all of them. In the second chapter, Lily's step-mother, Hetty, claims not to recognize her when she arrives in from the station. This part of the ritual that they enact. When she asks Hetty whether her brother Paddy has returned home, her response is: "'Paddy? Paddy?' she repeated vaguely, 'What Paddy?'" (*TF*, 11) The ritual began with Paddy's murder of the politician. Here the parts are being

---

[14] Jacques Lacan, *The Seminar Book VII,* p.212.
[15] Jacques Lacan, *Écrits,* (1977) pp.24/25.

played out accordingly. If past events are repressed from memory, they return by expressing themselves in actions; when the subject does not remember the past, therefore, he is condemned to repeat it by acting it out. For Lily: 'No matter how often she rehearsed her meetings with her step-mother the old woman always defeated her. It was no good knowing exactly how she would act' (*TF*, 10). From a Lacanian perspective, the basic definition of acting out is true but incomplete; it ignores the dimension of the Other. Thus, while Lacan maintains that acting out results from a failure to recollect the past, he emphasises the intersubjective dimension of recollection. For Evans:

> Recollection does not merely involve recalling something to consciousness, but also communicating this to an Other by means of speech. Hence acting out results when recollection is made impossible by the Other to listen. When the Other has become 'deaf', the subject cannot convey a message to him in words, and is forced to express the message in actions.[16]

Hetty's questions are 'deceptively simple', and the old woman has 'a genius for confusion' (*TF*, 10). If memory is the past, trying to recall it presently could be perceived objectively – we always recall objectively because we do it through language. The inability to recall because of repression causes us to act it out and through this we witness the distance between past and present, symbolic and real. That distance highlights objectivity and proves the universality of language.

In chapter 3, Lily enters into her aunt's room and again, memory is invoked in the opening three lines: '"I heard your step on the stairs and you went across to the drawing room door, didn't you? Don't you remember that everything can be heard in this house?"' (*TF*, 12). Her aunt calls her 'child' and during her first encounter with her brother, she is treated as such:

> 'Shut up, will you? He rasped at her, leaning forward and pounding the table with his fists. 'Shut your mouth. Do you expect me to tell you things like that?'
>
> 'I'm sorry Paddy,' she said humbly, plucking nervously at the tablecloth. 'I didn't think. It's just that I can't grasp this yet. I think Aunt Kate feels the same. It's too big for us, too terrible.'
>
> 'Women are all the same,' said her brother scornfully. (*TF*, 23)

---

[16] Dylan Evans, *An Introductory Directory of Lacanian Psychoanalysis*, p.3.

Mother-Father-Son-Sister-Brother-Lovers

Yet on other occasions, Lily appears as a surrogate wife and mother. Paddy was 'ten years younger than she was and she had always mothered him' and in the sentence after that, she upbraids her brother: '"I thought you didn't drink, Paddy," she said, with a touch of her old maternal severity"' (*TF*, 20). Later in the novel, Paddy forces himself onto Lily: 'Before she realized what he was doing he had seized her by the arms, imprisoned her in his arms and kissed her on the lips' (*TF*, 55). She says of the incident: 'It was as if she were groping in the darkness half-asleep and touched something at once repugnant and pleasurable' (*TF*, 56). Thus the sexual relationship between brother and sister blurs into paternal/maternal concern and even crosses over, breaching the incest taboo. In chapter 7, Ward is first introduced with his hand resting on Paddy's arm. When Ward removes the hand, he removes it 'from the boy's arm' (*TF*, 34). Her concern for her brother is described by Ward as 'pragmatic': 'Wives, sisters and mothers are always pragmatists' (*TF*, 36). Ward duly steps into this relationship with the words: 'One may as well complete the circle' (*TF*, 35). Ward thereafter becomes a father figure to Paddy: '"It's my job to see that no harm comes to you." His hand slid around the boy's shoulder in a protective gesture. He was smiling now, affable, paternal' (*TF*, 38).

The effect of castration, which is to say the incest taboo, is to divide the set of all women into two categories: accessible and inaccessible. However, the mythical father of the primal horde is said not to have succumbed to castration and thus knows no limits. According to Lacan, the primal father lumps all women into the same category: accessible. As Bruce Fink states:

> The fact that every single man is nevertheless defined by both formulas – one stipulating that he is altogether castrated and the other that some instance (*Instanz*) negates or refuses castration – shows that incestuous wishes live on indefinitely in the unconscious. Every man, despite castration, continues to have incestuous dreams in which he grants himself the privileges of the imagined pleasure finding father who knows no bounds.[17]

Insofar as the ego-ideal serves to anchor one's sense of self, to tie it to the approval or recognition of a parental Other, its absence leaves one with a

[17] Bruce Fink, *The Lacanian Subject*, p. 111.

precarious sense of self, a self-image that is liable to deflate at certain critical moments. When Lily passes her brother's bedroom door in chapter 8, she hears 'intimate laughter' (*TF*, 43) between Paddy and Ward. In chapter 10, Paddy partially assumes the ruse of passing off Ward as his sister's fiancé and throws a drunken party where he kisses his sister on the lips. He also queries Ward's heterosexuality when he exclaims: '"Go on, give her a kiss, Hugh... what sort of man are you? Don't you like women?"' (*TF*, 55) In chapter 14, again Lily and Ward assume familial relations, Ward states, in a paternal fashion: '"Do you think we ought to be getting back? We've been out the whole afternoon. Paddy might be worried"' (*TF*, 77). In chapter 16, these roles are again reversed when Ward attempts a clumsy seduction of Paddy: 'caressing his wrist with his thumb' (*TF*, 90) Rebuffed, he goes in search of Lily and in their ensuing conversation, the following lines are again significant:

> 'You're very fond of your brother aren't you?'
> 'Most people have some family feelings', said Lily flippantly
> 'Not often as much as you have for Paddy...' (*TF*, 96)

Paddy's appearance in chapter 4 confirms his essential femininity: 'his long, delicate fingers', 'ivory skin', 'he had always been careful about his clothes', a smile 'at once sweet and slightly mocking' (*TF*, 20). Lacan suggested that the masculine structure is related to a kind of 'totalization' brought on by the symbolic father, whereas feminine structure is related to a kind of 'nontotalization'; when the paternal function is missing from a boy's life, totalization does not occur and the boy takes on a certain element of feminine structure.[18] On other occasions, when a break in the structure occurs through fevered moments of anxiety, Paddy's imaginary identifications collapse, and his essentially feminine position re-emerges or forces itself upon him. The blurring of lines between brother, sister and father brings about an oedipal struggle re-enacted, and given that the 'true' father is palpably absent in this drama, the law which regulates human relationships is un-enforced – indeed it is dangerously revoked. Paddy's behaviour and mannerisms are akin to Ward's, the surrogate father, in particular his sadism:

> Suddenly Paddy was at her side. His voice was sharp and ugly: she was reminded of the voice of the stranger (Ward) in the shop two days ago.

[18] Jacques Lacan, *Écrits* (1977), p.206.

> 'What did you do that for?' He grasped her arm and dug his fingers into the flesh.
>
> 'You're hurting me Paddy. What do you mean? I thought you didn't want her to know?' (*TF*, 21)

What is covered over by the sadist's fantasies, Lacan tells us, is that he is seeking to isolate 'Object a', which comes into being due to the law that is applied to it.[19] Anxiety is not like fantasy, it always indicates that the object is about to be lost and the sadist's aim thus is not anxiety itself, but what it attests to: the object to which the law applies. The sadist believes that is would be the symbolic Other's will to wrest the object from him, to take away his *jouissance,* if only the Other really existed. The sadist, for whom the law has not operated, plays the part of the Other in his scenario in order to make the Other exist, and seeks to isolate for his victim the object to which the law applies. Thus the sadist plays both parts of the law; he is legislator and subject of the law and the one on whom the limit is imposed. Paddy remains something of an object for m/Other's desire, never becoming someone who can see himself as valued for his symbolic achievements. As Aunt Kate states: "'I don't know Lily,' she murmured brokenly. 'All I know is that nothing we can do will ever help Paddy'" (*TF*, 137). It may be argued, that because castration was never fully completed, it is the ever-repeated staging of castration that brings Paddy a quasi-form of *jouissance.* The object of his desire is his sister, the surrogate mother, and while Lacan argues that one is always faced with a choice – to accept or deny castration – Paddy appears to choose a middle away, normalising his relationship with the actual mother and transferring the potentiality of desire onto his sister, forever on the cusp of seeking out that absolute *jouissance* which is never fully regained despite all attempts on his behalf to do so.

Women

In chapter 6, there is a rather loaded sentence which begins: 'She loved to drift, filling in her empty days with the deferred luxury of a visit to the cinema, a walk in the park, a new book, a gramophone record' (*TF*, 32) and in the next paragraph: 'She thought of taking a job again; but she had become too accustomed to idleness' (*TF*, 33). Lily's character is akin to that of Julia Glynn from *The Pilgrimage*, a hedonistic creature, who

[19] Jacques Lacan, *The Seminars. Book XI,* p. 183-186.

associates: 'love with luxury, with pleasure given and accepted lightly, almost casually.'[20] Julia too was educated in a very old tradition: 'that of the sensitive courtesan to whom the luxury of idle days is the very breath of life.' Ultimately, these characters are sensualists: 'products of years of rich foods, over-heated houses, soft beds, fine linen and financial security' (*WR*, 81).

The common equation between these two women is money. It is a recurrent concern for the author who stated in an interview: 'I came from a very highly respectable family because they had money. That was the way to achieve respect in Ireland: to have money.'[21] The most obvious feature of the theory of money is that it appears to be subsumed within a general theory of exchange in which the act of giving imposes an obligation upon the recipient. The process of exchange is of key importance in the story – Lily exchanges sex for financial security in much the same casual way that Hetty exchanges gossip with Mrs Langan while Aunt Kate exchanges one form of ascetic life for another – her room is likened to 'a convent cell, except that no religious objects, no crucifix, statue or rosary were to be seen' (*TF*, 13).

There is, of course, no satisfaction drawn from these exchanges. Lily is no happier in London than she is in Athlone, despite her best efforts to disguise this fact – her decision to embark upon an affair with Tom is merely a way in which she can avoid making any choice whatever. For example, when she begins a letter addressed to Tom, she finds that: 'she could think of nothing to say' (*TF,* 33). According to Lacan, men and women are defined differently with respect to language – that is, with respect to the symbolic order. While men are defined by being wholly hemmed in by the phallic function, women are defined as the exact opposite – a woman is not split in the same way as a man and, though alienated, she is not altogether subject to the symbolic order. A woman's pleasure is only partially determined by the signifier and they are no less 'whole' than men except when considered in terms of the phallic function. Masculine or feminine structures, as related to the different sides of Lacan's formulas of sexuation, are able to situate themselves either side of the rigid level of sexual identity. These two levels, which often come into conflict, correspond to the ego and subject. At the level of ego identification, a woman may well identify with her father whereas at the

[20] John Broderick, *The Pilgrimage*, p. 21.

[21] Julia Carlson, *Banned in Ireland: Censorship and the Irish Writer*, p.43.

level of desire and of her subjective capacity of *jouissance*, she may be characterised by a feminine structure.

A woman's sexual identity can, in fact, involve many different possible combinations, for unlike masculine and feminine structure, which in Lacan's view constitute an either/or, there being no middle ground between them, ego identifications can include elements from many different persons, both male and female. In other words, the imaginary level of sexual identity can be extremely self-contradictory. The exchange between Lily and Tom, as described in chapter 6, is fairly perfunctory: 'a sop to her conscience, and exactly the sort of sensible arrangements he wanted' (*TF*, 31). Contrast this arrangement to her pursuit of Ward or her sexual encounter in the alley, where she assumes the masculine/mentor's role: '"No, no, not like that… yes, yes, that's it. Like that"' (*TF*, 134). Lily's sexual dichotomy again resembles Julia Glynn, who scolds her lover Stephen with the words: '"You must learn to make love properly. Who's been making love to you? That's not the way to live. If ever I saw a body made for it you've got it. From now on you're going to learn what to do with it."' These are almost the exact same words that one of Julia's lovers, Kurtz, spoke to her during an early affair.[22]

It seems then, that Broderick's fiction affirms the subjectivity of women in a patriarchal society. The only positive female representation in the entire novel is that of Mrs Finan - 'If anybody ever put their purgatory over them in this world it was poor Tessie Finan' (*TF*, 105) or Mrs Foley's daughters Maggie and Peg: 'giving up every minute of their lives in the convent' (*TF*, 46) – while the rest are 'kept-women' (Lily) silly, foolish girls (Eileen Foley), sadistic and bitchy gossips (Hetty, Mrs Langan, Mrs Foley) or frigid ascetics (Aunt Kate). For Broderick, it would appear that women are conservative creatures of enclosed claustrophobic spaces, associated with treachery, and, in particular, death:

> The little knots of watching women in the street outside lingering with glassy eyes fastened on the dying woman's windows, their mouths parted in a half smile of sensual excitement. They were preparing for the age old ritual of death (*TF*, 112).

And in chapter 21:

---

[22] John Broderick, *The Pilgrimage*, p. 166.

> The men… stealing surreptitious looks at the drawn blinds, behind which the ritual was being enacted: the ritual which like birth, and bed, belonged they knew to the women (*TF*, 118).

And again in chapter 26: 'Every woman who has been scorched by the fires of sensuality will always choose death rather than lack of love' (*TF*, 148). Paddy's attitude towards women is akin also to those expressed by Ward:

> 'Women are all the same' said her brother scornfully. 'They can never understand anything except what's happening yesterday or the day before, or every day for the last thousand years. That's why they all gang up with the priests: they're all terrified of change' (*TF*, 23).

It is a statement that echoes, in some way, Lacan's comments on the *rapport sexuel*: 'The most naked rivalry between men and women is eternal.'[23] It is a claim that complements Freud's famous remark: 'We must reckon with the possibility that something in the nature of the sexual instinct itself is unfavourable to the realisation of complete satisfaction.'[24] Of course, Lacan did not mean that love cannot exist or that people do not revel in sexual pleasure. What does not exist is a romantic love that allows individuals to complete each other, making one of two, like the fabled creatures in Plato's *Symposium*. The impossibility of sexual relations is thus largely structural, our fates as subjects being divided by the unconscious. In *The Fugitives*, Lily is a kept woman, in a relationship that could be scarcely described as harmonious, but convenient perhaps. When Hetty and Mrs Langan speak about relations between the sexes, Mrs Langan states: 'Marriage is catching you know, like death' (*TF*, 67), and later, when discussing another neighbour, Mrs Finan, states:

> Oh will I ever forget! Six months in mortal agony. And all those poor little children running and crying about the house and that sot of a husband coming home drunk every single night (*TF*, 105).

As Lacan states:

> We know that sexual division, in so far as it reigns over most living beings, is that which ensures the survival of the species. Whether, with Plato, we place the species among the Ideas, or whether we say, with Aristotle, that it is to be found nowhere but in the individuals that support

[23] Jacques Lacan, *Seminar II,* p.263.
[24] Jean-Michel Rabaté, *The Cambridge Companion to Lacan*, p.229.

> it, hardly matters here. Let us say that the species survives in the form of its individuals. Nevertheless, the survival of the horse as a species has a meaning – each horse is transitory and dies. So you see, the link between sex and death, sex and the death of the individual, is fundamental.[25]

In a quasi-biographical article on Broderick, Patrick Murray would state: 'The novels also suggest that their author was a misogynist: he seems to have had little or no belief in the possibility of female virtue…his single female characters tend to abandon decent standards with alarming promptness.'[26] As Bowie states:

> There is no such thing as a sexual relationship, Lacan repeatedly announces at this time, because, although each partner plays the role of Subject to the other's Other, this dispensation can never produce symmetry and reciprocity: language always creates between them an intractable and unsheddable surplus of cargo of otherness…[27]

According to Bruce Fink: 'the phallus is the missing relationship between them.'[28] That is, there is no reciprocity between the male and female position because the symbolic order is fundamentally asymmetrical and the signifier that Fink refers to, the phallus, governs the relations between the sexes. The clear divide is again evident in *The Fugitives*: 'The men stood about scraping their heavy boots on the path, segregated with their own kind' (*TF*, 118). But it is in Broderick's third novel, *Don Juaneen*, where his views on sexual relations are best expressed through the pretentious and somewhat ridiculous Sybil Quill:

> Men were men and women were women. They came together for a brief period in the marriage bed; something that a woman had to put up with, since that too was the order of the universe. Otherwise the less time they spent together the better, in her opinion.[29]

Ritual and Sexual Desire

An issue of note in chapter 4 is the use of the word 'ritual': 'little knots of women stood about, occasionally glancing up at the window where the

---

[25] Jacques Lacan, *The Four Fundamental Concepts of Psycho-Analysis*, p.150.
[26] Patrick Murray, *Eire-Ireland*, p. 31.
[27] Malcolm Bowie, *Lacan*, p.154.
[28] Bruce Fink, *Lacan to the Letter – Reading Écrits Closely*, p.84.
[29] John Broderick, *Don Juaneen*, p. 112.

ritual of death was being enacted' (*TF*, 24). The word ritual also opens chapter 5: 'It was a ritual'. (*TF*, 25). Thereafter, the word frequently reappears: 'I suppose the only thing that can save you is ritual' (*TF*, 53); 'Going through the ritual movements of everyday life' (*TF*, 106); 'A progress as familiar to them as the ritual of a neighbour's funeral' (*TF*, 114); 'The ritual had been too long enacted for her to attempt to break it now' (*TF*, 144) and so on. I feel that the word ritual has two connotations in this novel – the ritual of expulsion and the ritual of religion, which I shall explain later. René Girard has argued in *La Violence et le sacré* that the expulsion of the scapegoat has a culturally stabilising function; to sacrifice him may be the way of ending what Girard calls a vicious circle of violence in the community and to make possible structuring processes and social differentiations.[30] Social harmony extends no further than the imitation of other people's desires; one needs to know what is desirable, at the same time that one needs to eliminate others in order to possess the objects which they have designated to the individual's parasitic appetites – this is what I would term the ritual of expulsion.

Desire is a threat to the form of realistic fiction that Broderick was trying to portray. Patrick Murray attests: 'As a novelist, he was firmly in the premodernist tradition.'[31] Broderick's fiction, akin to the nineteenth century novel, is haunted by the possibility of subversive moments, and it suppresses them with a brutality both shocking and eminently logical. In formal terms, disruptive desire could be thought of as a disease of disconnectedness in a part of the structure which rejects being defined by its relations to other parts and asserts an affinity with elements alien to the structure.

Realistic fiction admits heroes of desire in order to submit them to this ritual of expulsion. The hero, the embodiment of desire, is an intruder in a world of significantly related structures, of unambiguous beginnings and definitive conclusions. He is alien to the world of realistic fiction and that incompatibility is largely an *a priori* choice on the part of the novelist in favour of a particular kind of world which he severely judges but also – perhaps unintentionally – he supports. In Broderick's fiction, the punishment for desire is revelation, as Lily reveals in chapter 2: 'But Lily knew that the street was alive; coiled up, immobile, with hooded eyes; awake and watchful' (*TF*, 9). This idea is, perhaps, more explicitly expressed by Julia Glynn in Broderick's first novel, *The Pilgrimage*: 'She

---

[30] René Girard, *La Violence et le sacré,* p.78.
[31] Patrick Murray, *Éire-Ireland*, p.20.

had committed the ultimate sin: she had been found out.'[32] With revelation comes the ritual of expulsion, which, unless acted upon quickly, progresses into a drawn-out process of humiliation. In the Broderick novel, the community is habitually encapsulated in one or two elderly women, who provide a sort of Greek chorus behind the narration. In *The Fugitives*, we are introduced to Hetty Fallon and Mrs. Lagan with the loaded sentence that I referred to earlier: 'It was a ritual' (*TF*, 25). The two women represent the watchmen of society, taking perverse delight in scoring points over each other by dropping subtle hints and innuendoes on the other's affairs. Nothing escapes the Medusa's gaze. In particular, desire is ridiculed and any attempt to forego the deep-seated rituals of the community is met by a stern rebuke. As Hugh Ward epigrammatically states: 'Murder, if you like to call it that, has a long and honourable history in this country. Love has not' (*TF*, 61).

The ritual that Broderick speaks of has deeper connotations. Before they begin their bating match with one another, the Rosary is said, though probably with little conviction. In the McGahern novel, the Rosary was a symbol for family unity, something that drew the family together at the close of the day, whereas in the Broderick novel it has little meaning save as a sideshow for the theatre to come. The fear of desire in Broderick's fiction can be discussed as a fear of psychological fragmentation – after all, we first experience desire in our lives as naive confusion of the self with the world. In the scenic mode of desire, the theatricalized self is a series of pictures of the world. But are desires are also – and perhaps primarily – repressed. A sense both of the forbidden nature of certain desires and of the incompatibility of reality with our desiring imagination makes the negation of desire inevitable. But to deny desire is not to eliminate it; in fact, such denials multiply the appearance of each desire in the self's history. In denying a desire, we condemn ourselves to finding it everywhere. Repressed desire is repeated, disguised and sublimated – for Ward, his homosexuality is: 'the filthy thing he was looking for' (*TF* 167); for Lily: 'brief bouts of sensuality, followed by self-reproach and a sharp sense of guilt' (*TF*, 32), the 'curious sensation, half-pain, half-pleasure' (*TF*, 78) which overcomes her from time to time. Its reappearances in various forms at different levels of mental life create the intelligible structures, the psychic continuities which can be formulated as an individual's personality or character. The disguised repetitions of inhibited desires constitute the coherent self.

---

[32] John Broderick, *The Pilgrimage*, p.29.

The viability of the structured self depends on the impoverishment of desire. The desiring imagination's contacts with the world are limited by the need for preserving the intelligibility of a psychic structure. Even more dangerously, the renunciation of desire may increase our guilt instead of assuaging it. In a later scene in *The Fugitives*, when Ward attempts a forceful seduction, he is defeated by his own hypocrisy:

> 'All that bunkum about love. That's no game for a man. There's no such thing as love, you said so yourself.'
>
> 'Yes,' repeated Ward dully. 'I said so and a lot of other things I knew you wanted to hear. Oh, I said them all right.' (*TF*, 91)

Heightened guilt welcomes the potentially ferocious punishments of conscience and of external moral authority. An important psychological consequence of sublimated (civilized) desire may be suicidal melancholy. Paddy displays such a tendency, as Ward states: '"All the same Paddy does not want to be taken alive"' (*TF,* 63). But the endless repetition of desires suppressed by guilt and angry frustration ultimately leads to the fantasy of death as the absolute pleasure, which is why Paddy seems so willing to die for the cause. Ward lives out his fantasies through Paddy – he is like one of those toy soldiers he lines up into columns and divisions on his bed (*TF*, 92-93) – and this is recognized by Lily's Aunt Kate: '"What I mean is that some people live through adapting themselves to others. Ward is like that"' (*TF*, 126). The repeated refusal to confess their desires gives them a kind of criminally immoral activity from which only the definitive immobility of death might rescue Paddy, and through proxy, Ward himself. Once the ritual of death/expulsion has taken place, the containment of desire is announced as a triumph for social stability, and at the novel's close, we return once more to Hetty and Mrs Lagan ensconced in the snug, proclaiming Lily a 'dirty rotten slut' (*TF*, 169) whose sexual impropriety, when revealed: 'was the worst punishment she could have got' (*TF*, 170).

Ritual and Religion

According to Jung, the consciousness of primitive man was so little developed that the performance of rituals was necessary to focus his will to do anything other than the purely instinctual.[33] As Eugene O'Brien states:

---

[33] Carl Gustav Jung, 'Psychology and Religion', in *Psychology and Religion: West and East*, Vol. XI of *The Collected Works of C.G. Jung*, p.19.

> Catholicism has generally seen desire, especially sexual desire, as a negative human quality, in need of repression. The adequation of desire with sin has long been part of the Irish: the corollary of this ethico-moral equation – desire+sin=guilt – has led to serious consequences for individual development in Ireland.[34]

O'Brien has astutely linked the patristic structure of the Church with Lacan's 'Catholic' Symbolic order. The symbolic is, after all, the realm of movement rather than fixity, heterogeneity rather than similarity. And given that it is also the realm of language, culture, death and the unconscious, it wields a huge influence on the day-to-day activities of the subject. For Benvenuto and Kennedy:

> Language belongs to the Symbolic Order and in Lacan's view, it is through language that the subject can represent desires and feelings, and so it is through the Symbolic Order that the subject can be represented, or constituted.[35]

In post-modern Ireland, when one is asked to think of primary law-giver, one may naturally think of the father. It is through the father that the Law in Lacanian terms is underpinned and though primarily a linguistic construction, it is the structure that governs all form of social exchange, whether gift-giving, kinship relations or the formation of pacts. The legal-linguistic structure is basically the whole symbolic order and it is the father who imposes this law on the subject in the Oedipus complex.

However, in our day-to-day lives we find ourselves surrounded by a number of prohibitive agencies, and we are duly bound by a plethora of socio-judicial regulations. It is difficult today to image that the Church could have been one of these agents, irrespective of how closely it is linked with the patricidal/symbolic order. Its word no longer holds any significant cache today but in the period when the novel was written, it could be accurately described as one of the pillars of the 'symbolic system' of the new State.[36] And yet, despite its omnipotent presence in Irish society only a quarter century later, the historian J.J. Lee could write:

---

[34] Eugene O'Brien, '"Kicking Bishop Brennan up the arse…": Catholicism, Deconstruction and Postmodernity in Contemporary Irish Culture,' in Louise Fuller et al (eds), *Irish and Catholic? Towards an Understanding of Identity*, pp.50-51.

[35] Bice Benvenuto & Roger Kennedy, *The Works of Jacques Lacan*, p.81.

[36] The quote is from J.J. Lee in James Whyte, *History, Myth and Ritual in the Fiction of John McGahern*, p.95.

> The more comforting conclusion that 'what the Church is experiencing is less a crisis of faith than a crisis of culture' may be optimistic in a society where faith and culture are so intimately intertwined. It is precisely this close connection that leaves civic culture so vulnerable to rapid decline in the role of institutional religion. If religion were to no longer fulfil its historic civilising mission as a substitute for internalised values of civic responsibility, the consequences for the country no less for the Church could be lethal.[37]

Lee's comments were prescient and foresaw some of the changes which occurred in Ireland over the past twenty years. The sense of security and meaning offered by rituals and ceremonies conjures up, in some fashion, a careful delineation of safe psychic spaces, but in return it does not tolerate individuality and demands total conformity. This can be best explained in the following passage:

> Nothing would ever happen in that secret town that would divert the people from their slow, inexorable progress towards death; a process as familiar as the ritual of a neighbour's funeral. They were born with the curse of the future: they sat down with it every morning at the breakfast table; it was hung with the scapular, the holy medal round their necks; it was pinned up on the Church porch among the memorial cards. (*TF*, 114)

Broderick's representation of the institutional Church is generally negative, and formal religion is little more than a set of empty rituals, adhered to out of blind faith and deprived of all spiritual significance. It would seem that Aunt Kate's comment: 'Like the doctors and the priests… people are afraid of a hidden force they cannot understand' (*TF*, 40) reflects Lily's (and the rest of the population's) religious convictions, which are a 'rigid set of hieratic beliefs, accepted without thinking, without any real conviction, because they were the custom of the country' (*TF*, 32). Ward's comments in chapter 10 merely reinforce this:

> 'What do people do on a Sunday afternoon? Die?' He tapped the window lightly with the tassel. 'What makes it possible to live through a few thousand of them without going mad? The football match, the family rosary, the dirty book? I suppose the only thing that can save you is ritual. The same thing in the same place, day after day, year after year. And to go through with it you have to believe, or at least be afraid not to believe.' (*TF*, 53)

---

[37] J.J. Lee, *Ireland 1912 – 1985*, p. 657.

The Rosary, typically a central family ritual, is instead used by Hetty and Mrs. Langan as the opening parley in a near perpetual slagging match between the two. When Lily attends the funeral of Mrs Fagan, the funeral procession is likened to taking part in some 'ancient and terrible rite', 'a macabre spectacle' where everything was 'ritualistic, pre-ordained, at once familiar and deeply mysterious' (*TF*, 118-119). The author's own views on the Catholic Church are fraught with contradictions. In one interview, he railed against 'the zealots, the narrow-minded Opus Dei, Legion of Mary people' who 'took over' the running of the state.[38] Yet he was deeply upset by the changes that took place after Vatican II and the various liberalising trends which were adapted into the liturgy: 'It was scandalous enough to banish an ancient and beautiful liturgy with a complete disregard for the feelings and wishes of ordinary Catholics.'[39] In a later article for *The Irish Times*, he would develop this theme:

> It is intolerable that this Easter the same old congregations will kneel and sit through the same ceremonies, conducted in pidgin English by clergymen who for the most part can neither walk, talk, nor remain silent in a manner befitting the solemnity of the occasion…we are told that pop masses appeal to the young; which is like saying that Barbara Cartland should be encouraged because she appeals to more readers than Jane Austen.[40]

For Broderick: '[t]his attitude of forging change and a particular brand of liberalism on the laity was really the same old Curial method put behind a different policy.'[41] His attitude towards the clergy similarly reflects his frustration at the direction the Church was taking: 'The average priest, intoxicated…drunk with the power of the charismatic idea, loses no opportunity to express his ego, which is usually an inflated one.'[42] It appears that what appealed to the author was the smoke and mirrors of the Latin mass, the age-old ritual which, in *The Fugitives*, he so closely aligns with death and apathy. However, it is important to remember that the Church, as Broderick saw it, was divided into two separate spheres: there was the Church as extension of the community and the Church as the

---

[38] Julia Carlson, *Banned in Ireland*, p.48.

[39] John Broderick, 'Proper Studies – Review of Aldous Huxley's *The Human Situation'*, in *The Irish Times*, 4 February 1978.

[40] John Broderick, 'A Curate's Egg at Easter', in *The Irish Times*, 14 April 1979.

[41] John Broderick, 'A Man for all Seasons – Pope John XXIII', in *The Irish Times*, 15 November 1980.

[42] John Broderick, 'A Curate's Egg at Easter'.

extension of one's private faith. The former was damned by association, while the latter was instinctual and deeply personal.

This concept can be best examined through a theory developed by Ludwig Binswanger, a psychiatrist working in Switzerland at turn of the 20th century.[43] He developed Existential analysis to show relatedness between the environment (*Umwelt*), and the world of signals (*Mitwelt*) and a world of actions (*Aliticwelt*).[44] He argued that we are 'thrown' into the world in that we do not choose but we are obliged to accept this 'throwness', and derive meaning from that into which we are 'thrown.' Out of 'throwness', and awareness of a relation that is 'with-the-world' (*Mitwelt*), it argued that we gain understanding of our relationships with a world that is 'social' and that differentiates us from each other. We seem to move from being 'anonymous', through a period where our identity as part of a group (e.g. the family), to assume individual identity which separates us from the group. With further understanding, we assume a 'mode of being', which is reflective of our dual state of being-there (i.e. both physical, and spiritual). We seem to come to understand what it might be like being-there with ourselves (i.e. *Eigenwelt*), from our understanding of what it might be like being with others.

As such, we can use this classification to distinguish between the three areas of human living – the *Umwelt* is the world of social pressures and a major focus of the author. In *The Fugitives*, Ward duly describes how religion and community react against each other:

> Did you look round you at Mass this morning? A few thousand people going through a lot of mechanical movements, mouthing prayers they have forgotten the meaning of years ago… a decadent religion. Without thought, or any real feeling. A religion of organization. That's all that's necessary – join the regiment and toe the line. And for the man who says he will not serve there isn't even hell any more. That's too simple. They've laid that off now, you know, it's too dramatic, too romantic. No, they just leave you behind, outside the herd, in the desert. (*TF*, 53)

In contrast to the *Umwelt*, the *Eigenwelt* is the world of the self, the source of meaning and awareness within an individual while the *Midwelt* is the

---

[43] Michael Paul Gallagher also touched upon this theoretical distinction when discussing the early novels of John Broderick – see Michael Paul Gallagher, 'The Novels of John Broderick', in *The Irish Novel In Our Time,* pp.236-245.

[44] Ludwig Binswanger, *Being-in-the-World: Selected Papers of Ludwig Binswanger: Translated and with a Critical Introduction to His Existential Psychoanalysis,* pp. 84-102.

more intimate world of personal relations. There are certain close connections between these Hegelian classifications and those of Lacan's triumvirate – the real, the imaginary and the symbolic – but Binswanger's schema is particularly useful in ultimately explaining Broderick's complex religious plerophory.

Broderick's stance was a by-product, no doubt, of his staunchly 'Catholic' influences; in particular, Francois Mauriac. It is important to note that Mauriac also differentiated between the common-law believers whose substantiations were afflicted with 'intellectual poverty, base credulity, hatred, the fear of strange alluring passions, and, under the guise of edification, prejudice against the noble works in favour of false and foolish rhapsodies' and the more daring proponents of a internalised Christian faith – the *Eigenwelt*.[45] At the time of Mauriac's 'conversion', Catholicism in England and France was no longer the force it once had been. Mauriac railed against the dying of the sacramental light, and thus brought into being an intrinsic tenet of his philosophy: to be a true Christian is to suffer; we all have a cross to bear and we bear it, for the most part, alone. As Aunt Kate states:

> The whole of Catholicism is based on the need to atone, to suffer, to sacrifice. What is the mass but just that? It runs through all the Gospels. There are other things, of course, but that is the fundamental thing. (*TF*, 128)

The Church in Ireland, during the early 1950s, had reached its zenith. It was in stark contrast to the crumbling edifice in France, but because it was not being persecuted, because it did not seem to be struggling against the tides of agnosticism, because it was so closely associated with the community, Broderick did not correlate the Church with that of Mauriac's time. There was no struggle, no pain, in being an isolated Catholic in Ireland. After all, in a population that was ninety-five percent Catholic, of which ninety percent went to Mass on a Sunday, the similarities to the increasingly secular France of Mauriac's novels were scant indeed.[46] Thus, Broderick linked the Church with the community, the *Umwelt*, or, as he said in an interview with Julia Carlson: 'The people in power in Ireland in the twenties and thirties were very narrow-minded, and I think they got the

---

[45] François Mauriac, *The Stumbling Block*, p.166.

[46] The figures were taken from F.S.L. Lyons *Ireland Since the Famine*, pp. 688-690.

Church they wanted.'[47] The true Church represents an internalised faith – the realm of *Eigenwelt* – which Broderick certainly believed in, and bore no parallel to the post-Vatican II 'sideshow'.

The Undermining of Ritual

The key reason why I choose to examine *The Fugitives* is that it foreshadows a number of key trends in Irish society. I have explained how the family unit, based upon a supposedly immutable patriarchal structure, is undermined in the novel. The 'real' father is absent from the text and the surrogate father, Ward, is duplicitous rather than domineering, destructive rather than protective, effeminate rather than masculine. The Church, again a supposedly patriarchal edifice, is dominated by women and beleaguered by hypocrisy and spiritual indifference. The third great symbol of Irish patriarchy – nationalism – is a central theme in the novel and again, it is found wanting. Ward is the embodiment of the nationalist cause but Lily appears to sum up the essential shallowness of its chief acolyte:

> 'Do you know what he thought you were, do you, Paddy? He doesn't give a damn about Ireland, or freedom, or martyrs or all the rest of that nonsense. He only wanted you…' (*TF*, 167).

The cause is thus as empty or opportunistic as the Church and the grand narratives of Irish society are shown up as false and misleading. In the early 1960s, given the triumphant nature of the State's celebration of the 1916 Rising, backed by the seemingly omnipotent nature of the Church, this was scarcely apparent. But by the 1970's, the Easter Rising was no longer celebrated for the ironic fear of being associated with or hijacked by the Provisional IRA while the Church began to falter, collapsing under the weight of its own obduracy. Thus the violence in the North destroyed the fig-leaf of southern proto-nationalism; an act made palpable by the tragic-comic proceedings that was the Arms Trial. The Church meandered onwards, caught in a cul-de-sac of outmoded theocracy, but by the early 1990s it had imploded, giving to rise to Mary Kenny's comment, when she 'marked 1992 as the year when Catholic Ireland began to slide into retreat and decline, the year when Irish Catholicism was seen as being wrong.'[48]

---

[47] Julia Carlson, *Banned in Ireland – Censorship and the Irish Writer*, p. 39.
[48] Mary Kenny, *Goodbye to Catholic Ireland*, p.373.

In 2006, the following statistics fully reveal the collapse in the Church's standing:

> Not quite half of Ireland's adults attend Mass each week, according to a survey conducted by the state's RTE broadcast network. The survey found that 13% of Irish people attend daily Mass, and another 35% go to Mass every Sunday. The total of 48% attending Mass at least weekly represents a sharp drop from 1990, when a survey put the figure at 81%.[49]

The role of the Irish male in the family unit has also become more ambiguous, with the rise of single mothers, house-husbands and dual income families. One of the key symbolic events of this time was the ascension of Mary Robinson as President of Ireland in what had been a stubbornly male-only club, and in its way, it seemed to reflect the changing nature of Irish society as a whole – within five years, the Church's moral standing had disintegrated under a welter of sexual abuse charges, the birth of the Celtic Tiger economy brought in a new wave of secularism and unabashed materialism which finally put to rest De Valera's notion of frugal yet virtuous comfort, while in the North, the Downing Street Declaration heralded the first, and soon to be lasting, IRA ceasefire. Thus, *The Fugitives* acts as a weathervane for the changes to come, neatly dissembling and discrediting the Irish sociological strata, which ultimately manifests itself in the closing lines of the novel, where we witness Hetty attending a dying woman who might as well stand for pre-modern Catholic Ireland as a whole (*TF*, 173).

The Waking of Willie Ryan

First published by Weidenfeld and Nicolson in 1965, the novel is centred on the character of Willie Ryan, wrongly committed to an asylum for twenty years, who makes a dramatic return to the lives of his brother and sister-in-law, the petit-bourgeois Ryans. It is a traumatic return, because Willie had been imprisoned by his family, in collusion with the Parish Priest, Father Mannix. Willie had been involved with a group of homosexual men and in particular a gentleman farmer called Roger Dillon, whose existence had threatened the corporate respectability of Irish small-town society. Society had closed ranks and offered him up as a scape-goat for its own hypocrisy. Recovering from the initial shock, every effort is

---

[49] Catholic Culture website:
http://www.catholicculture.org/news/features/index.cfm?recnum=44521.

bent on reconciling him to his religion – if Willie will make this outward act of submission, then he will have publicly acknowledge the error of his ways and face will have been saved all round.

But Willie will not submit. Father Mannix now comes round every evening to convert him. The priest engages in a battle of wills with Willie, of which the priest is at first confident of victory: for this, he relies upon Roger Dillon's apparent conversion to convince Willie to return to the flock. Willie, however, has yet to play his trump card. Roger's 'conversion' was no more than a piece of showmanship; he continued on the affair with Willie whilst attending Mass, taking apparent pleasure in misleading the Catholic mob which he held in disdain all his life. Willie moves in with his nephew Chris and partner Susan, both of whom, through their friendship with Willie, attempt to defy the hypocrisy of the community.

Father Mannix's final manoeuvrings become increasingly desperate. He is shocked by Willie's admittance that he is attending the Mass arranged ostensibly for the benefit of blessing the new house, as a sop to Susan, whom he did not wish to upset. Fr. Mannix learns that Willie accepted the sacrament without confession; he is incensed, describing Willie as 'insane,' 'disgusting,' finally, with a hoarse shout, condemning him as 'evil.' Willie's check-mate, his revelation, is enough to stop him in his tracks:

> 'Roger never gave up what you like to "vice". If it's of any interest to you now I never wanted it, not with him anyway. It was he who – how would you put it? – seduced me. Yes, that's how you'd put it. I hated it; but I did it because I loved him' (*WR*, 152).

Certainly, Willie is not the only one due a reawakening. Father Mannix alone offers an apology for his actions, and Willie, though embittered, turns the other cheek: 'he pressed his hot cheek against the glass' and the two men appear partially reconciled at the last. (WR, 160) *The Waking of Willie Ryan* is akin to Broderick's first novel, *The Pilgrimage*, in that Willie receives a final grace in the form of a Mrs Whittaker, who reveals that her brother, Roger, was distraught that Willie would never forgive him for his hypocrisy.

When she reveals that knew all about their affair, that 'some good can come out of evil,' because she was able to help her brother at the last, Willie is finally able to come to terms with the past. (*WR* 184-185) If the miracle of Michael Glynn's rehabilitation is grounded in a sceptic's belief, then the reconciliation of Willie Ryan is more a temporal concordance with the living and the dead.

Colour

In contrast to *The Fugitives*, *The Waking of Willie Ryan*, opens in a riot of colour – 'the white hen', 'red as a sea snapper', 'blue line of the Slieve Bloom Mountain', 'gold in the summer', 'green in the spring', silver in the winter' (*WR*, 9), 'purple in summer', 'black as a night beast', 'golden only for a brief time', 'tongues of flame', 'white hair', 'white hand' (*WR*, 10), 'white coiling hand', 'red to purple', 'light and yellow as brimstone' (*WR*, 11), and so on. The use of colour is omnipresent, but then colours do play a significant role in the epistemological, personal and social lives of human beings. Colours are important epistemologically, as natural signs or indicators for the identification and re-identification of physical objects. Lacan defines the sign thus: 'the whole ambiguity of the sign derives from the fact that it represents something for someone…any node in which any signs are concentrated, in so far as they represent something, may be taken for a someone.' The sign duly stands in contrast to the signifier, which is 'that which represents a subject for another signifier.'[50] The signs are either natural or conventional, the latter being ones designed for various social purposes. The purposes are equally well served even if objects do not have colours, but have the right appearances. From a social point of view, colours serve a variety of purposes. While retaining their function as natural signs, they also serve as conventional signs, for example as badges, uniforms, in ceremony, ritual, etc.

Religion and superstition are close expressions of the same sense of the spiritual. These forces are all contained, shaped and made safe in the social forms imposed upon them. Rituals, with their patterns of sequences and precedence, cause things to become interrelated; they create form and schemes which order life and make it meaningful. Lacan presented religion as a denial of the truth as cause of the subject and argued that the function of sacrificial rites is to seduce God, to arouse His desire: 'At this level, the artist is operating on a sacrificial plane – he is playing with those things… that may arouse the desire of God.'[51] The nature of sacrifice is a common theme throughout all the texts that I am exploring – in *The Fugitives*, Paddy sacrifices himself for a false ideal, in *The Leavetaking*, Moran is sacrificed by the hypocrisy of the Church, in *Cold Heaven*, Marie is supposed to sacrifice her individuality and spiritual freedom for her

[50] Lacan, *The Four Fundamental Concepts of Psycho-Analysis*, p.207.
[51] Ibid., p.113.

husband's life. But in *The Waking of Willie Ryan*, Willie is sacrificed for money, nothing more and nothing less.

Money

In *The Four Fundamental Concepts of Psycho-Analysis*, Lacan brought up the question 'Your money or your life!' to illustrate how money and life concern the relation between rule and possible exception. Lacan states: 'Your money or your life! If I choose the money, I lose both. If I choose life, I have life without money, namely, a life deprived of something.'[52] At first, life and money are complementary; Lacan implies that real life is with this something (money). Life without it is life deprived of something: 'The choice, then, is a matter of knowing whether one wishes to preserve one of the parts, the other disappearing in any case.'[53] It is not free choice, because there is no way to give up life and to keep money. The only option is to lose both life and money, or only money. In Lacan, life-money-death forms a triad. Money and life do not contradict each other, nor is money a metonym for life. Rather, money is on the side of life, which, however, one must surrender. Surrendering money, as opposed to surrendering life, has nothing to do with death. The victims' only choice entails losing life's most precious thing. Lacan places freedom on the side of death and states:

> Because death comes into play, there occurs an effect with a rather different structure. This is because, in both cases, I will have both… you choose freedom. Well! You've got freedom to die… in the condition in which someone says to you, freedom or death! The only proof of freedom that you can have… is precisely to choose death, for there, you show that you have freedom of choice.[54]

Since money is not just "something" but the most precious thing – more precious, perhaps, than life itself yet secondary to it – Lacan's treatment also illustrates the relation between the rule and the exception. He recognizes that the rule has an exception by demonstrating that the relation between them is structural: the exception to the rule is a constitutive exception generated by the rule. In *The Waking of Willie Ryan* it is money that drives the ostentatious Ryans and Carrolls. A passage from

[52] Ibid., p.212.
[53] Ibid., p.211.
[54] Ibid., p.213.

Broderick's third novel, *Don Juaneen*, offers perhaps the best description of the attitude to money among Broderick's characters:

> They were snobbish, purse-proud and devoid of enthusiasm… their whole life was permeated with a profound and largely unconscious hypocrisy. Money was the only God they worshipped; although pious and bigoted Catholics as they were they would have been horrified if anybody had told them so…honest, hardworking, frugal, sexless, hating every exhibition of emotion, they possessed all the virtues which cost nothing to maintain.[55]

For Mary Ryan, money is the key equation in life – when she describes a potential 'match' for her son, the following quote is indicative of her outlook: '"Look at Susan Carroll, two pubs and a hotel, and a nice refined girl into the bargain."' (*WR*, 14) Susan is indeed a 'bargain', as Chris infers in a later conversation with Susan:

> 'You're quite a valuable property.'
> 'Yes, quite. Property is the word.' (*WR*, 88)

The families engage in vulgar bartering, not only for their offspring, but in the realms of spirituality too:

> 'Well anyway… will you put it up to Mannix?'
> 'It's my duty. And his too. Afterall he is the parish priest. It's his duty to call on the old sick people of the parish'
> 'Instead of playing golf and driving round in that big yoke of a car he has. That's where all our money goes. Robbed we are…'
> 'Isn't it terrible! But what can we do? Business is business.' (*WR*, 37)

As I mentioned earlier in the chapter, it was Broderick's belief that the people got the Church they wanted, so the Church in *The Waking of Willie Ryan* is not only avaricious, it is also deeply hypocritical, as we can see in this exchange between Willie and Father Mannix:

> 'God, God, God,' said Willie… 'You all talk about Him, the whole lot of you. I'm tired of hearing about God. He's a convenient excuse for the hypocrites to get their own way.'
> 'And now you're the biggest hypocrite of them all,' retorted Father Mannix. 'I've noticed that we always accuse other people of our own vices.'
> 'Hypocrisy seems to pay. Have you noticed that too?' (*WR*, 156)

---

[55] John Broderick, *Don Juaneen*, p.38.

Lacan posed the theory of the desiring subject, who always desires to enjoy more to the point of wanting to transgress his prohibitions.[56] But more enjoyment is a structural turning point where enjoyment turns into suffering. One always desires more enjoyment – in this instance, money – but in reality there is no such thing as full enjoyment. In terms of enjoyment, the thing is a material object raised to a status beyond what enjoyment of a mere object can bring. It is raised to the status of impossible enjoyment – to 'more enjoyment' beyond the pleasure principle. The 'thing' designates the structural impossibility of the subject to fully enjoy. To posit an impossible enjoyment, Lacan is forced to introduce essentialist terms. While he does not want to return to pre-existential notions of transcendental essence, he makes clear that existential terms alone cannot account for impossible enjoyment. This enjoyment is impossible only in reality, that is, on the existential level, but not on the psychic level, where human beings are embedded in language. The quest for money in *The Waking of Willie Ryan* becomes self-perpetuating, endless, as we witness in the closing chapter where Mary Ryan begins grooming Kathleen O'Neill to take her place:

> 'Don't worry', said Chris with a little smile, 'I'll make an honest woman out of you.'
>
> 'Now look here, you,' shouted Kathleen furiously, 'I won't be talked to like that… and while we are on the subject I want to talk to you about this place…'
>
> Mary stood up and looked at her watch.
>
> 'I'm exhausted,' she said in a faint voice, but with an encouraging look in Kathleen's direction, 'I'm going home to lie down.' She gave another meaningful look at Kathleen and smiled gallantly. 'And for heaven's sake don't start arguing about your problems before your marriage. You'll have quite enough of them to face afterwards…' (*WR*, 189)

Kathleen is, in Willie's words: '"[t]he worst of them all, narrow-minded, bigoted, and with an inferiority complex to boot"' (*WR*, 157), but she is an imminently suitable match once Susan Carroll is discredited. Lacan argued that the child must detach himself from the imaginary relation with the mother in order to enter the social world and failure to do so can result in any one of various peculiarities ranging from phobia to perversion. While Chris' character is largely untainted by abnormality, there is little doubt

[56] Jacques Lacan, 'Responses to Students of Philosophy Concerning the Object of Psychoanalysis,' in *Television: A Challenge to the Psychoanalytic Establishment*, pp. 107-114.

that it is his mother whom he seeks to marry. The following conversation between Willie and Susan is illustrative of Chris' maternal attachment:

> 'What he wants (Chris) is a woman who makes him feel superior, and who'll not let him touch her until it's sanctified by bell, book and candle. Then she can take over. A girl who knows the rules, and can mould her man without wielding an inch.'
>
> 'Like Kathleen O'Neill?'
>
> 'And Mary.' (*WR*, 134)

Since the agent who helps the child to overcome the primary attachment to the mother is the father, these peculiarities may also be said to result from a failure of the paternal function. As an agent of paternal authority, Michael Ryan is a staggering failure. As Willie states: '"Oh, Michael was never any kind of man. He did what he was told"' (*WR*, 115). I shall return to the subject of oedipal attachments within the family unit later on in this section, but for the moment it is sufficient to say that Chris' brief rebellion peters out by the close of the novel and the linearity of the community duly rights itself.

The perpetual quest for monetary gain brings no personal happiness for either Mary Ryan or Kitty Carroll – their happiness exists in material comfort and while their desire for money is insatiable, they desire also to surround themselves with expensive furniture and gaudy artworks in vast, overstuffed rooms. Again, their desire for 'things' is incessant, and the impossible enjoyment they thirst for is forever outside their reach. Simply put, they will never have 'enough' money.

Another aspect to the their materiality is the curious way in which the inhabitants of the town seem to ape their former colonial masters – the ugly Victorian villa which the Ryans own is referred to as 'the hall', the family are ridiculed as having pretensions akin to 'the Royal Family', Mrs Ryan herself is nicknamed 'the Queen Mother' (*WR*, 41). Pinkie White, another of Broderick's malevolent gossips, openly proclaims her love for the Queen (*WR*, 40); Kathleen idles away her time reading *Forty Years at Court* by the Marchioness of Malahide so as to 'improve her mind' (*WR*, 45). We are told by Pinkie White that 'Lady Fitzharold looked after her father for years and years' and 'naturally the Ryans' copy everything in that line' (*WR*, 79). The Ryans' front room is 'loaded with the loot of crumbling mansion houses' (*WR*, 85) and so on.

The obligation on the part of the colonized to mirror back an image of the colonizer produces neither identity nor difference, merely a version of a 'presence' that the colonized subject can only assume partially. Thus the mimic man who occupies the impossible space between cultures is the effect of a flawed colonial mimesis in which to be Anglicized is emphatically not to be English.

The flight from colonial discourse only served to extenuate the divide between the so-called elite and the working class. The relationship between these two classes, the elite and the working classes, is a major preoccupation for Broderick, with the *nouveau riche* often representing the worst traits in society – brash, hypocritical, parsimonious and mean-spirited – while the working class are Church-ridden, vulgar, at times depraved, usually impoverished. The only group in Irish society who escape the author's wrath is the crumbling Ascendancy class, as is the case here with Mrs Whittaker and later, the aged spinsters inhabiting the Big House in *The Pride of Summer*. The curious dialectic between the working classes and the social elite reminds me of Lacan's use of the master and slave dialectic, which he borrowed from Alexandre Kojéve's reading of Hegel: that is, after an initial conflict when one side gives up his desire for recognition, the victor – the master or *maître* – sets the slave to work for him. The slave works by transforming nature in order that the master may consume and enjoy it. However, the slave is partly compensated for his defeat by the fact that, by working, he raises himself above nature by making it other than it was. In the process of changing the world the slave changes himself and becomes master of his own destiny, unlike the master who changes only through the mediation of the slave's work. The master duly ends up in a dissatisfying 'existential impasse' while the slave retains the possibility of achieving true satisfaction by means of 'dialectically overcoming' his slavery.[57]

The dialectics of the master/slave relationship goes some way in explaining the relationship between Britain and Ireland, and after independence, the native elite and the working classes. Thus, in *The Waking of Willie Ryan*, neither the Ryans nor the Carrolls attain any degree of satisfaction. They hoover up the resources of the town but their children have no ambition, they are heartily disliked but assiduously served by the working classes while their vulgar attraction to the trappings of the vanquished colonizer serves only to further alienate them from society, where they withdraw behind the walls of their 'local version of Buckingham Palace' (*WR*, 25).

---

[57] Alexandre Kojéve, *Introduction to the Reading of Hegel*, p.52.

Oedipal Attractions

In the opening part of this section, I made reference to the oedipal triangle between Lily, Ward and Paddy – the surrogate father, mother and son. This is a theme which is again broached in *The Waking of Willie Ryan* where the father becomes Roger Dillon, the mother Mary Ryan and the son Willie Ryan. In the Oedipal Complex, as Lacan casts it, the subject passes from a register of imaginary fusions with the world and with others (the Imaginary) into language (the Symbolic). Lacan almost describes this as a fall from Edenic presence and fusion into a post-lapsarian world of subject and object, division and desire. As Bruce Fink states:

> Despite the infinite permutations allowed by language in the constitution of desire, man can be seen as bounded or finite with respect to the symbolic register. Translated in terms of desire, the boundary is the father and his incest taboo: man's desire never goes beyond the incestuous wish, impossible to realize, as that would involve overstepping the father's boundaries and thus uprooting the very "anchoring point" of neurosis.[58]

By loving and identifying with the father who has the phallus, the boy runs the risk of maintaining a feminine and homosexual position in relation to him. In *The Waking of Willie Ryan*, Willie states: '"You see, in the beginning Roger was more or less like a father to me. I never had anybody like that. I suppose that was what I was looking for"' (*WR*, 111). Thus Roger assumes the role as surrogate father and law-giver in much the same way that Ward assumed a similar role in *The Fugitives*. Mary Ryan was, according to Mrs Whittaker, 'very keen on Roger, and I think he did consider it (marriage) for a while' (*WR*, 74). Lacan considers that in the second stage of the Oedipus complex – where the forbidding father intervenes and where the relation to the child should be dissolved –where the mother is particularly dominant, making the homosexual child discover that the mother holds the key to the solution of the Oedipus complex, as it is she who lays down the law. Many homosexuals deal with rivalry with the father by identifying with the mother who has laid down the law to the father. This would be Mary Ryan, who had helped bring down the 'law' upon Roger. Willie's attempt to kiss Mary is perhaps doubly significant if we think of the act in these terms (*WR*, 115).

Turning to psychosis, failure to comply with symbolic castration and the name of the father results in profound disturbances in the Symbolic

[58] Bruce Fink, *The Lacanian Subject: Between Language and Jouissance*, p.106.

Order. Entering into this paradigmatic triangular structure appears Willie's brother, Michael. It was Michael who first began to sexually abuse Willie and it is Michael who joins forces with his wife and banishes his brother to an asylum (*WR*, 112). The figure of incest occupies a complex but critical position within this structure. Following Saussure, Lacan argues that the relation between signifier and signified was an arbitrary one. The paternal Law, he thus insists, is the law not necessarily of the biological father (whose paternity, in any event, is always open to doubt) but of a 'neutralized' paternal signifier (the Phallus) which represents the Law of the Name-of-the-Father. By the same token, the primordial absence or 'structural defect of being' upon which the Lacanian subject is founded – that ontological condition of lack that triggers the substantive movement of desire in discourse – is not necessarily the irrecoverable maternal body.[59] Incest, nevertheless, remains a privileged figure for that conceptual knot or 'lack of a fixed point' at the centre of the Lacanian symbolic order, where according to the standard Lacanian narrative (in which the subject is assumed to be male) a pre-oedipal state of Imaginary fusion with the m/Other is disrupted under the sign of the father's Name and Law. In Lacan's words: 'the interdiction of incest' that 'primordial Law…which in regulating marriage ties superimposes the kingdom of culture on that of nature abandoned to the law of copulation,' constitutes the 'subjective pivot' of the Symbolic order.[60]

What occurs in the novel then is the total deconstruction of the family unit and what replaces it instead is chaos – Michael as brother/abuser/jailer, Roger as father/lover/abuser and Mary as the dominant mother who lays down the law of the father in the absence of a significant paternal figure. What occurs in *The Waking of Willie Ryan* is not the subtle undermining of patriarchy but the immolation of order in itself and what results is an extended family abandoned to the laws of copulation. The grotesquery of cowering, brow-beaten men, dominant libidinal females, and disingenuous figures of authority (Father Mannix is such an example) makes us question whether there is any hope for salvation in Broderick's fiction.

---

[59] Jacques Lacan, *The Seminar. Book II*, p.223.

[60] Jacques Lacan, *The Language of the Self: The Function of Language in Psychoanalysis*, p.40.

Chastity as an Ideal

In an interview with Julia Carlson, John McGahern would state:

> There was a cultivation of sexlessness here (in Ireland) as well because of the bachelor, simply because it wasn't possible for him to marry until the parents grew too old. Celibacy was admired because of economic necessity, and of course, the Church copper-fastened that.[61]

The notion of celibacy as an ideal state is one that McGahern would return to in *That They May Face The Rising Sun*. In this scene, Rutledge is speaking about his unmarried uncle, The Shah:

> 'He wanted to be on his own. He didn't want to be married,' Rutledge said. 'The priest, the single man, was the ideal of society, and with all the children we saw looking up at us from the floors of those bungalows, who can blame him?' (*TRS*, 46)

In the same collection of interviews with Julia Carlson, Broderick, in reference to Catholic attitudes towards sex, had this to say:

> It (Irish society) wasn't intellectually biased, but it was very biased as regards sex, which was the *verboten*, forbidden thing in Ireland when I was growing up.[62]

Broderick, sarcastically, saw the ideal Irishman as 'sober then, chaste in mind and body, studious and well informed on matters of importance.'[63] For Séan McMahon: 'Broderick's particular interest… is in the "outsiders" which include… the sensual who cannot lead celibate lives.'[64] However, in reference to Broderick's sixth novel, *The Pride of Summer*, Patrick Murray had this to say:

> In its context, this extended use of pornographic material is an index not of Broderick's permissiveness but of his inherent Puritanism. The female penitent is as heavily satirized for her unbridled passion as the "enlightened" priest for encouraging it.[65]

---

[61] Julia Carlson, *Banned in Ireland: Censorship and the Irish Writer,* p. 64
[62] Ibid., p.39.
[63] John Broderick, 'God Save The Queen', in Kingston (ed.), *Stimulus of Sin*, p.145.
[64] Séan McMahon, 'Town and Country', in *Eire-Ireland*, p.87.
[65] Patrick Murray, 'Athlone's John Broderick', in *Eire-Ireland*, p.28.

There is a complex ambiguity at work in Broderick's fiction, the curious dichotomy between what appears to be a libertine attitude towards sexuality and Murray's accusation that Broderick was, in reality, a stuffy 'puritan.' This is played out in two significant scenes between Chris and Susan:

> 'It's not that,' he (Chris) mumbled, sitting down on the high-backed chair Father Mannix had used the night before, and crossing his legs. 'You're not that sort of girl. I don't know what came over me.'
>
> 'But I am that sort of girl, Chris. Most girls are. I like it when you make love to me' (*WR*, 106).

In the second scene, which appears later in the novel, Susan's overtures are severely rebuked by Chris:

> 'Is that the kind you are?' he whispered hoarsely, leaning over her threateningly, holding his bandaged hand stiffly behind him. 'You!'
>
> She looked up at him searchingly: taut, composed, cold-eyed.
>
> 'I love you and I want you,' she said in a clear distinct voice.
>
> 'Christ!' he swore savagely, digging his fingers into her flesh. (*WR*, 132)

Some of the more colourful or engaging anthropological (in certain cases, partly fictitious) accounts of Irish sexuality emerged in the late sixties and early seventies – notably *Irish Peasant Society* (1968), edited by K.H. Connell, a new edition of Conrad Arensberg and Solon T. Kimball's classic *Family and Community in Ireland* (1968), Michael Sheehy's *Is Ireland Dying?* (1968), John Healy's *Death of an Irish Town* (1968), J.C. Messenger's *Inis Beag: Isle of Ireland* (1969), Hugh Brody's *Inishkillane: Change and Decline in the West of Ireland* (1974) and Nancy Scheper-Hughes' *Saints, Scholars, and Schizophrenics* (1977). Arensberg and Kimball's study predates the other aforementioned books in that it was first published in 1940, but it does offer a rather striking picture of rural society in the 1930's:

> Men and women are much more often to be seen in the company of other members of their own sex than otherwise, except in the house itself. Except upon ceremonial occasions in family life… in Clare at least they go to mass, to town, or to sportive gatherings with companions of their own sex. Till recently and even now, in remote districts, a peasant woman

> always kept several paces behind her man, even if they were walking somewhere together.[66]

The clergy were the chief regulators of contact between the sexes and the supposed result of this clerical vigilance was that by the age at which most men would marry, young Irish adults had established a comfortable social life that did not involve emotional intimacy with members of the opposite sex, much less sexual relations. J.C. Messenger's book paints an even grimmer picture of sexual repression, stating:

> The *marriageable* man in his late twenties and thirties is usually repressed to an unbelievable degree… several bachelors or spinsters almost have married several times, only to find that the sexual commitment on each occasion too difficult to make at the last moment.[67]

The men of Inis Beag (the fictitious name of an island Messenger chose for his studies) seem to favour marriage without sex, for it was chiefly an unwillingness to accept the sexual responsibilities of marital status that resulted in late marriage and high rates of celibacy amongst them. This viewpoint led one contemporary critic to state:

> If Messenger were to be believed, the average Irish islander's knowledge of sex was so woeful and limited that it is difficult to understand how the country could have been populated at all.[68]

Like Messenger, Nancy Scheper-Hughes was interested in the high incidence of celibacy and late marriage and in particular, the relationship between these and mental illness. According to the author, her psychological tests revealed a lovelessness and lack of warmth and an ambivalence towards intimacy composed of both longing and fear, an attitude she considers 'quintessentially Irish' in its 'suspiciousness of the flesh and sexuality.'[69] According to Thomas Wilson:

> Ethnographers refer to socio-economic factors like late inheritance, the teaching of the Catholic Church, and the deep religiosity of the rural Irish to explain… conservative and repressive attitudes towards the body and

---

[66] Conrad Arensberg & Solon T. Kimball, *Family and Community in Ireland*, p. 196.

[67] J.C Messenger., *Inis Beag: Isle of Ireland*, pp.68-9.

[68] Thomas M Wilson, *The Anthropology of Ireland*, p.45.

[69] Nancy Scheper-Hughes, *Saints, Scholars, and Schizophrenics – Mental Illness in Rural Ireland*, p.118.

> sexuality, and though others have argued that the Irish obsession with land and religion… were a strategic response to the asymmetrical power relations characteristic of the colonial experience, it has generally been on the role of religion that the wider discussion has been fixed.[70]

Instances of sexual repression and celibacy are rife in the novel. We have the example of Michael's incestuous relationship with his brother.[71] Mary, his wife, has shown interest in only two men, both of whom were homosexuals. Chris, as we have seen, 'wants a woman who'll not let him touch her until it is sanctified by bell, book and candle' (*WR*, 134). Susan Carroll's parents appear to have lived an asexual life together for some fifteen years (*WR*, 88). Willie is largely asexual and when he attempts some gesture of affection towards his sister-in-law: '"[s]he got hysterical and accused me of trying to rape her"' (*WR*, 115). Father Mannix was complicit in Willie's incarceration because he 'didn't fit into the scheme of things' (*WR*, 115).

The Catholic Church, as recognized by McGahern, Wilson and the other authors that I have mentioned, was the main arbiter in guiding the public's perception of 'morality'. The following extract from a Catholic Truth Society pamphlet titled *Can I Keep Pure?*, published in the nineteen-fifties, is indicative of the attitude at work in the Church:

> Hence, the pleasure of sex is secondary, a means to an end and to make it an end in itself, or to deliberately to do this, is a mortal sin… let a tiger once taste blood and he becomes mad for more… the poor victim is swept off his feet by passion, an decides, for the time being at any rate, that nothing matters except this violent spasm of pleasure…[72]

Within the Christian aesthetic tradition, sexuality came to be seen as largely incompatible with religious practice. In particular, sexual enjoyment is a specific threat to any attempt to create a systematic religious response to sinfulness. The solution was to make the religious orders an elitist group which withdrew from the world in order to abstain from sexual promiscuity which remained embedded in the "profane" world of everyday society. As F.S.L. Lyons states:

---

[70] Thomas M Wilson, *The Anthropology of Ireland*, p.47.

[71] There is a very telling passage on page 36 where Chris reveals his age as twenty five and then, in the next paragraph, he speaks of his family 'forgetting Uncle Willie for twenty-five years.' The fact that Willie is involuntarily committed around the same time as his nephew is conceived cannot be entirely accidental.

[72] Quoted in Breandán O'hEithir, *The Begrudger's Guide to Irish Politics*, p.124.

> The convincing proofs of Irish devotion lie less in these outward evidences than in the underlying reality of a simple faith early inculcated but tenaciously retained, and in the special position which the parish priest still holds in his community…given the penal discrimination against Irish Catholicism in the eighteenth century… the priest found himself in the position where he and he alone supplied the necessary local leadership, not just in matters of religion, but in all sorts of other matters as well.[73]

In *The Waking of Willie Ryan*, the priest, Father Mannix, is a figure of mock authority. In his actions, he reflects some of the worse vices of the community, in particular the hypocrisy and money-grubbing antics of the Ryans. Morality is seen as something that can be bought and traded – the nuns are proposed as a solution to the problem with Willie, 'How many times have I seen them ease out of this life with the pure power of prayer' with a cost that 'very reasonable too' (*WR*, 95) while the priest himself can be bought with a five pound note. (*WR*, 99) The façade of sexual propriety is something of a sham. Lyons' argument that the priest 'alone' supplied the necessary local leadership is not entirely accurate. The play between the community and its spiritual leader was, rather, a balance of colluding interests.

For Broderick, the priest supplied a 'service', no more remarkable that the one provided by the petit-bourgeois Ryans. The service he provides is simple enough – he simply helps to maintain the status-quo. His celibacy demarcates his authority – that sets him apart from the community and the quasi-religious role he holds merely copper-fastens that authority. As a spiritual leader, Father Mannix is an abject failure but the role he plays – whiling away his hours playing golf, trading absolutions for hard cash and exorcizing the community of its hidden sins – this is what is truly expected of him and he perform the role admirably.

Michel Foucault, in his *History of Sexuality*, stated that human desire is distorted by cultural constraints, which once lifted, would liberate desire and permit its natural, harmonious fulfilment, thereby eliminating the various neuroses that beset our civilization. For Lacan, it is always the signifier which is repressed, never the signified.[74] Signifiers are what allow drives to be represented, in a way *presented* to us as beings of language. The primary mechanism that defines repression is neurosis which, according to Freud, leads to a separate recording of perception that once occurred in the subjects mind. Repression cannot occur unless the

---

[73] F.S.L Lyons, *Ireland Since the Famine*, p.689.

[74] Lacan, *The Four Fundamental Concepts of Psychoanalysis*, p.218.

reality in question has been affirmed on some level. This is in contrast to psychosis where reality is rejected or foreclosed. Serge Leclaire summarizes the difference between neurotic repression and psychotic foreclosure in the following terms:

> If we imagine common experience to be like a tissue, literally a piece of material made up of criss-crossing threads, we could say that repression would figure in it as a rent or a tear, which nonetheless could still be repaired; whilst foreclosure would figure in it as a gap… a primal hole which would never again be able to find its substance since it would never have been anything other than the substance of a hole.[75]

Our understanding of repression is through the acceptance of reality on a basic level but subsequently pushing these thought out of our consciousness. This goes in some way to explaining why the word 'forgotten' recurs so often in *The Waking of Willie Ryan*. Chris states that "'[w]e've forgotten Uncle Willie for twenty-five years, refused to think about him'" (*WR*, 36), whereas Father Mannix states: "'It's all such a long time ago, I've… I've almost forgotten'" (*WR*, 102). In a later reply to Father Mannix's lapse, Willie notes: "'And then of course one forgets. And after all appearances have been preserved'" (*WR*, 126). Even in trivial matters, such as Michael's memory of the smoking fire or in Willie's sense of direction on the Esker road, memory is unstable and the characters are forever in the process of remembering or half-remembering events or occurrences.

Freud made a distinction between two forms of repression – primal depression or, in German, *urverdrängung* and secondary repression or *verdrängung*. Primal repression is, for Lacan: '[t]he alienation of desire when need is articulated in demand.'[76] This is a sort of mythical forgetting of something that was never conscious to begin with can be partly seen in Mary Ryan response to her son's question on whether Willie's incarceration had anything to do with her (*WR*, 39). The rejection of this thought is not like repression *par se*, where there was no judgement upon the question of its existence, but it was the same as if it did not exist. Secondary repression is the conscious expulsion of some thought or idea, a psychical act by which a signifier is elided from the signifying chain. Since repression does not destroy the memory, it can resurface in a

[75] Serge Leclaire, quote taken from Bice Benvenuto & Roger Kennedy, *The Works of Jacques Lacan – An Introduction*, p.153.
[76] Jacques Lacan, *Écrits* (1977), p.286.

distorted form, in symptoms, dreams or in unintentional humour – what Lacan refers to as 'the return of the repressed.'

For Lacan: 'The motives of the unconscious are limited… to sexual desire… the other great generic desire, that of hunger, is not represented.'[77] The symbolic order of the nineteen sixties may have been changing but as Eugene O'Brien states: 'Catholicism has seen desire, especially sexual desire, as a negative human quality, in *need* of repression.'[78] O'Brien would go on to suggest an analogy between the structure of the Catholic Church and Lacan's symbolic order: 'This order is patriarchal, fixed and stratified, within temporal and spatial structures, not unlike the hierarchy of the Church itself.'[79] The symbolic order, however, is open to change and remains anchored only through points which Lacan terms 'master signifiers.' This is the order in which the subject as distinct from the ego comes into being, and into a matter of being that is always disjointed and intermittent. As Lacan observes: 'Nothing exists except on an assumed foundation of absence. Nothing exists except in so far as it does not exist.'[80] Finally, the rules and restrictions that make up the symbolic are regulated by the fundamental signifier, the Name-of-the-Father.

In the novel, the Church is the true representative of the social order; in essence it plays the role of the master signifier, the father who regulates desire and lays down the law. In Bowie's terms: 'It (the symbolic father) was the inaugurating agent of Law, but also gave birth to the mobility and the supple interconnectedness of the signifying chain.'[81] However, Lacan suggests that certain fathers – often ones who are socially successful – are characterized by an unrestrained ambition or 'unbridled authoritarianism.'[82] Whereas the symbolic father can be conciliatory towards his son, the imaginary father can act as agent of privation, punishing without reason, imposing his will irrespective of the consequences. According to Bruce Fink, a father who acts in such a fashion:

> Is perceived as a monster, and Lacan suggests that the only relationship possible is an imaginary relationship characterized by rivalrous, erotically

---

[77] Ibid., p.142.

[78] Eugene O'Brien, ''Kicking Bishop Brennan up the Arse…'Catholicism, Deconstruction and Postmodernity in Contemporary Irish Culture', p.50.

[79] Ibid., p.53.

[80] Jacques Lacan, *Écrits* (1977), p.392.

[81] Malcolm Bowie, *Lacan,* p.108.

[82] Jacques Lacan, *Seminar III – The Psychoses*, p.230.

> charged tension. No triangulated Oedipal relation can form, and the child assumes a feminine position in relation to the domineering, monstrous father – the imaginary father.[83]

The connection with the novel is all too clear. The Church had been reduced by the people from the symbolic father to an imago, the imaginary father, the 'father who has fucked the kid up.'[84] As Fink states, the child assumes a feminine position in relation to the domineering father – in *The Waking of Willie Ryan*, this is the central image in the novel. All the men are weak-willed, sexually ambivalent and entirely dominated by their wives and mothers. That is one of key reasons why I chose the novel – it undermines the common perception that in post-independence Ireland, the Irish male 'was constructed as active, a fighter and earner, occupying the public and political realm outside the home.'[85] This may have been how they were perceived, but in reality they were merely humoured in this fantasy.

Conclusion

As we have seen from the quotes I presented in the opening part of the last section, the symbolic order of 1960 Ireland is vastly different from the one in evidence today. There are some reasons for this. In the 1960s, sexuality as presented by the Catholic Church was seen as something base, in the words of The Catholic Truth Society: 'A means to an end', nothing more. But the repercussion for breaking this taboo had far greater, and sometimes more sinister consequences. In the case of Willie Ryan, a kiss is enough to seal his fate and resulted in his incarceration for twenty five years.[86] And as Pat Brennan wrote: 'It wasn't all that long ago that the choice facing many single women who became pregnant was emigration, prostitution or incarceration.'[87] This is a reference to the Magdalen homes which were set up for single women who had become pregnant and consequently, were often rejected by their families. Not all the women

---

[83] Bruce Fink, *A Clinical Introduction to Lacanian Psychoanalysis*, p.99.

[84] Jacques Lacan, *Seminar VII: The Ethics of Psychoanalysis*, p.308.

[85] Gerry Smyth, *The Novel and the Nation*, p.55

[86] In case I may be accused of hyperbole, according to the Athlone poet Desmond Egan, the character of Willie Ryan was based on a cousin of John Broderick's who was incarcerated for an equally spurious offence. Interview with Desmond Egan, conducted on 22 September 2006.

[87] Gene Kerrigan & Pat Brennan, *This Great Little Nation*, p. 217.

who entered these institutions were pregnant, however; some were sent because they were headstrong, or mildly retarded, or orphaned, or simply because they were thought to be in moral danger. Although legally they were free to leave at any time, many had nowhere to go and consequently stayed locked away as Magdalen women until they died.

The collapse of Church authority in Ireland, as I outlined in the opening chapter, occurred over a thirty-year period but the defining moment for many people was the 1991 revelation that Bishop Eamon Casey broke his vow of celibacy and fathered a child. Sexual repression existed so long as the façade of clerical celibacy remained and this set in store many of the controversies that raged throughout the sixties, seventies and eighties all of which were of a "repressive" nature – contraception, divorce, homosexuality and abortion. Once the fig-leaf of moral probity was removed, the power of the Church was weakened to a considerable degree. The new symbolic order of the nineties ushered in another index of the primacy of desire. The desire for commodities and modes of instantaneous gratification.

Thus, *The Waking of Willie Ryan* offers us a valuable insight into the nature of Irish society in the sixties. The Church acted as the repressive father, the *ur*-father who dominated and withheld any recourse to debate with the result that all the central male figures in the two novels I discussed are psychologically repressed in some fashion and what occurs during this period is stasis and a debilitating counter-dependence. It would be thirty years before the rebellion against the master signifier of this order – the Church – would run its course and the after-effects are still being felt to this day.

CHAPTER FOUR

JOHN MCGAHERN

JOHN MCGAHERN (1934 – 2006) was born in Dublin and reared in County Roscommon, the eldest son of a Garda Sergeant who left an indelible impression on the author and his fiction. His second novel, *The Dark*, caused something of a sensation when it was banned in 1965, for he subsequently lost his job as a primary school teacher (this episode became the basis for his next novel, *The Leavetaking*) and his case became so controversial that it was raised in Dáil Éireann. After residing for a time in both London and Connemara, he returned to Leitrim, where he remained until his death in March 2006.

McGahern regarded solitariness as an unavoidable feature of modern life though he seemed to give it the spiritual and artistic awareness which he associated with a positive moral value. Through this coda, we may at first tentatively discern McGahern's literary outlook. David Coad, one of McGahern's most forceful critics has said: 'I think one should be careful about using philosophical terms for a writer who is as unphilosophical as McGahern.'[1] He would go on to state: 'McGahern's style has hardly altered in thirty years. There is always the same monotonous, paratactic, uninventive string of non-periodic sentences, often bordering on cheap melodrama, or Barbara Cartland-type sentimental romance.'[2] On this point, Eamon Maher would argue:

> Whereas I can see a reason for the reservations he expresses when comparing McGahern to some of the giants of modern literature, as Sampson does, I can find no justification whatever for the criticism of McGahern's style.[3]

What then is McGahern's style? David Malcolm would suggest:

---

[1] David Coad, "One God, one disciple: the case of John McGahern", p.61.

[2] Ibid., p.61.

[3] Eamon Maher, 'Disintegration and Despair in the early Fiction of John McGahern', p. 85.

> Most critics see McGahern as intensely particular and local writer, deeply interested in individual existential experiences while, at the same time, pointing beyond the particular and individual to a more general level of reference.[4]

Dennis Sampson's assessment of those 'general levels of reference' is noteworthy:

> McGahern will hardly be accused of nostalgia, but he has frequently been found deficient of a related version of self-congratulation, of failing to take Ireland's progress into account, of writing only of the forties and fifties and sixties, of being out of date in his personal obsessions and social observations.[5]

Nonetheless, McGahern was conscious of the difficulty facing the Irish novelist: 'the Irish novelist has to create his own forms', as he states in an interview with James Whyte, and his work and literary style therefore defy any simple elucidation.[6] In an interview with Eamon Maher, McGahern comes close to delineating his own definition of art:

> One of my favourite definitions of art is that it abolishes time and establishes memory and, if you reflect on it, you couldn't have the image without memory. The image is at the base of the imagination and it's the basic language of writing.[7]

What then is this image? McGahern establishes a definition in his Prologue to a reading at Rockefeller University:

> When I reflect on the image two things from which it cannot be separated come: the rhythm and the vision. The vision, that still and private world which each of us possesses and which others cannot see, is brought to life in rhythm...[8]

The 'still and private world' that McGahern refers to draws similarities to the Proustian *moi profond*, the profound and deep-seated 'I', juxtaposed against the ritualistic milieu. Explicitly, the solitary artist in society is the one who transforms the subjective world of the imagination into the

---

[4] David Malcolm, *Understanding John McGahern*, p.6.

[5] Denis Sampson 'The Lost Image: Some Notes on McGahern and Proust', p.57.

[6] James Whyte, *History, Myth, and Ritual in the Fiction of John McGahern*, p.228.

[7] Eamon Maher, *John McGahern - From the Local to the Universal*, p.146.

[8] John McGahern, 'The Image: Prologue to a Reading at the Rockefeller University', p.12.

objective world of social identity and form. Implicitly, McGahern's vision of that 'private world which each of us possesses and which others cannot see' is echoed in *A La Recherche du Temps Perdu*: 'The life of all various lives we lead concurrently, is the most episodic, the most full of vicissitudes, I mean the life of the mind.'[9] McGahern continues:

> Art is an attempt to create a world in which we can live if not for long or forever, still a world of the imagination over which we can reign, and by reign I mean to reflect purely on our situation through this created world of ours, this Medusa's mirror, allowing us to see and to celebrate even the totally intolerable...[10]

Thus, the vision of the author is the basic element in McGahern's fiction – it precedes the material which it transforms and is given shape in form. In an interview with Ciaran Carty, he describes the form as 'the social clothes of the material.'[11] The shaping of this vision in language is, then, the point at which the artistic self is given social identity. Lacan, however, had a partial mistrust of the imagination as a cognitive tool. He insisted on the supremacy of pure intellection, without dependence on images, as the only way of arriving at certain knowledge. For Lacan, the use of the symbolic was the only to dislodge the disabling fixations of the imaginary: '[t]he imaginary is decipherable only if it is rendered into symbols.'[12]

However, the opposition between the imaginary and the symbolic does not mean that the imaginary is lacking in structure. On the contrary, the imaginary is always structured in the symbolic order. In his discussion of the mirror stage, Lacan refers to the relations in imaginary space, which therefore imply a symbolic structuring of that space. The imaginary will always resist this structuring and behind both there is the real which is both beyond language but can also only be partially accessed by language.

Among the many traits McGahern shares with Broderick is his complex relationship with the Catholic Church. Whereas Broderick harked back to the symbolic mysteries of organized religion, McGahern carefully differentiated religion, which was how we interact with the world around us, from morals, which concerns our relationship with other people. For McGahern, prayer was essentially a private activity (such as in the case of

---

[9] Marcel Proust, *Remembrance of Things Past - Swann's Way*, p. 237.

[10] John McGahern, 'The Image', p.12.

[11] Carty, Ciaran 'Sex, Ignorance and the Irish', in the *Sunday Tribune*, 29 September 1991.

[12] Jacques Lacan, 'Fetishism: the symbolic, the imaginary and the real', in *Perversions: Psychodynamics and Therapy*, p.269.

the Moran family in *Amongst Women*) while the Church was more of a theatrical experience: in this regard, McGahern reminds us of Proust's distinction 'between the spire of the church and the church politic.'[13]

The proliferation of religious themes and rituals is one of the many reasons I chose McGahern for this book. Similarly, Lacan borrows heavily from Christian theology; the most obvious example is the phrase 'Name-of-the-Father', a metaphor for the fundamental signifier whose foreclosure leads to psychosis. Later, in the seminar of 1972-73, he used the term 'God' as a metaphor for the big Other and compares feminine *jouissance* to the ecstasy experienced by Christian mystics such as St Teresa of Avila. As Bruce Fink states:

> The idea of an Other *jouissance* is closely related to the idea of God. There is a kind of fantasy at work here: the fantasy that we could attain such perfect, total, indeed, we might even say spherical, satisfaction. [14]

Thus for Lacan God is the 'One' that male sexuality ordains, and the 'Other' that comes between partners in a sexual relationship, a relationship that cannot exist in Lacan's eyes because each partner plays the role of subject to the other's Other. As Lacan states:

> Why should the materialists, as we call them, be indignant that I place God as third party, and why not, in this affair of human love? After all, doesn't it ever happen even to materialists to know something about the *ménage à trois*?[15]

The connection here with McGahern can be found in, amongst other examples, *Amongst Women*. Links between Catholicism and patriarchy are forged in the novel by its most repetitive narrative ritual and the family prayer from which it derives its title. Moran's devotion to the Rosary is explicable on familial and patriarchal grounds, the idea that the family that prays together stays together. The Rosary in the Moran household is a public prayer that reinforces a hierarchal social structure: it is presided over by the head of the family and the five decades are allocated from eldest to youngest in descending order of importance – in essence, an attempt to create a 'big Other.'

---

[13] James Whyte, *History, Myth, and Ritual in the Fiction of John McGahern*, p.230.
[14] Bruce Fink, *Lacan to the Letter*, p.157.
[15] Jacques Lacan, *Seminar XX*, p.66.

Although the Rosary repeatedly pronounces Mary as 'blessed... amongst women', because she was chosen to be the mother of Christ the redeemer, in the Moran household, the character blessed 'amongst women' is Moran himself. Indeed, this is where the title of the novel comes from – Moran being blessed means that the women around him represent his big Other but the structuring of the imagery is very much his own – he is like the god figure in their universe and the relationship is symbiotic as well. It is to this relationship between the patriarch and his charges that I shall devote the rest of the chapter – if his daughters eventually 'win out', if the novel is as much a play on the trumping of modern Irish women over the old order as is part suggested by critics such as Antoinette Quinn and Siobhán Holland, at what cost do these changes come about and to what extent do Moran's daughters need him for some sense of validation?[16] Indeed, is Moran (and what he represents) a necessary catalyst for change or has he been made redundant by it? Or else, a more pertinent question might be: can the two orders co-exist without each other?

For anyone with an interest in the high aesthetics, the cultural form and minute familial details of Irish society during the period in question, John McGahern makes for essential reading. In the context of this investigation, McGahern's preoccupation with sex, the family, the dual roles of father as lawgiver and tyrant, can be explained anew through a Lacanian re-reading and it is my hope that it offers a fresh perspective on both a complex author and a period in Irish history where patriarchy, the Church and the family were the dominant forces in society.

The Dark

First published by Faber and Faber in 1965, the genesis, development and publication of *The Dark* is worthy of a chapter in itself. After McGahern's first novel, *The Barracks*, was published to critical acclaim, the author was awarded a Macauley Fellowship which afforded him a year's leave of absence from his job as a schoolteacher in Clontarf. He moved to London, where he subsequently married the Finnish theatre director Annikki Laaksi. With the publication of the novel in 1965, McGahern notes:

---

[16] Antoinette Quinn, 'A Prayer for my Daughter: Patriarchy in *Amongst Women*', in *Canadian Journal for Irish Studies*, pp. 78-90; Siobhán Holland, 'Re-citing the Rosary: Women, Catholicism and Agency in Brian Moore's *Cold Heaven* and John McGahern's *Amongst Women*', pp. 56-76.

> I was made several approaches on the grapevine not to come back to the school, that I would be doing everybody a favour. It was called doing the decent… since I was a good teacher, I got every encouragement that they'd write glowing references for a job in England, but not to come back there and disturb. That made me twice as determined.[17]

The Dark made for uncomfortable reading. It is easy to see why people were shocked by the novel. It presents graphic depictions of masturbation, violence, incest, clerical apathy and the implication of sexual abuse. An anonymous reviewer in *The Times Literary Supplement* censures McGahern's failure to establish whether the Mahoneys' lives are individual or representative, declaring that the protagonist: 'remains a bit of a suffering machine.'[18] Nor did the book find favour with the Catholic Archbishop of Dublin, John Charles McQuaid. As McGahern states: '[t]he archbishop was behind the whole thing, and he had an absolute obsession about what he called impure books.'[19]

James Whyte would argue that: 'Much of the controversy surrounding the novel centred on the question of whether or not it presented a realistic picture of Irish society.'[20] Vivian Mercier in the *New York Review of Books* argued: 'No work since Joyce has presented Irish adolescence with such freshness and objectivity.'[21] Contrarily, an editorial in *The Irish Independent* stated: 'It seems to us that the novel is unreal…unreal in its concentration on problems within a tiny group, unreal especially in its picture of provincial Ireland today.'[22] James Cahalan suggests that the choice of the *Irish Independent* as the paper over which Mahoney masturbates is deliberate because it was 'then the most staid newspaper in Ireland.'[23] It is hardly surprising then that the *Independent,* who evidently never got the joke, stood foursquare behind the banning.

McGahern's predicament took a more sinister turn on his return – the headmaster of his school haphazardly informed him that he was no longer employed, and when the author took this matter up with the school manager:

---

[17] Julia Carlson, *Banned in Ireland*, p.56.
[18] David Malcolm, *Understanding John McGahern*, p.30.
[19] Julia Carlson, *Banned in Ireland*, p.56.
[20] James Whyte, *History, Myth and Ritual*, p.5.
[21] Vivien Mercier, 'Growing up in Ireland', Review of *The Dark*, p.50.
[22] Anon, 'Banned', editorial in the *Irish Independent*, 3 June, 1965.
[23] James Cahalan, *Double Visions: Men and Women in Modern and Contemporary Irish Fiction*, p.123.

> He asked me what did I want to write books for and why did I want to bring trouble, that their phone had been annoyed with journalists and that he heard that I was married and didn't get married in the church. It took me a long time to get any letter of why I was dismissed, and the only letter I got said: 'Mr. McGahern is well aware of the reason of his dismissal.' It was priceless![24]

Certain agencies approached McGahern to see whether he would be interested in taking the case to the high court, Beckett was approached in Paris and a petition was mooted, the case was even raised in the Dáil by Brendan Corish, leader of the Labour Party. But the author was aware of the futility of such an approach, made palpable perhaps by the reaction of one INTO member, in a much recounted tale, where he said:

> If it was just the banned book, then we might have been able to do something for you, though it would have been difficult. But with marrying this woman you're an impossible case… by the way McGahern, what entered your head to go and marry a foreign woman when there are hundreds of thousands of Irish women going around with their tongues out looking for a husband![25]

However, the banning of *The Dark* would prove to be a Pyrrhic victory for the Church. Like the Mother and Child scheme fifteen years before, it served only to hold the clergy and their dogmatic supporters up to ridicule. As Dermot Keogh says:

> The climate of tolerance improved for the arts about two years after the McGahern case. It must have precipitated the sense of urgency for legislative change… the Minister for Justice, Brian Lenihan… brought in legislation in 1967 to provide for the unbanning of books after twelve years…the result was the release of 5,000 titles, and re-banning has since proved the exception.[26]

The novel itself is in the classical tradition of the *Bildungsroman* and concerns a young unnamed protagonist whose complex and evolving relationship with his tyrannical father becomes the central motif in the narrative. It opens with a shocking scene of domestic abuse, where the elder Mahoney forcefully imposes his authority on the household. The first five chapters span some three or four years in the life of the narrator – at

---

[24] Julia Carlson, *Banned in Ireland*, p.57.
[25] Ibid., p. 59.
[26] Dermot Keogh, *Twentieth Century Ireland – Nation and State*, p.258.

sixteen, he considers a vocation in the priesthood but a visit to his cousin, Father Gerald dissuades him from the course. He spends the rest of the year devoted to his studies, in spite of his father's frequent acts of petulance, and ultimately wins a scholarship to university in Galway. But during his first week there, he is seized by doubts and a sense of inadequacy. Therefore, when offered a secure clerk's position with the ESB, he gives up his place in university. The closing chapter witnesses a scene of reconciliation between father and son, which appears partly insincere and yet, strangely touching.

A number of details concerning the family are undisclosed – the number of sisters the protagonist has, both his own or father's Christian name, how or when his mother passed away – such details are either immaterial to the plot or add to the narrator's anonymity, a foreclosure of his life ahead. Another technique that is utilized is the shifting narrative, where the chapters switch between a third and second person narrative and later in the novel, in chapters 22 and 23, into the first person narrative. The final chapter uses a combination of all three. Neil Corcoran would argue that such a technique makes the text both 'autobiographical and generic' by fusing the different points of view on the protagonist.[27] In contrast, Stanley van der Ziel would argue that *The Dark* is: '[a] product of the post-Beckettian era, the uncertainty as to the identity of the narrator is not only present in the reader, but is extended to the narrator himself.'[28]

It is important to recognize however, that the text only drifts into the first person on the eve of his exams – the prospect of forthcoming independence is distinct, the boy has found his voice. But the following chapters return to the alternate second and third person narrative. University life offers no escape from patriarchal constraints, however: feeling like an impostor from the dark heart of rural Ireland, young Mahoney retreats to the sanctity of the familiar, where anonymity in the ESB is preferable to thwarted ambition in the professional sphere. The big Other designates a radical alterity, an otherness which transcends the imaginary because it cannot be assimilated through identification. The shifting narrative in the novel represents young Mahoney's attempt to escape the law of cultural signification, to break free from the locus in which speech is constituted. It shifts radically until the voice of narrator is unified in the closing chapters – he speaks of himself as a subject and his

[27] Neil Corcoran, *After Yeats and Joyce: Reading Modern Irish Literature*, p.89.
[28] Stanley van der Ziel, 'All This Talk and Struggle: John McGahern's *The Dark*', in *Irish University Review*, p, 110.

belief that you could 'begin again and again all your life' (*TD*, 188) is merely, in his words, a 'cliché' – there is no freedom to choose, only a choice of limited freedom.

F-U-C-K – Objects of Verbal Offense

The Dark opens with the elder Mahoney forcing a confrontation with his son, who has uttered a swear word - 'F-U-C-K…that profane and ugly word' – and he will receive a mock beating as a result. (*TD*, 7) Anne Goarzin has made an astute observation concerning this opening scene:

> By refusing to speak the word because he judges it to be morally inconceivable, the father refuses the function of the word as a shield or barrier, a naming which would defy the strangeness of the world… he tries in vain to prevent it from signifying by breaking it down into letters but in doing so he creates another object-word, conferring onto it an unexpected 'materiality' giving it a new stake which eludes him.[29]

For Lacan, meaning is not found in any one signifier and the play between signifiers along the chain is unstable. Signifiers are the base units of language, subjected to 'the double condition of being reducible to ultimate differential elements and of combining according to the laws of a closed order.'[30] Those who search for meaning at its source have to travel by way of language and, as Goarzin rightly observes, when the signifying word is negated and reduced into letters by Mahoney senior, it dissolves into yet more signifiers. Thus, when Mahoney uses language as a system common to other subjects, the use he, as subject, makes of it is to signify something quite other than what he says. His meaning is always veering off or being displaced. The verbal slip that occurs – 'I didn't mean it, Daddy. I didn't mean it, it just slipped out' (*TD*, 8) – is indicative of the unstable relationship between the signifier and the signified. The signifier anchors itself to the subject, marking its place with a letter, and whether or not the subject knows, reads or denies it, the subject will function like a signified and will always 'slip' under the signifier, temporarily pinned only by the *points de caption*.

In chapter 6, Mahoney once more attempts to negate the signification of the word, 'always': '"Did you know that there's only one thing you

---

[29] Anne Goarzin, ''A Crack in the Concrete': Objects in the Works of John McGahern', in *Irish University Review*, p.29.
[30] Jacques Lacan, *Écrits* (1977), p.152.

should use ALWAYS about and that's God"' (TD, 35). It is a crucial passage in the novel. In the opening scene, Mahoney senior imposes his will upon his son but in this episode, set some years in the future, the son responds to his father's fevered beating of his sister by stating: '"Hit and I will kill you"' (TD, 36), and in consequence: 'Mahoney fell back without striking, as if he sensed, mixture of incomprehension and fear on the face. The world was a shattered place' (TD, 36). In *Seminar III: The Psychoses*, Lacan makes reference to lineage, which indicates that the father establishes an order, not natural, but mathematical. By structuring descendence into a whole series of generations, patrilineality introduces an order: 'who structure is different from the natural order.'[31] In this way, he establishes a relationship among the symbolic chain, between the father and the signifier.

The function of the father's name constitutes the law of the signifier and it is through articulation that the subject inscribes himself in the signifying chain. The presence of the signifier in the subject is ordered according to two 'slopes': metaphor and the metonymy. Metonymy is the relationship of one word with another, as Benvenuto and Kennedy state:

> Metonymy refers to the linear syntagmatic connection of one word and another. In metonymy, a 'paradigm', in the case, a linear structure in which one word follows another which according to the linguistic order, takes the place of the subjects lack of being.[32]

Metonymy is primary and makes metaphor possible and constitutes 'the passage of the signifier into the signified, the creation of a new signified.'[33] Metaphor of the father's Name is the metaphor that substitutes the Name first symbolized by the mother's absence. The signifier of the father's name constitutes the law of the signifier where the phallus is the signifier of the Other's desire. Lacan suggests that certain fathers are characterized by 'unbridled authoritarianism' and establish a relationship which is not a mutual pact of harmonious co-existence but instead one of rivalry and antagonism.[34] In *The Dark*, Mahoney Senior assumes the role of the monstrous father, the imaginary father, whose relationship with his son is characterised by erotically charged tension. The element that is foreclosed in psychosis intimately concerns the father. In psychosis,

---

[31] Jacques Lacan, *Seminar III*, p.320.
[32] Bice Benvenuto & Roger Kennedy, *The Works of Jacques Lacan*, p.118.
[33] Dylan Evans, *Dictionary of Lacanian Psychoanalysis*, p.112.
[34] Jacques Lacan. *Seminar III*, p. 230.

because of the failure of the operation of Negation, the subject is not under its phallic significance – he does not inhabit the language, rather he is inhabited *by* the language.

For Lacan, the murder of the father is a narrative of the emergence of the modern Oedipal structure of the subject. Mikkel Borch-Jacobson argues that 'the modern form of the Oedipus, characterized by 'an ambivalent and devouring identification with the real father' produces a subject that engages in aggressive rivalry with the father.'[35] The monstrous father is thus transformed into the symbolic father whose position the son usurps through his incorporating identification in a way that he cannot do in reality. With that identification, the son commits a symbolic murder of the father. In *The Dark*, we witness this Oedipal drama played out:

> You watched the hand come up to hit, your own hands were ready and watching the raised hand and the throat. You knew or felt nothing, except one the raised hand moved you'd get him by the throat, you knew you'd be able, the fingers were ready. No blow could shake you, only release years of stored hatred into that one drive for the throat. (*TD*, 36)

However, the blow does not come. This is significant as the act mirrors the imaginary beating meted out to the boy in the opening chapter. This process is identification of the order of 'wanting to be like.' That identification process incorporates what Lacan describes as the single mark, the unifying trait of the phallus of the father, which functions as a representative of the Law of the Father and of a cultural order which privileges him. However, the boy's neurosis, which we shall examine later, could be construed as part of this inadequate resolution of the Oedipal drama and the symptomatic decline of the paternal function in general. It is also important to note that despite the symbolic murder of the father, the fraternal social order does not indicate the end of patriarchy, because it does not represent a post-patriarchal order. Rather, it represents a different form of a phallic social order. The following passage exemplifies this argument:

> "Get up Joan" you stooped to get her to her feet and help her to the big armchair. The others stood as stones about. They knew something strange and different had happened in the house. (*TD*, 37)

---

[35] Mikkel Borch-Jacobson, *Lacan: The Absolute Master,* p.40.

In the opening chapter, as Goarzin observes: 'The object of verbal offence transforms itself into a monstrous object'[36] – 'the heavy leather strap he used for sharpening his razor' (*TD*, 7). In chapter six, the object of verbal offence, the word 'always' is transformed into 'strands of … black hair… tangled in his fingers. By spreading them he thought the hair would fall loose but it didn't' (*TD*, 36). Lacan, by re-psychologising Saussure, posits a linguistic stimulus-response of the most radical kind. In other words, Lacan assumes that language combines and recombines itself apart from the speaking subject. Whatever his other changes from Saussure, he keeps the premise that words are the active ones in the psychological or, more precisely, the psycholinguistic process. It is language that 'means' – not the readers or hearers who make meaning. The chain of signifiers, running along according to its own laws, determines the 'I', and the determinism is total. The chain of signifiers is constantly in play and there's no way to stop sliding down the chain.

This is what the unconscious looks like – a continually circulating chain or multiple chains of signifiers, with no anchor or, to use Derrida's terms, no centre. This is Lacan's linguistic translation of Freud's picture of the unconscious as this chaotic realm of constantly shifting drives and desires. Lacan would argue that the process of becoming an adult, a 'self,' is the process of trying to fix, to stabilize, and to stop the chain of signifiers so that stable meaning – including the meaning of 'I' - becomes possible. Mahoney's shifting narrative reinforces this – he becomes a character in desperate search of a 'voice' of his own. However, Lacan would say that this possibility is only an illusion, an image created by a misperception of the relation between body and self.

Father – Son – Son – Father

Like Joyce's *A Portrait of the Artist as a Young Man*, the novel strongly evokes the *Bildungsroman* tradition. Both novels chronicle the intellectual, emotional, and moral development of an increasingly alienated young protagonist, exposing the institutionalized pressure of family, religion, and education – in other words, the big Other. In addition, both novels counter the negativity within the culture by using exile to subvert the traditional reconciliation of the novel of apprenticeship: the protagonists flee from

[36] Anne Goarzin, ''A Crack in the Concrete': Objects in the Works of John McGahern' in *Irish University Review*, p.29.

their homes in an attempt to leave hegemonic control behind. They serve a programmatic educational function, furthermore, by reflecting social restriction and by providing models of extrication. According to Shaun O'Connell: '*The Dark* is a cautionary tale, dramatizing the defeat of young Irelanders.'[37]

The Dark, then, performs an educational function contrary to that of the traditional *Bildungsroman*. Specifically, it teaches separation rather than integration. As Anthony West states: 'McGahern has omitted details… with the intention of presenting a picture of spiritual barrenness – a wilderness that can only be lived in clinging to cold and detached non-involvement; by growing an exoskeleton and keeping the soft parts inside.'[38] This significant generic alteration reflects the severity of the pressure on the apprentice and, in particular, the relationship between father and son.

As David Malcolm attests: 'The son's relationship with the father lies at the heart of *The Dark*.'[39] In the first three pages, the word 'teach' appears on eight separate occasions, and again on three occasions in chapter six, where the father's dominant role is established. However, in the case of John McGahern, we have someone who has tended to concentrate on what Judith Butler has called the 'promising ambivalence' of violent and patriarchal speech.[40] This ambiguity accounts for the likelihood that speech can sometimes fail to act, or act in ways that counter the meaning of the speaker. Butler argues that all cultural discourses share a volatile correlation with the intentions that accompany their deployment, and that it is this unpredictability which can provide the impetus for the undermining of the patriarchal order.

Even before the apocalyptic row with his son, Mahoney's position as head of the family is a precarious one. In the opening pages of chapter 2, we witness how the children unite to 'make him suffer':

> They all got beaten, often for no reason, because they laughed when he was in foul humour, but they learned to make him suffer – to close their life against him and to leave him to himself. (*TD*, 11)

---

[37] Shaun O'Connell, 'Door into Light: John McGahern's Ireland', in *The Massachusetts Review*, p.260.

[38] Anthony West, 'Morning Twilight', in *The Nation*, p.488.

[39] David Malcolm, *Understanding John McGahern*, p.38.

[40] Judith Butler, *Excitable Speech: A Politics of Performance*, p.91.

In chapter 4, the children begin to mimic their father, '"God, O God, O God," they started to mimic, it was an old game between them, it brought relief' (*TD*, 28), and while the boy realizes that no person can be just a 'walking mirror' (*TD*, 94) for another, it is precisely that which McGahern's fathers require; they insist that their children 'mirror' their feelings or echo their utterances. In his short story, "Bomb Box", for example, the hypochondriac sergeant, who tells his children that he is dying, wants 'to see his life in the mirror of the pain of need.'[41] Significantly, the children's most effective means of subverting the authority of the father is mimicry, which distorts rather than reaffirms the self-image he wishes to project. In this, it becomes a form of language itself – a subverting of the big other.

The mirror image, the whole person the baby mistakes as itself, is known as an 'ideal ego,' a perfect whole self who has no insufficiency. This 'ideal ego' becomes internalized – we build our sense of 'self,' our identity, by misidentifying with this ideal ego. By doing this, according to Lacan, we imagine a self that has no lack, no notion of absence or incompleteness. The fiction of the stable, whole, unified self that we see in the mirror becomes a compensation for having lost the original oneness with the mother's body. In short, according to Lacan, we lose our unity with the mother's body, the state of 'nature,' in order to enter culture, but we protect ourselves from the knowledge of that loss by misperceiving ourselves as not lacking anything – as being complete unto ourselves – in essence the imago as image of the self with emotions. An unconscious prototype of personae, the imago determines the way in which the subject apprehends others. It is elaborated based on the earliest real and fantasmatic intersubjective relations with family members.

The imago is linked to repression, which in neurosis, through regression, provokes the return of an old relationship or form of relationship, the reanimation of a parental imago. This regression is linked to particular quality of the unconscious, that of being constructed through historical stratification. In his 1938 article entitled *Les Complexes familiaux dans la formation de l'individu* (The family complexes in the formation of the individual), Jacques Lacan drew the connection between imago and complex. It was at this time that he advanced his first theory of the Imaginary. The imago is the constitutive element of the complex; the complex makes it possible to understand the structure of a family institution, caught between the cultural dimension that determines it and

[41] John McGahern, *Nightlines*, p.62.

the imaginary links that organize it. Lacan described three stages in the process: the weaning complex, the intrusion complex (in which the mirror stage is described), and the Oedipus complex. This complex-imago structure prefigured what would become his topology of the Real, the Imaginary, and the Symbolic. Whereas for Jung and Klein imagos have equally positive and negative effects, in Lacan's work they are weighed towards the negative, being fundamentally deceptive and disruptive elements.

In *The Dark*, Mahoney Senior has the egotism of a child, and on numerous occasions in the novel, he is portrayed as such. In chapter 2, when he asks whether 'anyone wants a game of cards', the children mimic their father, and with a 'grim smile of understanding', collectively state: '"Let him play alone"' (*TD*, 15-16). In chapter 9, as he sits in the old Morris car seat, he 'looked suddenly an infant enclosed in its pen chair' (*TD*, 50). By the close of the novel, Mahoney Senior has become something of a tragic-comic figure, his authority reduced to a bit part being played out on a greater stage. 'This is my life, and this kitchen in the townland of Cloone is my stage, and I am playing my life out here on', he groans, before adding bitterly: '"And nobody sees me except a crowd of childer"' (TD, 128).

Slavoj Zizek defines the paternal function as three-fold: the 'father-jouisseur', the symbolic father – the big Other – and the tyrannical father. The tyrannical father is described as the father who strikes the disobedient with his vengeance, whose will is absolute and requires no justification. In the Oedipal drama, the 'father-jouisseur', the pleasure-seeking father, is killed off and the empty place he vacates is invested with what the father now symbolically stands for. Deprived of his virility, he needs to ignore his impotence to carry out the paternal function without a sense of ridicule. The child, equally, is forced to forget that the 'father-jouisseur' is already dead in order to preserve the Oedipal efficiency. As Zizek states: 'So when, today, one speaks of the decline of paternal authority, it is this father, the father of the uncompromising 'No!' who is effectively in retreat.'[42]

The absolute father can no longer impact the child with his threat of vengeance and is effectively disempowered. Modern Irish society at this time was beginning to be dominated by the culture of the virtual, of the simulacrum of the real, where the inclination was towards belief in the symbolic functions – words, images – rather than relying on the veracity

---

[42] Slavoj Zizek, *The Ticklish Subject*, p. 322.

of sensory information. The decline of our belief systems directly correlated with 'the notion of belief, of symbolic trust, of credence, of taking others 'at face value.'[43] And without belief, Zizek thinks that symbolic efficiency would fail – we would become a society that behaves as if the father was still out there. Knowing the death of the father means the end of transcendental function, by degrees of 'lying sincerity' the symbolic contract is maintained.[44]

In chapter 24, the son becomes conscious that 'He was a man. He was among men. He was able to take a man's place' (*TD*, 149). But one wonders about the conviction of the statement. Such religious doubts as he might have are extended in kind to the paternal metaphor: he no longer believes in Mahoney's symbolic function but remains wary of liberating himself from his presence:

> He watched him (Mahoney Senior) there old, and remembered. The looking moved from the cruelty of detachment out into the incomprehension, no one knew anything about himself or anybody, even moods of hatred and contempt were passing, were of no necessary consequence. (*TD*, 150)

A similar theme is explored in McGahern's short story, "Wheels", which in some ways could be regarded as a sort of sequel to *The Dark*. In this story, a son, estranged from his father, comes back home for a brief visit. The young Mahoney character is now clearly an adult but has not put the conflict with his father behind him. The son invents a speculative excuse to avoid having to live with and care for his ageing father. When this point of conflict is brought up, the son brings his visit to an end:

> I knew the wheel: fathers become children to their sons who repay the care they got when they were young, and on the edge of dying fathers become young again; but the luck of a death and a second marriage had released me from the last breaking on this ritual wheel.[45]

In *The Dark*, the father dreams also of selling the land and coming to live with his son. However: 'That was his dream, but there was no response. He grew aware of his own voice and stopped. He'd be given nothing' (*TD*, 46). The breaking of this 'ritual' is of crucial importance in *The Dark*. As young Mahoney states later in the novel:

---

[43] Ibid., p.323.
[44] Ibid., p.329.
[45] John McGahern, *The Collected Stories*, p.8.

> If you married you would plant a tree to deny and break finally your father's power, completely supplant it by the graciousness and marvel of your life, but as a priest you'd remain just fruit of the cursed house gone to God. (*TD*, 84)

Home and Back Again

When discussing Broderick's *The Fugitives*, I drew attention to the use of the word 'ritual', suggesting both the religious and symbolic referents in the novel. McGahern's approach to ritual, however, is more closely attuned to the act of repetition, namely in the tendency of his characters to expose themselves again and again to distressing situations. Lacan suggests that enjoyment comes from the repetition of the past because doing so represses the anxiety of lack. Lacan theorizes that the act of repressing a sense of lack gives rise to desire, which can drive subjects to repeat outmoded and even dangerous behaviour or, in more open conditions, lead to changes in signification.

A subject's relationship with the symbolic order 'is not simply equivalent to a conscious sense of agency, which is a mere illusion produced by the ego, but to the unconscious.'[46] That is, people relate to each other not in their full complexity as living, feeling individuals, but in terms of significations that have come to represent them in their essential absence. A subject thus only appears in relation to a socially constructed or cultural symbolic community. This cultural symbolic, defined through history and thus welded to the past, reinforces psychic structures of repetition and repression. The cultural symbolic is part of the greater signifying chain of Irish culture and for young Mahoney the impetus is to 'pass the exam. Learn the formula. Thing would come out that way' (*TD*, 113). That the formula involves cramming 'further rubbish by the ton, cram it into the skull' is a moot point, as by the early sixties most of the totems of our symbolic order – nationalism, economic autonomy, the Irish language – had become largely irrelevant to the general population (*TD*, 114). As James Whyte states:

> Yet if religious rituals have, in many cases, been worn down to the level of meaningless habit, by the same token, many habitual actions acquire the status of ritual, through their ability to give shape to experience.[47]

[46] Dylan Evans, *Dictionary of Lacanian Psychoanalysis*, p.194.
[47] James Whyte, *History, Myth and Ritual in the fiction of John McGahern*, p.107.

In McGahern's fiction, the disaffected son's continual home-coming becomes 'a bad habit.' For example, in the short story "Gold Watch" the protagonist goes on to describes his reasons for returning as 'sinister', stating: '"I've gone home for so long that I'd like to see it through."'[48] In *That They May Face The Rising Sun*, Jamesie's brother, Johnny, returns home from England every summer and is welcomed as if he were 'a god coming home to his old place on earth.'[49] Of course, the reality is rather different – his annual return is merely a ritual, one that both Jamesie and his wife dread, but they cannot be seen to act uncharitably and turn him away:

> They could not live with him and they could not be seen – in their own eyes or in the eyes of others – to refuse him shelter or turn him away. The timid gentle manners, based on fragile interdependence, dealt in avoidances and obfuscations.[50]

Why Johnny subjects himself to this ritual is another matter – he cannot be seen to lose face, to tear down the fabric of the deceit to which both parties have become accustomed and so perpetuates this comedy of manners. In *Amongst Women*, Moran's daughters: '[o]n the tides of Dublin or London… were hardly more than specks of froth but together they were the aristocratic Moran's of Great Meadow, a completed world.'[51] They need to return again and again to Great Meadow in order to be affirmed and re-affirmed by Moran but in doing so they forfeit their autonomy. The bond that exists between father and daughter is an indissoluble bond and the mechanics of patriarchy continues until Moran falls into ill health. But like the hen pheasant in the hayfield whose legs are amputated by Moran's tractor, his daughters are so emotionally crippled by him that they literally can never fly away from Great Meadow (*AM*, 159). Luke is unique in the McGahern oeuvre and by remaining steadfast in his refusal to compromise his independence he is cast in a rather unflattering light. Of all of McGahern's creations he is perhaps the most enigmatic, though the novel gives credence to the possibility that his behaviour is merely a mirror image of his father's truculence.

In *The Dark*, young Mahoney assiduously follows this pattern of morbid co-dependence, forever repelled yet drawn to the imago of his

---

[48] John McGahern, *The Collected Stories*, p.215.
[49] John McGahern, *That They May Face The Rising Sun*, p.5.
[50] *Ibid.*, p.186.
[51] John McGahern, *Amongst Women*, p.2.

omnipotent father. In the third chapter after his father masturbates against him in the bed they share together, young Mahoney finds it 'impossible to lie close… he lay far out on the bed's edge.' But he is eventually drawn to his father, 'the sleeping heap of warmth' (*TD* 21). There follows a curious episode – partly comic, partly sinister – where father and son are attacked by fleas and they join together in 'the hunt' (*TD*, 22). Mahoney senior remarks on his battle scars as: 'your blood and mine.' Once they return to bed, there was no longer any 'repulsion as their flesh touched deep down' (*TD*, 23).

The scene executes an almost primitive depiction of rural life and the repeated reference to animals in the novel cannot be ignored. Mahoney's belt is like: 'an animal's tail' (*TD*, 8) during the first simulated beating; young Mahoney is described as a 'broken animal' (*TD*, 9), while the rest of the children are described as 'a vicious litter of pigs' (*TD*, 37). When young Mahoney triumphs over his father, the latter states: 'the pup is stronger than the dog' (*TD*, 37). When Joan is about to depart with Father Gerald, her father observes: 'So the first bird is leaving the nest?' (*TD*, 48); and later, when young Mahoney suggests that the priest may help him with his seminary education, his father retorts: 'He meant he'd buy the calf when it was reared a bullock' (*TD*, 51). These repeated references may allude to savagery or kinship; 'pig' ignorance or 'foxy' insight; rural deprivation or the triumph of a bucolic existence over an urban one. It is left to the reader to decide, although it is noteworthy that the only time young Mahoney appears truly happy in the novel is when he spends his 'last' summer working with his father on the farm.

Again, when young Mahoney chooses to spend a summer with his cousin, Father Gerald, he returns home after only a short space of time – a mere three days. During his punishing regime preparing for his exams, young Mahoney again attempts to distance himself from his father: '"Can you not shut up. Can you not leave me alone for these few months?"'(*TD*, 114). However, once his exams are over, he once more attempts some form of reconciliation with his father and spends the summer working with him in the fields. The day of his exam results, he is humiliated by his father's boasting: 'Resentment grew with hot embarrassment. He was beginning to hate the Scholarship' (*TD*, 157), but by the time they return home: 'He wanted to laugh with him and say, "You are marvellous my father"' (*TD*, 160). Finally when 'the dream was torn piecemeal from the University' (*TD*, 172), Mahoney again returns to his father for advice by sending a telegram asking for his consent.

The obstacles now facing Mahoney are mirrored in the text. To begin with, there are constant references to boundaries in the novel: 'The hedge around the orchard' (*TD*, 76); 'A green prison' (*TD*, 85); 'Grass, concrete, shade, strands of wire running between concrete posts' (*TD*, 135); 'Imprisoned by the high netting wire' (*TD*, 137); 'White railings around the lawns' (*TD*, 143); 'Wet iron railings'; 'Four walls of your room' (*TD*, 170); 'Green oaks lined the boundary wall' (*TD* 173). We may infer from the constant repetition of these words and images that the obstacles facing young Mahoney are everywhere so his decision to return again and again to his father's sphere of influence and the final reconciliation between the two in a boarding house in Galway led one exasperated critic to proclaim: 'There is an inconsistency of character and incident here… the novelist fails utterly to justify this particular epiphany.'[52]

One can understand Cronin's arbitrary dismissal of the final scene between father and son. Eamon Maher suggests that 'what happens at the end of the novel was outside of McGahern's control.'[53] It is an interesting point – why, when the young protagonist has suffered so much at the hands of this man, when he has striven to escape the 'boundaries' of rural Ireland, would he keep returning to his father for guidance or re-affirmation? Is it that he is simply, in the words of the anonymous *Times* critic: 'a bit of a suffering machine.'[54] For Freud, the 'compulsion to repeat' – also referred to as the 'repetition complex' or '*Wiederholungszwang*' – is related to the death drive and the desire to return to an inorganic state. Lacan would define repetition as insistence, or, more specifically, the 'insistence of the letter', the compulsive repetition of certain signifiers despite the subject's attempt to repress them.

According to Lacan, the pleasure we gain through repetition derives from the impulse to avoid this sense of lack:

> Desire is a relation of being to lack. The lack is the lack of being properly speaking. It isn't the lack of this and that, but lack of being whereby the being exists… relations between human beings are really established before one gets to the domain of consciousness. It is desire which achieves the primitive structuration of the human world, desire as unconscious.[55]

Lacan suggests that the need for repetition is a 'form of behaviour staged in the past and reproduced in the present in a way which doesn't conform

[52] John Cronin, 'The Dark is not Light Enough: The Fiction of John McGahern', in *Studies*, p.429.
[53] Eamon Maher, *John McGahern: From the Local to the Universal*, p.29.
[54] Anon, 'Swotting out of the Farm – Review of *The Dark*', in *Times Literary Supplement*, p.365.
[55] Jacques Lacan, *Seminar II*, p.223.

much with vital adaptation', and in turn, this causes repetition to 'emerge beyond the pleasure principle. It vacillates beyond all the biological mechanisms of equilibration, of harmonisation and of agreement.'[56] Both Freud and Lacan examined how behaviour originating in the past but performed in the present is repeated despite the fact that it produces suffering. Such repeated behaviour on a communal level forms the symbolic structure of one's own culture. Desire is embodied in speech; it is an effect of symbolic articulation and this articulation, notes Lacan: 'is the discourse of the circuit in which I am integrated.'[57] He further develops this argument, stating:

> It is the discourse of my father for instance, in so far as my father made mistakes which I am absolutely condemned to reproduce.... I am condemned to reproduce them because I am obliged to pick up again the discourse he bequeathed to me.[58]

With this in mind, a paragraph in chapter six takes on a new meaning: '"Get her a drink of water", you asked and one of the girls obeyed as decisively as if you were Mahoney and you didn't care or know' (*TD*, 37) and again, in chapter 26 when father and son are passing by the graveyard on their way home from the exam celebrations, Mahoney senior states:

> 'And you wouldn't mind only there's people dying to get into it,' *everybody repeated themselves* but suddenly at the old joke he wanted to laugh with him and say, 'You are marvellous my father.' (*TD*, 160 – my emphasis)

Finally, in the closing scene of the novel, one should take note of the discourse between father and son, each sentence being an echoed refrain from one to the other – 'I can look around then', 'take a good look…'; 'not what counts much', 'it's not what counts'; 'that was one good day', 'it was a good day'; 'We'd better try…', 'We'd be better.'; 'Good night so', 'Good night, my son' (*TD*, 190-91). Desire structures a subject's socially constructed unconscious and the cultural symbolic of Irish patriarchy accounts for the persistence of an ideology which is tied to a historical past. Young Mahoney unconsciously assumes this role, installing himself in his father's place and the mechanics of patriarchy are thus renewed:

---

[56] Ibid., pp.89-90.
[57] Ibid., p.89.
[58] Ibid., p.89.

> "Can you not go easy? How can I get much work done in this racket?" They'd stop, go to their places or their school bags, sit in suppression. You were their tyrant in place of Mahoney now, and you'd be too disturbed after to be able to concentrate again. (*TD*, 111)

Cultural demands dictate what is necessary or desirable for the community. Thus, the demands of the symbolic order produce a monotonous programme of repetition, a drive that cannot be satisfied because: 'No object ... can satisfy the drive.... the drive moves around the object… its aim is simply this return into circuit.'[59] As Malcolm Bowie states:

> Each drive, if and when it is individually considered, bears the mark of impossibility. Each is desire seeking and failing to find its point of satiation. Failing to find this point, it pursues or half-pursues its own extinction: 'every drive is virtually a death drive.'[60]

It is the repetition of this closed circuit that produces enjoyment and it is only when the cultural symbolic is understood to be the irrational desire of one's culture, can one re-examine it in order to discover one's own desires. If we look at the closed townland community of Cloone in *The Dark* as a microcosm of Irish society, a number of key features emerge – sexual repression, patriarchy, clerical dominance and staunchly entrenched class divisions. Because of repression, forbidden desire serves only to perpetuate our sense of lack. When the characters project their desire elsewhere, it is an attempt to preserve homeostasis.

Young Mahoney's fantasises can be seen as both a violent extension of his father's sexual frustration and as a means to escape his power. In one fantasy, he dreams of raping a penitent in the confessional. In another he dreams of: 'peace and loveliness, charm of security: picture of one woman, the sound of wife. A house with garden and trees near the bend of a river' (*TD*, 82). As I have illustrated in an examination of celibacy in the previous chapter, sexual austerity was held in high regard, seen as an ideal state in the Ireland of the 1940's and 50's. In an interview with Julia Carlson, McGahern states:

> One of the things that I resent about my upbringing is that the doctrine was taught to us by celibates, and the very nature of abstinence is that it makes food or whatever more attractive if you have too much of it… I think it

---

[59] Jacques Lacan, *Four Fundamental Concepts of Psychoanalysis*, p.167-168.
[60] Malcolm Bowie, *Lacan*, p.162.

> was a very dangerous thing and a very twisted thing: the whole attitude to sexuality.[61]

In *The Dark*, it would appear that young Mahoney cannot escape his past; he becomes, to paraphrase Joyce, trapped in the nightmare of history. Ultimately, our past comes to represent a symptom, a type of suffering that seems to be freely chosen, providing psychic enjoyment that supports the ego, even as it causes the ego and others to suffer. It is only by coming to terms with one's relationship to desire and its implied lack that one can let go of a dysfunctional past and create an alternative future, yet another example of the repetition complex.

The pessimism in the novel emanates from Mahoney's inability to be liberated from the cultural symbolic's desire, to make himself a subject and pursue his own independent desires. When he thinks about sex, it exists either as a violent and punitive fantasy or as an extension of the cultural symbolic. As young Mahoney states:

> Lives were lived through this rathole of security… you must get the same bus at the same time on the same road each morning, hang your hat on the same hook, have three pennies for the same newspaper which the newsboy would hand you without asking. That was the height of the exam. (*TD*, 136)

Later in the novel, Mahoney's dream is shattered when he recognizes that University is simply an alternative means to reinforce the cultural symbolic:

> And money was dream enough to soldier on too. Choice of car and golf club and suburban home, grade A hotel by any sea in the summer, brandy and well-dressed flesh.
>
> 'Security. Security. Everyone is after security. And the only gilt-edged security to be had is the kingdom of heaven,' the Reverend Bull Reegan thumping at the old annual retreats in Carrick. (*TD*, 184)

While Mahoney is capable of verbalizing his relationship to the cultural symbolic, he cannot relate any differently to it; he submits and joins the ESB, for 'A steady job has a lot to be said for it' (*TD*, 184). He can articulate his desires but for him, sex either remains a shameful act or acts as an extension of security. This again reinforces the cultural symbolic where in Ireland it was taught that sexual congress was reserved for the

---

[61] Julia Carlson, *Banned in Ireland – Censorship and the Irish Writer*, p.63.

procreation of children, a speculative duty rather than a biological need. Any outward demonstration of libidinous behaviour was condemned and so the society which created this warped ideology is one that Mahoney appears doomed to sustain.

Eros and Thanatos

The expression of sexual desire in *The Dark* is directly concomitant to a desire for death and closure. The spectre of death is utterly pervasive. Young Mahoney dreams of the 'dead days' (*TD*, 17), whereas Father Gerard insists: 'We'll all be buried' (*TD*, 25). The moment of confession 'would be a kind of death' (*TD*, 40); joining the priesthood would mean: 'You'd die into God the day of your ordination' (*TD*, 56); while the priests wear the 'black vestments of the dead' (*TD*, 78). For young Mahoney, 'The moment of death was the one real moment in life' (*TD*, 69), for his life moves 'in the shade of a woman or death' (*TD*, 127). For his father, 'there's people dying that never died before' (*TD*, 125). Finally, young Mahoney experiences his last day at University as 'the death of the day, and the same habitual actions of the funeral as always, and no matter what happened all days and lives ended this way' (*TD*, 171).

The death drive occupies each of us; it is within us all from the start of our lives. The death drive leads us to destroy our Symbolic and Imaginary objectives. In the Symbolic we desire and pursue meaning, something to fill up the lack in the self and in language; and if in the Imaginary we anticipate and pursue a concrete, coherent image of identity, then the death drive wants us to abandon the search for meaning and identity. In explaining the connection between the death instinct and aggression, Freud would note: 'During the oral stage of the organization of the libido, the act of obtaining erotic mastery over an object coincides with that object's destruction.'[62] The death drive aims not to fill in but to preserve the void in the self. According to Lacan, the death drive finds its most intense manifestation in the sexual act, and in particular, in the moment of orgasm.

In young Mahoney's masturbatory fantasies, in this moment: 'everything is as dead as dirt, it is as easy to turn over' (*TD*, 31); 'a drifting death from hole to hole' (*TD*, 56); 'The body dead as ashes' (*TD* 118). In French, a term for orgasm is 'le petit mort,' which means 'little death.' It is precisely the 'little death' of orgasm for which the death drive strives. The death drive thus directs human subjects away from Symbolic and

---

[62] Sigmund Freud, *Beyond the Pleasure Principal*, p.39.

Imaginary coherence and towards the single goal of sexual satisfaction. And since the experience of *jouissance* shatters, if only momentarily, our sense of self, the death drive is contrary to every attempt to confer identity upon the subject and meaning upon the world. The death drive is that which always threatens to undo one's sense of self in favour of sexual gratification, 'the drive, the partial drive, is profoundly a death drive and represents in itself the portion of death in the sexed living being.'[63] Sexual satisfaction and identity are thus completely contradictory. The death drive aims for sexual satisfaction, for *jouissance,* and *jouissance* is precisely what shatters identity. For Lacan:

> Pleasure as that which binds incoherent life together, until another, unchallengeable prohibition arises from the regulation that Freud discovered as the primary process and appropriate law of pleasure.[64]

For Lacan, 'the sexual' is antithetical to identity. And the structure of identity is endangered by the sexual. What this suggests is that 'sexual identity' has nothing to do with 'sexuality.' These two concepts are so radically separate that one cancels out the other. Where identity prevails, the sexual, the death drive, and *jouissance* become obscured. And where sexuality erupts, identity categories fall apart. As Lacan puts it: 'That's what love is. It's one's own ego that one loves in love, one's own ego made real on the imaginary level.'[65] Sexuality – which contemporary culture associates most closely with one's 'true' self – has nothing at all to do with one's self at all. Sexuality, for Lacan, radically destabilizes the self and threatens to undo all the structures within which we try to make meaning of the world.

The neurotic illusion that enjoyment would be attainable were it not forbidden ties in the prevailing attitudes of the closed communities and the greater cultural symbolic. Prohibition creates a desire to transgress it and this stands for both *jouissance* and the puritanical attitudes prevalent in *The Dark.* This can be witnessed in part through the sheer number of perverted relationships in the novel: namely that of Mahoney senior and his incestuous relationship with his son; that between Father Gerard and his effeminate servant John and that between the shopkeeper Ryan and Mahoney's sister, Joan. When young Mahoney arrives at the Ryans' house, he is immediately cognisant of the fact that something is amiss and

---

[63] Jacques Lacan, *The Four Fundamental Concepts of Psychoanalysis*, p.205.
[64] Jacques Lacan, *Écrits* (1977), p.319.
[65] Lacan, Jacques. *The Seminar of Jacques Lacan, Book I*, p.142.

he finds himself staring out the window at Ryan's daughters, dressed in swimsuits, 'lobbing a tennis ball over and back across a loosely strung net' (*TD*, 91). Ryan stands behind him and whispers in his ear, 'Tempting?' The biblical analogy between the garden, the 'apple-green' swimsuits, and the serpentine Ryan cannot be overlooked. Mahoney reacts violently:

> You wanted to smash Ryan's face in, to defile and slash the stripped girls in the garden, to kick into the trunks of thighs that opened under the newspaper in the deck-chair. But all you could do was clench hands and wait till Joan came. (*TD*, 92)

Mahoney is again led in temptation on the night of the jibs dance but his attempts at forming a 'natural' relationship are once more thwarted for he views it as a 'world of sensuality from which you were ready to lose your soul' that it would not be 'so easy to drag… your mouth either for that one destructive kiss'. Rather, it would be 'as hard to lose your soul as save it' (*TD*, 177-78). The biblical analogies are again evident and Mahoney's attempt to transgress the cultural symbolic, to view sex as a simple biological function fails utterly. He may well be an 'oddity' all his days (*TD*, 176).

While Denis Sampson asserts that the boy '[r]elies increasingly on his absolute need to preserve his own integrity,' this is an optimistic view of what is, essentially, a devastating précis on a sick and morbidly desexualized society.[66] Eamon Maher would state: 'The jerky style and fluctuating points of view could be a means to translate the uncertainty and insecurity of a young man who is unable to embrace change.'[67] But change, true social change, is not apparent in the novel. Young Mahoney is the first member of his family to attend University but a scheduled meeting with the Dean firmly puts him in his place:

> There seemed to be contempt in his voice, you and Mahoney would never give commands but be always menials to the race he came from and still belonged to, you'd make a school teacher at best. You might have your uses but you were both his stableboys, and would never eat at his table. (*TD*, 188-87)

The cultural symbolic would remain monolithic for some years to come. The novel was written at a time when second level education was neither free not within the means of the majority of the population – a Department

---

[66] Denis Sampson, *Outstaring Nature's Eye*, p.81.
[67] Eamon Maher, *From the Local to the Universal*, p.28.

of Education survey of a cohort of 55,000 students who began primary school in the early sixties found that only 2,000 eventually entered University.[68] The Church's attitude on sexuality would remain a guiding principle for politicians and would consequently shape the lives of many other confused adolescents like young Mahoney.

The closing chapters of *The Dark* reinforce the pervading sense of despondency. Thrown out of a lecture by a petty and supercilious lecturer, Michael Foley writes: 'The professor's bullying, the boy realizes, is the mirror of his father; and he sees tyranny as the way of University life. Riddled by doubt, he uncertainly makes a bid for freedom.'[69] Whether the oppressor is father, priest, or professor, all discourage integration in their obsessive need for authority, rather than encouraging the emergence of an engaged citizen. At that precise moment he receives a letter from the E.S.B. offering a job in Dublin. Mahoney takes the position and the freedom and economic safety it offers – he cannot see it as a defeat for 'You just couldn't go home defeated to Mahoney' (*TD*, 179).

As Foley suggests: 'The victory of the imagination over oppression… is the only real victory.'[70] For young Mahoney, he comes to an epiphany of sorts:

> One day, one day, you'd come to more authority than all this, an authority that had need of neither vast buildings or professional chairs nor robes nor solemn organ tones, an authority that was simply a state of mind, a calmness even in the turmoil of your passing.
>
> You couldn't go to the E.S.B. If it was no use you could leave again and it didn't matter, you could begin again and again all your life, nobody's life was more than a direction. (*TD*, 188)

Both Eamon Maher and John Cronin exclaim dissatisfaction with young Mahoney's sudden *volte-face*, as well as with his new found *dégagé* perspectives and softening attitude to his father. Both as already mentioned, maintain there is no justification for the epiphany, but what happens may have been outside the novelist's control [71]

However, I feel it could be best explained thus: in a healthy environment, young Mahoney might have taken the risk, both with University and, in part, with entering the Aula for the jibs dance. He would

[68] Dermot Keogh *Twentieth Century Ireland – Nation and State*, p.273.
[69] Michael Foley, 'The Novels of John McGahern', in *The Honest Ulsterman*, p.36.
[70] Ibid., p.36.
[71] Eamon Maher, *From the Local to the Universal*, pp.28-29.

do this knowing failure would not have the same devastating results. But that is not the case. He must play it safe to make his escape: he must conform to the cultural symbolic and subscribe to his part in the farce, Rather than being a *volte-face*, it is perhaps the most devastating indictment of all. It is an escape from the responsibility of making any decision whatsoever and is fully in keeping with the prevailing mood of this dark and disturbing novel.

Amongst Women

Amongst Women was first published in 1990 and was subsequently short-listed for the Booker prize. In it, we are introduced to Michael Moran, a farmer and one-time officer in the Irish War of Independence in the 1920s. A competent and effective officer, he felt displaced, unwilling to continue in the military during peacetime and unable to make a good living in any other way. '"The war was the best part of our lives," Moran asserts. "Things were never so simple and clear again."'[72] While the army provided the security of structure, rules, and clear lines of power, Moran's life after the war consisted of raising two sons and three daughters on a farm and scraping out a living through hard manual labour. A widower, Moran confuses his identity with the communal identity of his family in a gesture that divides and conquers. Moran's daughters are 'a completed world' separate from 'the tides of Dublin or London' (*AM*, 2).

As such, he can control them, as is shown when he discourages one from accepting a university scholarship. No longer powerful, Moran is repeatedly described as withdrawing into himself 'and that larger self of family' in order to channel his aggressions into a shrunken realm he attempts to control (*AM*, 12). His adjustment from guerrilla fighter to father is never complete, and the question of how to maintain authority over his children while allowing them room to grow is central to the novel.

Nowhere is this struggle between dependence and independence more pronounced than in the character of Luke, the oldest son who runs away from Moran's overbearing authority, never to return. Rejecting his father, Ireland, and all of the violence and provincialism he associates with both, Luke flees to England. He reacts in a noncommittal manner to all of Moran's many letters, and he doesn't return to Ireland except at the end of the novel when his sister gets married. '"Please don't do anything to upset

[72] John McGahern, *Amongst Women*, p.6. All future references to the novel will be marked by *AM*, with the page number in the text.

Daddy,"' one of his sisters pleads, typically trying to placate her father. '"Of course not. I won't exist today," Luke replies' (*AM*, 152). His best weapon against Moran's control is absence. Whereas the daughters, 'like a shoal of fish moving within a net', find individuality painful compared to the protection of their familial identity, Luke gains strength in his departure (*AM*, 79). "I left Ireland a long time ago", Luke announces gravely (*AM*, 155). As it does for many of James Joyce's characters, life in Ireland seems like imprisonment for him.

His sisters, on the other hand, not only fail to break away from the family, but their identification with and loyalty to Moran threaten to subsume them. However, it also gives them a kind of strength, as Michael seems to understand: 'In the frail way that people assemble themselves he, like the girls, looked to Great Meadow for recognition, for a mark of his continuing existence' (*AM*, 147). The patriarchal structure is undermined in the novel in other subtle ways and shall be explored in depth in the following pages. In *Amongst Women*, while Moran accepts that the domestic authority of the Irish mother figure is an 'old story' (*AM*, 156) he is also obliged to use it to his own benefit – notably when he remarries and is forced to acknowledge the importance of the central female figure in the family:

> He saw each individual member gradually slipping away out of his reach. Yes, they would eventually all go. He would be alone. That he could not stand. He saw with bitter lucidity that he would marry Rose Brady now. (*AM*, 22)

The family home, the new fragility of which helped to challenge the stability of Moran's power, now comes to signify the authority of benevolent mothers rather than that of powerful patriarchs. In this sense, they each create a big Other for the separate factions in the family – Great Meadow, at the beginning of the novel, is in essence a small imaginary community. One could see the development of the novel as the gradual erosion of the imaginary by the symbolic order. Moran, akin to Lear, forfeits his Kingdom to his daughters and 'For the first time in his life Moran began to fear them' (*AM*, 178).

He has always been in the driving seat – like Mahoney Senior in *The Dark*, he sits in 'a car chair meditatively rotating his thumbs' (*AM*, 45) – and ironically, although he rallies his 'troops' to 'seize the day', as Denis Sampson attests: 'Moran's lifelong inability to seize the day is finally revealed to be at the heart of his egocentric inability to accept the reality of change.'[73] Due to a combination of fear of penury, a loathing of the professional class and aversion to outsiders, he has retreated into Great Meadow and will give no further ground. But he is helpless in dictating to his grown children and it is they who finally open up Great Meadow to the world. Towards the end of the novel, Moran, helpless in the face of change, reluctantly resigns himself to the back seat: 'He still went to the post office to post letters but Rose drove him there and waited outside in the rain' (*AM*, 172).

In the context of this chapter, Declan Kiberd's analysis of the novel is worth recalling:

> McGahern *Amongst Women* was published within a year of Mary Robinson's accession to the presidency. In both its opening and closing passages, it refers to the trumping by modern Irish women, back in the late 50's, of their father's old heroic world of ambushes and flying columns – as if the advent of Mary Robinson were over three decades in the gestation.[74]

This is a prescient appraisal. On the surface, the novel appears to be anything but subversive – Moran is firmly entrenched in his role as patriarch, his wife and daughters clearly demarcated in a subservient role. In recounting the Monaghan Day episode, we find Moran 'in and out of the house like a devil' and his daughters sinking 'into beseeching drabness, cower as close to invisible as they could' (*AM*, 8). On the night of their marriage, Rose is shown about the kitchen by her step-daughters: 'They showed her the places and secrets of the kitchen, the room was now her room' (*AM*, 45). Victoria Glendinning's critique is of interest here: 'I abandoned my trite feminist furies about why none of the women argued with Moran or challenged his authority. It is not an option.' Accepting that Moran's selfishness and the women's subservience 'were socially approved and cultural determined', she refused to explore the degrees in which the novel participated in this process of approval because 'to use such phrases would rob the novel of its quality.'[75]

Glendinning's critique captures, in essence, the prevailing opinions of those who reviewed the novel. As John Banville states: 'It is an example of the novelist's art at its finest, a work the heart of which beats to the

---

[73] Denis Sampson, *Outstaring Natures Eye: The Fiction of John McGahern*, p.240.
[74] Declan Kiberd, *The Irish Writer and the World*, p. 277.
[75] Victoria Glendinning, Review of *Amongst Women*, in *Literary Review,* vol. 10, May 1990, p.5.

rhythm of the world and of life itself. It will endure.'[76] But the question I wish to turn to now, is how does one make the leap from Glendinning's view, that we must accept the misogyny in the novel as being 'socially approved', through Banville's assertion that the novel is, in itself, timeless through to Kiberd, who regards it as the 'trumping' of Irish women over the past? Indeed Kiberd would suggest that *Amongst Women* resonates very much with the period in which it was published – on the eve of Mary Robinson's accession to the Presidency which seemed to spell the end of the old, patriarchal order.

Fathers

In Ireland, as in any decolonizing nation, the idea of gender remains a crucial concept. During the nineteenth century, both Ireland and Britain were figuratively viewed in binary opposition to one another – essentially as masculine and feminine entities. This allowed British colonial discourse a framework in which to enact a master text that set into opposition a natural division of the sexes. Visibly, the Irish were indistinguishable from their colonial masters. Yet, the master text of English literature needs this 'other' to construct itself. The obligation on the part of the colonized to mirror back an image of the colonizer produces neither identity nor difference, only a version of a presence that the colonized can partially assume. What was inherent in Irish expression soon became mirrored in Irish psyche – the carnivalesque, playful society (what Ernest Renan called the 'essential feminine' nature of the Celtic race) was set against the staid, pragmatic British discourse of science and culture.[77]

As Franz Fanon illustrated in *The Wretched of the Earth*, anti-colonial nationalism was locked into Western imperialist modes of thought. The intellectuals and social elite that were responsible in leading the nationalist drive were the ones who, once they came to power, quickly reinstated the systems of hierarchy and privilege that had characterised the colonial policy.[78] As Moran states in *Amongst Women*:

> 'What did we get for it? A country, if you believe them. Some of our own johnnies in the top jobs instead of a few Englishmen. More than half of my

---

[76] John Banville, '"In Violent Times" Review of *Amongst Women*", in *New York Review of Books*, p.22.

[77] Ernest Renan, quoted in Mary Storey, *Poetry and Ireland since 1800: A Source Book*, p.58.

[78] Frantz Fanon, *Wretched of the Earth*, p. 147.

> own family work in England. What was it all for? The whole thing was a cod.' (*AM*, 5)

The nexus of colonialism and gender left a deep impression on the Irish cultural imagination. Uncritically adopting the divisions imposed by colonialism, Irish decolonization attempted to deny its representation as this 'essentially feminine race', by reconfiguring the natural division of the sexes along specific and patently unequal lines. Thus, in post-independence Ireland, the Irish male was constructed as active, a fighter and earner, occupying the political realm outside the home; the Irish woman was passive, a nurturer, mainstay of the family, bastion of the domestic realm of home and hearth. In *Amongst Women*, though the girls 'had never been taught to cook or housekeep' they were able to 'cook vegetables and meat simply, deal with eggs and bacon and porridge, and they were able to bake and housekeep, learning as they went along. They didn't need to know much more' (*AM*, 48).

That final sentence, 'They didn't need to know much more', whether intentionally or not, gives the reader a snap impression that housekeeping should be the extent of their ambition. If circumstances change, attitudes perhaps do not. Later in the novel, when Shelia is showing off her new suburban home in Dublin, she frets: 'Sean is worried we spent too much', to which Rose replies: 'Don't pay a bit of attention… men are all like that. Get everything you need while you have the chance' (*AM*, 151). In the house, Moran is 'at a loss' and 'anxious to get away' while Sean, Shelia's husband-to-be, is notably absent from this scene. That Shelia is the one who showed off each room with 'touching pride' is, perhaps, significant (*AM*, 151).

The men in the novel do not sit easily in the house: 'Even on very wet days Moran seldom hung around the house' (*AM*, 63). Towards the end of the novel: 'He wanted to escape, to escape the house, the room, their insistence that he get better, his illness' (*AM*, 178). After his first visit to Great Meadow, Maggie's husband Mark remarks: '"I feel as if I've just gotten out of jail"' (*AM*, 141). If Michael is better able to adapt to the confines of the home, it may be on account of his effeminate nature. Growing up, he 'had no liking for physical work and he was slow to give Moran any help on the land' (*AM*, 64). His flower garden both 'amused and irritated' Moran, leading him to comment to his son: '"I suppose one of these days you'll be getting yourself a skirt"' (*AM*, 65) and in a later aside: '"They've mollied you for far too long. You'll have to grow up and fight your corner"' (*AM*, 91). However, even Michael eventually finds life in the home impossible: 'The fiercest urge was to break out of his life as it was. He could not endure his life in the house any longer' (*AM*, 110).

While commentators such as Denis Sampson have suggested that the home acts as Moran's 'fortress' or 'the boundaries of his kingdom', I would argue otherwise – it is in the home where Moran suffers his greatest setbacks.[79] The loss of his friend McQuaid, Rose's assertion of her equal status in the marriage and his physical altercation with Michael which ends in defeat – all these incidents take place in the kitchen. It is only in the fields and in war that Moran regains his primacy: '"For people like McQuaid and me the war was the best part of our lives. Things were never so simple and clear again"' (*AM*, 6). Thus, it would not serve our purpose to view Moran merely as a domestic tyrant, waited on hand and foot by subservient womenfolk.

When McQuaid quits the house for the final time he states: '"Some people just cannot bear coming in second"' (*AM*, 22). It is, perhaps, as good an explanation for the inherent weakness of patriarchy as has yet been given. As I illustrated in the opening chapter, the monologic discourse of the past century was collapsing in the face of modernizing trends which were beginning to undermine the whole symbolic/patriarchal order. As society began to fragment, the Irish male proved incapable of dealing with his loss of centrality. Conversely, Irish women, better equipped as they were with compromise rather than conquest, eventually supplanted the male as the head of the household in this new society where interdependence (individual responsibility to the mutual benefit of all) took precedence over an autocratic (and often self-serving) male dominated one. As Declan Kiberd states:

> There is a strong implication that it is the women who really impel the narrative from start to finish and that it is the men's inability to live for long at peace with the feminine principal of life that leaves them at war among themselves.[80]

When Luke states: '"Only women could live with Daddy"' (*AM*, 133), he makes reference to the central dichotomy in the novel. Moran, who prides himself on his individualism, who rejects the 'outside', an outside he 'refused to accept unless it came from the family' (*AM*, 93), is nonetheless reliant upon outside forces – in the shape of his second wife, Rose – to preserve his authority. For his children however, Moran's authority comes not through his physical presence but through their demand for

---

[79] Denis Sampson, *Outstaring Nature's Eye*, p.230.

[80] Declan Kiberd, 'John McGahern's *Amongst Women*', in *Language and Tradition in Ireland: Continuities and Displacements*, p.207.

satisfaction. The agent of demand goes beyond necessity – it is the desire for the absolute and unshared signifiers of the desire for the big Other or, in this instance, the desire by Moran's daughter's for Moran himself. When The Thing or object of desire is displaced by the phallic signifier, the symbolic phallus is uncoupled and leaves its place to the signifier – the Name-of-the-Father – that which introduces the subject to the symbolic system. Yet we mourn for our lost *jouissance,* we seek ultimate satisfaction. But satisfaction always leaves a trace of disappointment: there is something missing in the object that the Other offers – it is never enough.

Once he brings Rose into the house, Moran finds himself compromised – he must share power with his wife and daughters and from the beginning: 'They were already conspirators. They were mastered and yet they were controlling together what they were mastered by' (*AM*, 46). The women in the novel are the ones who quickly realize that direct confrontation with Moran's authority is counter-productive. As Kiberd states:

> They can sense that the patriarchy epitomized by the father, far from being a sign of strength, is an outward covering of his male weakness. For he is a man who feels not at all at home in the world. Under Rose's benign and loving care, even his daughters come to seem like aliens, members of another species entirely.[81]

Both his friend McQuaid and eldest son, Luke, refuse to compromise their own authority and therefore depart, never to return. Rose attempts to instil the principal of conspiratorial cooperation into Moran's youngest son:

> 'You know your father. He'll not change now. All you have to do is appear to give in to him and he'd do anything for you after that. He wants nothing but good for the whole house.' (*AM*, 122)

But confrontation becomes inevitable and Michael also departs, though 'in a more sporadic way', he would keep returning. By then, however: 'Moran had given up trying to bend him to his will and was content to leave him to his own devices, glad to see him at all' (*AM*, 170). By the end of the novel, there is little doubt who has succeeded in this war of attrition. However, it is important to remember that the women in the novel *need* Moran, in a way that is explained in reference to Shelia who knew 'that her loyalty was probably ambiguous, that the deepest part of herself was bound to her

[81]Ibid., p.202.

sisters, this man and house. That could not be changed' (*AM*, 170). The mode of compromise that these women exert is all-encompassing. They try, vainly, to bring Luke back into the fold but as Luke explains to Maggie: "If he wants to meet me he could have come over for your wedding and we could have taken it from there. He just wants everything on his own ground" (*AM*, 143). Like Freud's repetition complex, what we don't understand we are doomed to repeat – in this, Luke is stating what is equally true of himself. Similarly, in the opening passages of the novel they attempt to resurrect Monaghan Day, but only after the death of McQuaid who doubtless would not have come back either. That it is left to the women in the novel to act as arbitrators between opposing factions is indicative of both their power and weakness. They look to the family as a mark of their 'continued existence' (*AM*, 147), meaning that their own fate is forever tied up in the mechanism of patriarchy. Why should this be so?

In Lacanian theory, it is essential to recognize the metaphoric nature of the father's role: he is installed in the position of lawgiver not because he has a superior procreative function, but merely as an effect of the linguistic system. The mother recognizes the speech of the father because she has access to the signifier of the paternal function, which regulates desire in a repressive manner. Thus, only by accepting the necessity of sexual difference and regulated desire can a child become socialized. A castrating acceptance of its sovereignty precipitates the child out of its ambivalent attempts to be the fully satisfying Thing for the mother. As Lacan quips, when the child accedes to castration, it accedes to the impossibility of its directly satisfying its incestuous wish. If things go well, however, it will depart with the guarantee that, when the time comes (and if it plays by the rules), it can at least have a satisfying substitute for its first lost love-object.

The Oedipal complex for girls, however, involves an extra, earlier, step. The girl transfers her love from mother to father, because she realizes that neither she nor her mother has a phallus, in a process that Freud famously termed penis-envy. The assumption of a sexual position is, in essence, a symbolic act which takes places on a symbolic plane:

> It is insofar as the function of the man and woman is symbolized, it is insofar as it's literally uprooted from the domain of the imaginary and situated in the domain of the symbolic, that any normal, completed sexual position is realised.[82]

[82] Jacques Lacan, *The Seminar, Book III*, p.177.

If there is no other signifier of sexual difference apart from the phallus on the symbolic plane, the female is thus 'required to take the image of the other sex as the basis of its identification.'[83] Moran's daughters see themselves as exactly that – not as individuals but rather by a collectivity directly linked with their father: 'On the tides of Dublin or London they were hardly more than specks of froth but together they were the aristocratic Moran's of Great Meadow, a completed world, *Moran's daughters*' (*AM*, 2). But if they need to identify with Moran to properly enter into the symbolic order, what is the basis of their love and loyalty – if indeed that loyalty exists as we perceive it? Lacan partially solved this question by linking the process through which women must give up an essential part of themselves in order to be the phallus with a concept he called masquerade. He stated:

> Paradoxical as this formulation may seem, I am saying that it is in order to be the phallus, that is to say, the signifier of the desire of the Other, that a woman will reject an essential part of her femininity, namely, all her attributes in the masquerade. It is for that which she is not that she wishes to be desired as well as loved.[84]

Thus, it is through the masquerade that a woman's 'not-having' the phallus is transformed into 'being' the phallus. While the closing pages of *Amongst Women* remain ambiguous it is nonetheless imbued with such an irony for it would seem that Moran's patriarchal legacy will continue, ironically through his daughters: 'It was as if each of them in their different ways had become Daddy' (*AM*, 183). As Lacan has suggested, women, paradoxically, are made to 'be' the phallus or 'embody' the phallus:

> Paradoxical as this formulation might seem, it is in order to be the phallus, that is, the signifier of the desire of the Other, that the woman will reject an essential part of her femininity, notably all its attributes through masquerade.[85]

What has occurred, in this event, is that the individual's imaginary identifications (or 'ideal egos') that exclusively characterised its infantile years have been supplemented by an identification of an entirely different

[83] Ibid., p.176.
[84] Jacques Lacan *Écrits* (1977), pp.289-290.
[85] Jacques Lacan, 'The Meaning of the Phallus', in *Feminine Sexuality: Jacques Lacan and the Ecole Freudienne*, p.84.

order: what Lacan calls a symbolic identification with an 'ego ideal.' This is precisely identification with and within something that cannot be seen, touched, devoured, or mastered: namely, the words, norms and directives of its given cultural collective. Symbolic identification is always identification with a normatively circumscribed way of organising the social-intersubjective space within which the subject can take on its most lasting imaginary identifications – for example, the hysterical-vulnerable female identifies at the symbolic level with the patriarchal way of structuring social relations between sexes, outside of which her imaginary identification would be meaningless. This point is repeatedly illustrated in *Amongst Women*: 'No matter how far in talk the sister's ventured, they kept returning, as if to a magnet, to what Daddy would like or dislike, approve of or disapprove of' (*AM*, 131).

Here we see that identification made whole – they were not the Moran sisters, they were Moran's daughters. Indeed, most tellingly, in reference to Moran's daughters: 'Together they were one world and could take on the world. Deprived of this sense they were nothing, scattered, individual things' (*AM*, 145). When Maggie brings her fiancé home for the first time, she insists on telling her father first about their engagement because: 'What she wanted most of all was Moran's approval' (*AM*, 133). When Mark quizzes Maggie on why she removed her engagement ring before meeting Moran for the first time, she replies:

> 'We didn't tell Daddy we are engaged. If I wore the ring it'd look as if we got engaged without his leave.'
> 'That's what happened.'
> 'It wouldn't look right.'
> 'What if the old boy can't stand me?'
> 'It won't matter love…' (*AM*, 134)

But even in this matter Maggie inverts traditional custom and effectively asks Moran for permission to marry. That it 'won't matter' whether Moran gives his leave or not further illustrates both the importance of the cultural collective and also its inherent immateriality. Shelia is faced with a similar choice when she decides to marry – again, according to tradition it would be 'a white wedding in June at the little village church' (*AM*, 150). This Moran 'would not endure' for it meant having 'to lead her up the aisle in front of people he spent his life avoiding' (*AM*, 150). Again, Shelia compromises in the face of her father's intractability: 'Faced with the choice, she wanted Moran more than any particular altar rail or beloved trees' (*AM*, 151).

To critique this analysis, Jane Flax would state:

> Woman is not identified with but relegated to the realm of the Other, the bearer of difference, the body, instinct, lacking a phallus, castrated. If we are in or enjoying our bodies, we are perpetually outside of this and all possible cultures. Woman, in Lacan's theory, is placed in a familiar double bind. She is charged with introducing "difference" in human experience. Yet as woman we literally cannot speak, we do not know what we experience, and we can say nothing to the men (signifiers?) who constitute culture.[86]

In so far as he is virile, a man is always his own metaphor. The father places himself, as locus of the law, above the signifying chain in a metaphorical position. For the male subject, it is a question of identifying himself with the father qua possessor of the penis and for the female subject it is a question of recognizing the man qua the one who possesses it. The Oedipus Complex can be seen, in short, as the conquest of the symbolic order through language. By the seventies, Lacan was developing a theory of the Other, not as the other of intersubjectivity or language, but as the Other of sexual relationship. He proposed a new theory on the specificity of feminine *jouissance* . He proposed to start again from the primary masochism as described by Freud. In *Beyond the Pleasure Principle*, Freud had already challenged the anteriority of sadism to masochism:

> The account that was formerly given of masochism requires emendation as being too sweeping in one respect: there might be such a thing as primary masochism—a possibility which I had contested at that time.[87]

The reason for specifying the primary nature of masochism was to underscore an early fusion of the death instinct through and with the life instinct occurring internally. Accordingly, primary masochism also becomes primal in psychic and instinctual life, prior to any object. Lacan's idea was that this concept of 'primary masochism' was inaccurate, and should be replaced by the idea that the sexual relationship does not exist. The sexual relationship, Lacan argued, does not exist in the unconscious because the Other of language stands between them as a third party: 'Between male and female beings there is no such thing as an instinctive relationship.'[88] Men are dedicated to phallic *jouissance,* a *jouissance* of the

---

[86] Jane Flax, *Thinking Fragments – Psychoanalysis, Feminism & Postmodernism in the Contemporary West*, pp.105-6.
[87] Sigmund Freud, *Beyond the Pleasure Principle*, p. 66.
[88] Jacques Lacan, *The Seminar of Jacques Lacan, Book XX: Encore*, p.64.

Oneness which separates them from women and allows them only a part-object access to the feminine body. Women, on the contrary, are on the side of the Other. They are directly confronted to the fact that the Other is incompatible with *jouissance* . This has a physiological correlate and also a logical one: the woman, as such, is 'not-all'; she is a stranger to herself insomuch as an other woman is always there to show her that she is incomplete, even if a man can bestow her a phallic equivalent. In this case, the logical structure of femininity replaces what the name of the father cannot do; the subject can elaborate something about the structure of the world on the basis that a woman represents the totality of the objects in the world, insomuch as she presents herself as not-all. As we shall see in the next section, Moran is his daughter's 'first man' and their love of him is indistinguishable from the fear he inspires in them (*AM*, 62). As much as the novel traces the incursion of the symbolic into the family's fragile, 'imaginary' world, Moran remains steadfast in this role. While two of his daughters will in time marry, it is their husband's that marry into *his* family, a break with the tradition of women going 'into' the family of their husbands. As Moran says to Maggie, '"I look on all my children as equal. Anybody they choose to bring into the family will get looked on in the same way. If you marry Mark, he'll be like any other member of the family, neither more or less"' (*AM*, 140).

Sons and Daughters

As we have seen, acceptance of the law of the father, and hence subjection to the law of society, is a crucial step in the formation of personality. McGahern's fathers do not carry any of these positive attributes. In *Amongst Women*, Moran's bullying of his teenage daughters is implicitly contrasted with his inability to maintain his ascendancy over his former lieutenant, McQuaid. McQuaid acts as another, different big Other to Moran, he deconstructs his ego and invades his imaginary identity. McQuaid once bolstered his ego as a freedom fighter, a killer independent of the community. That McQuaid is no longer willing to accept this role leads Moran to feel a 'wild surge of resentment' towards him (*AM*, 11). The military and its discipline, though he never romanticised it, is key to Moran's imperturbability, reinforcing the image of him as head of a small battalion rather than a family. His '[S]eparateness and pride' (*AM*, 23) is what first attracted Rose whilst he addresses his children as the 'troops' (*AM*, 3, 31, 59). McQuaid also make reference to the 'missing soldiers' (*AM*, 12). He tells his daughters: '"The closest I ever got to any man was when I had him in the sights of my rifle and I never missed"' (*AM*, 7).

During his second, major argument with Rose, he speaks to her 'as quietly as if he were taking rifle aim' (*AM*, 69). Mark, Maggie's husband, complains to her that his stay in Moran household was '[L]ike moving around in a war area' (*AM*, 135).

Finally, as James Whyte demonstrates, Moran's courtship of Rose is portrayed 'as a battle between two military strategists.'[89] Rose, on her way to the post office, exposes herself to the taunts of the local community which 'echoes out like firing' (*AM*, 25). This can be compared to McQuaid's memory of the ambush and 'the steady fire coming from the windows' (*AM*, 17). Rose eventually withdraws, forcing Moran's hand and in doing so 'She is no longer vulnerable… from a given and confident position she would be now able to move forwards' (*AM*, 30). Again, this resembles the situation in the countryside after the ambush: '"We had them on the run by then… we hadn't to hide any longer"' (*AM*, 15). There is little doubt that he is outmanoeuvred by Rose, which leaves him, on the day of his marriage, looking at his bride's back with violent puzzlement' (*AM*, 46). That McQuaid is now determined to break up this imaginary world, leaves Moran badly exposed. That his bride succeeds in besting him in the courtship, further underlines Moran's antipathy towards the outside world.

One scene which is of importance is set during the Monaghan Day section, where the daughters are frantically cleaning the house:

> No sooner had the door closed than Mona, released from the tension of his presence, let slip a plate from her hands…quickly they swept up the pieces and hid them away, wondering how they would replace the plate without being found out…anything broken had to be hidden until it could be replaced or forgotten. (*AM*, 10)

The plates act as a metaphor, in one way, for the fractured but outwardly coalesced Moran family, and on a deeper level, for Moran himself, broken but defiant, hidden behind the barriers of the family. Lacan also posited the idea of the *corps morcelé* – the fractured body – which referred not only to the image of the physical body but to any sense of fragmentation and disunity: 'He [the subject] is originally an inchoate collection of desires – there you have the true sense of the fragmented body.'[90] When the infant views himself in the mirror, he see his reflection as whole, a synthesis – this causes him to perceive his own body as divided and

[89] James Whyte, *History, Myth and Ritual in the Fiction of John McGahern*, p.173.
[90] Jacques Lacan, *The Seminar: Book III*, p. 39.

fractured in contrast. This anxiety is viewed positively – a step towards the disintegration of the rigid unity of the ego. The human subject oscillates between these two poles – the image, which is alienating, and the real body, which is, like the plates, in pieces. Lacan used the idea of the fractured self to explain certain symptoms of hysteria, reflecting in part the way the body is divided up by an imaginary anatomy. The structure of desire, as desire of the Other, is shown more clearly in hysteria that in any other structure – the hysteric is someone who appropriates another's desire by identifying with them. As Bruce Fink states:

> The hysteric also identifies with her male partner, and desires as if she were him. In other words, she desires as if she were a man. When Lacan says that "man's desire is the Other's desire," one of the things he means is that we adopt the Other's desire as our own: we desire as if we were someone else.[91]

Certainly, Moran's daughter's desire as if they were the Other – Moran in this case. Each have inherited his sense of separateness and in turn, dominate the men in their lives in the same sense of role reversal that Fink made reference to – Moran's desires are his daughter's desires – his distrust of femininity, weakness, the outside world, friendship tempered somewhat by his espousal of the family and patriarchy – such is the way his daughter's lead their life almost as if they *were* Moran. Maggie returns home to London to discover that her husband has squandered their savings: 'She put the children into day-care and went back to nursing. From then on she would always have her own money' (*AM*, 169). Mona 'had many admirers' who were 'content to move within the authority of her beauty without making any serious demands… if they did they were let go at once' (*AM*, 168). Moran remarks acidly to Shelia on her husband, '"Go and trim that poor husband of yours if you want something to trim. I'd say you were the man for the job"' (*AM*, 158).

Moran turns his family into a closed community and the absence of any intrusion from without further augments his own paternal supremacy. The primacy of the family is an idea also sanctioned by the Catholic Church where links between Catholicism and patriarchy are reinforced by its most repetitive narrative ritual – the rosary – which acts in part as an illustration of what is termed the repetition complex. In psychoanalytic terms, ideology and dogma constitutes a sort of repetition-complex that dooms us to perform the same destructive acts over and over without end.

[91] Bruce Fink, *A Clinical Introduction to Lacanian Psychoanalysis*, pp. 124/25.

Lacan linked the repetition of the unconscious repressed to the insistence of the signifying chain, where 'repetition is fundamentally the insistence of speech.'[92] Lacan used the word 'insistence' to express the notion of repetition or compulsion where in analytical terms, the chain of unconscious purposive ideas insists on being heard, beyond an attachment to the pleasure principal or the ego's attempts to stifle meaning. In Lacan's words:

> For its symbolizing function speech is moving towards nothing less than a transformation of the subject to whom it is addressed by means of the link that it establishes with the one who emits it – in other words, by introducing the effect of the signifier.[93]

In Lacan's view, the signifier dominates over the subject. In his seminar on Poe's "The Purloined Letter", Lacan emphasized how the path of the letter as pure signifier determines the destiny of the subjects – as such, the subject is transformed by the effects of the signifier. The Rosary in *Amongst Women* is such an example – it represents Moran's hold over the family:

> 'They say the family that prays together stays together… I think that families can stay together even though they're scattered, if there is a will to do so. The will is the important thing.' (*AM*, 137)

Even when he uses the Rosary to enforce his dominance over the family, the reality is that it is used merely as a device to impose his will rather than one which automatically confirms it. As Antoinette Quinn writes:

> The Rosary is peculiarly identified with Moran, an economical, realist device for connecting Catholicism, patrocentrism, and the mesmeric rhythms of shared family experience… the stability conferred by ritual and repeated phraseology implicitly underscores the disruptions and changes that the passage of time brings to Great Meadow.[94]

This can be seen in Maggie's return from London, where she becomes the centre of attention – 'She was the centre of the table' – displacing Moran from his self-assumed role (*AM*, 79). He attempts to supplant her primacy by starting the Rosary earlier than usual, but the formulaic manner in

---

[92] Jacques Lacan, *The Seminar. Book III. The Psychoses*, 1955 – 1956, p.242.
[93] Jacques Lacan, *Écrits* (1977), p.83.
[94] Antoinette Quinn, 'A Prayer For My Daughters: Patriarchy in *Amongst Women*', p.86.

which it is recited breaks down and rather than confirming his role as head of the family, it positively discourages it:

> This night Moran enunciated each repetitious word with slow clarity and force as if the very dwelling on suffering, death and human supplication would scatter all flimsy vanities of a great world; and the muted responses giving back their acceptance of human servitude did not improve his humour. (*AM*, 79)

Once he loses the physical strength which has helped him regulate the patriarchal power structure in the family, the words of the Rosary no longer contribute to, or endorse, his claims. Nonetheless, his daughters and younger son will return time and again, exposing themselves to Moran's approbation in attempt to reaffirm their own sense of identity. For example, the word 'came' or 'come' holds special significance in the opening pages of the novel – it is repeated no less than nine times on the first page: 'came at Christmas', 'came every weekend', 'her family to come with her', 'come regularly', 'come from London', 'not come', 'came every year'. It can also be seen as an allusion to Moran as the 'big Other.' (*AM*, 1)

Moran's final utterance in the novel further indicates that the Rosary holds no special significance to him save as a means to reinforce the hierarchal structure in the household. According to David Malcolm: 'He seems to have no religious belief himself, yet insists on the ritual, for he decides when the beads are to be told, and he controls the whole event. His patriarchal power is never more evident.'[95] It draws the family together but firmly places him as the centre of attention – but as his life slips away, his daughters take up the Rosary on his command. It is notable that by the end of the novel, the Rosary is only thing Moran has left to initiate – his daughters and wife have supplanted him in everything else. Conscious of this perhaps, it may be the reason why his final words are '*Shut up*!' If he can command them to pray, a final command to 'shut up' indicates that he is not willing to fully surrender, even on his death-bed. As Antoinette Quinn states:

> In view of the novel's critique of patriarchy, the desirability of the daughters' patrimony, however lyrically endorsed, is questionable. The power they derive from their father is founded on dominance, not on the metaphysical revelations of his final months. It is an empowering that will

[95] David Malcolm, *Understanding John McGahern*, p.113.

> enable them to live independently as adults, but it is also an assimilation of patriarchal values.[96]

Anne Goarzin draws attention to another recurring motif in the novel, that of the beach at Strandhill:

> Moran and Rose go there first, pp.58-59; then Michael and his lover Nell, pp.104-106; then Moran and Rose, who initiate the outing this time, pp.173-74. As one examines the three passages which differ syntactically and semantically, it appears that that the feeling of unity is not merely due to the recurring geographical location, but to more subtly pervasive images of liquidity which lie at the heart of the story… the sea makes for a homogenous image… this concrete yet moving 'line' helps one track down an elusive text that has neither beginning nor end and suggest a constant circulation of meaning as spatial and temporal impressions add up layers of meaning.[97]

If Moran's daughter's come to assimilate their father's patriarchal values, Michael also comes to resemble his father: 'From Moran he inherited a certain contempt for women as well as a dependence on them but it did not diminish his winning ways' (*AM*, 91). This is a trait his sisters have also inherited, for on their return from the funeral of their father, Shelia remarks of the men-folk: "Will you look at the men. They're more like a crowd of women" (*AM*, 184). He also strives to be the centre of attention – when he and his sisters visit the neighbours on St. Stephen's Day, he finds himself 'very much in their shadow… tired of being ignored he went home with ill-grace to Rose' (*AM*, 99). His narcissism is the cause for his being absent when his father dies: 'Being on the periphery of what was happening he had become bored and driven to town with his son' (*AM*, 180). When he goes to Strandhill with Nell he '[b]etrayed the same sense of separateness the father had instilled in the others' (*AM*, 106). He walks the same beachfront with his lover as his father did before him, further indicating Moran's pervasive influence – patriarchy is not so much supplanted as subsumed into a new symbolic order.

In *Amongst Women*, a large part of the fascination which Moran holds for Rose and his daughters is sexual. Rose loves him, his 'sense of separateness and pride that she found unlike any of the other local men she had known' (*AM*, 23). Before his marriage to Rose, Moran shares his bed

---

[96] Antoinette Quinn, 'A Prayer for my Daughter: Patriarchy in *Amongst Women*', p. 89.

[97] Anne Goarzin, 'Objects in the Works of John McGahern', p.35.

with his youngest son, Michael. Tellingly, McGahern writes: 'Tomorrow night Rose would lie in the boy's place' (*AM*, 39). His daughters have an oedipal attraction for him also. When Maggie departs for London for the first time, 'Moran turned and kissed her as if it were a last good night to all the nights she had come to him' (*AM*, 63). Later, 'The girls wanted to gather their father and the whole, true, heartbreaking day into their arms' (*AM*, 81). He remains the dominant figure in their life. Even after two of the daughters, Maggie and Shelia, marry, his control is secure as neither of their husbands posed a threat to Moran's authority. But what does it mean for Moran's daughter's to underwrite their father? In other words, how is it that we know his daughters only through the father? Indeed, it seems that he marks the founding auspices of female representation and that we have no way out.

The Electra complex, identified by Carl Jung, occurs where a triangle of mother-father-daughter plays out in a manner which is not a part of traditional psychoanalysis. Jung wrote:

> The oedipal conflict takes on a more masculine and therefore more typical form in a son, whereas a daughter develops a specific liking for the father, with a corresponding jealous attitude towards the Moran. We would call this the Electra complex. As everyone knows, Electra took vengeance on her mother Clytemnestra for murdering her husband Agamemnon and thus robbing her – Electra – of her beloved father.[98]

Jung suggested that when the girl discovers she lacks penis that her father possesses, she imagines she will gain one if he makes her pregnant, and so moves emotionally closer to him. She thus resents her mother whom she believes castrated her. The father symbolizes attractive power and a potentially hazardous male-female relationship is formed, with predictable jealousies and envy as the mother completes the triangle. The dangers of incestuous abuse add, and perhaps develop, the female position of siren temptation. Girls, as well as boys, need to find independence and their separation from the mother is a matter of creating a separate femininity. This is not as strong a separation as that of boys, and girls can sustain closer female-female relationships with the mothers. This perhaps explains something of why relationships with others are a more important part of a female life than it is for a male.

---

[98] Carl Jung and Carl Kerényi, *Essays on the Science of Mythology: the Myths of the Divine Child and the Divine Maiden,* p.154.

From the male perspective, most of the main players in this drama are absent – Moran's first wife is dead and Luke has departed. It is possible, however, to see an Oedipal drama played out between Rose, Michael and his father: 'Rose loved to see Michael home. He was more her natural child than any of the girls' (*AM*, 142). Since the symbolic is the realm of the law, and since the Oedipus complex is the conquest of that order, it has a normative function. We have no way of knowing when Michael's biological mother died. He would appear to compete for Rose's affection but Moran only intervenes when he begins a sexual relationship with Nell Morahan. One could be tempted to suggest that Nell stands as surrogate to Michael's absent mother and Maggie's comment: '"You'd think she had more to do than cradle snatch"' (*AM*, 102) is noteworthy in this context.

Moran intervenes once more as an omnipotent and prohibitive figure. An infant has little choice but to accede to the paternal position but Michael, at fifteen, resists and by this some part of the complex seems to be interrupted. A phobia arises when the subject cannot make the transition from the second time of the Oedipus complex to the third time because the real father does not intervene or, in this case, is thwarted in his attempts. The phobia then functions as substitute for the intervention of the real father thus permitting the subject to make the passage to the third time of the Oedipus complex in a somewhat more atypical way. He eventually marries an older woman - 'She's a good sensible age' (*AM*, 171) - and the incestuous link is emphasised by Moran referring to her as 'just another daughter' (*AM*, 172).

The father does provide a haven from female-female jealousies, and so a healthy father-daughter relationship may be built that also includes appropriate distance. As with mother-son, once the incest taboos are established, a uniquely satisfying opposite-sex relationship can be built, although secret desires for the father can result in the girl feeling some guilt about the relationship. The latently incestuous relationship which Moran inspires in his daughters is violated only when Shelia leaves him and the family in the hayfield to go indoors and make love to Sean. As a result, the family is united in its disapprobation:

> "You'd think they could have waited", Michael said quietly, in agreement with the resentment he felt all around him. It was as if the couple were together disregarding the inviolability of the house, its true virginity, with a selfish absorption. (*AM* 166)

Michael here shows a curious degree of hypocrisy – he is the most libidinous of Moran's children but in such matters he becomes curiously conventional. Like Mahoney in *The Dark*, he challenges his father for dominance in the household. But with victory, he does not assume his father's place – akin to his slightly feminine characteristics, he chooses compromise instead. Even in adulthood, as here, his daughters considered themselves Moran's inferiors and granted him a sort of paternal carte blanche. Around Moran a 'silence and deadness would fall upon them…if they had to stay they moved around the place like shadows' (*AM*, 53). Yet Moran also instils in his daughters the importance of family and the house:

> Beneath all differences was the belief that the whole house was essentially one…deprived of this sense they were nothing, scattered, individual things. They would put up with anything in order to have this sense of belonging. (*AM*, 145)

They need to return again and again to Great Meadow in order to be affirmed and re-affirmed by Moran, but in doing so they forfeit their autonomy. The bond that exists between father and daughter is an indissoluble bond and the mechanics of patriarchy continues until Moran falls into ill health.

New Ireland

In a recent study of contemporary Irish culture, Joe Cleary suggests that the backwards glance by some Irish authors indicated the traumatic nature of Irish history – it is the oppressive and restrictive nature of the recent past that '[a]cts as a negative validation of the present which, whatever else it may be, is understood as a lucky escape "from all that."'[99] A novel such as *Amongst Women* emphasized memory as part of a transcendental strategy, so that the way to the past is constructed as part of the subject. According to Lacan, there can never be an objective representation of history. Articulation of past events is influenced by that which has occurred in years between, and the verbalization of this experience brings with it its own distortions. He states: 'history is already producing itself on the stage where it will be played out, once it has been written down, both within the subject and outside him.'[100] Once an event takes place, it is transformed by the symbolic order through the languages and cultural context in which it is first interpreted.

---

[99] Joe Cleary, 'Modernization and Aesthetical Ideology', in Ray Ryan (ed.), *Contemporary Irish Culture:, Writing in the Irish Republic*, p.108.
[100] Jacques Lacan, *Écrits* (1977), p.57.

According to David Malcolm, readers '[m]ust come to their own terms with McGahern's picture of family life in mid-twentieth century rural Ireland.'[101] For Eamonn Wall: '*Amongst Women* is a mirror to the century… a chronicle of the fortunes of the nation in its progress through fifty years of change.'[102] We are given no indication of any time-line in the novel, however, and must assume by the reference to the post-war shortage of nurses, the fact that Maggie's first husband is a teddy-boy, and later, as we learn that Shelia's new home in the suburban sprawl of Dublin is 'a new estate of a couple of hundred bungalows exactly the same, the front gardens still raw with concrete' (*AM*, 151), that the period in question is roughly 1945 – 1965. These years, as I outlined in the opening chapter, witnessed a number of seismic events and yet the mind-set of the people was slow to change – women remained discriminated against, both in legislation and in the home. But from what we can see in this chapter, they had begun to restructure matters to suit their own predicament.

If they could not fight the old order it stood to reason that they could certainly rearrange matters in much the same way that Rose rearranges the Moran household when she first arrives. By standing deferential and yet resolute against Moran's instinctive conservatism, the women in novel achieve liberation of sorts – but only by taking on much of the machinery of patriarchy. Moran's withdrawal could act as metaphor of Ireland's policy of isolationism – his generation would give no further ground but in acting in such a fashion, left themselves no room for manoeuvre. With the advent of Lemass's brand of *Realpolitik* in the nineteen sixties, both Great Meadow and Ireland are opened up to the world: Moran's daughters 'brought the bracing breath of the outside, an outside Moran refused to accept unless it came from the family' (*AM*, 93).

The novel thus is a paean of sorts, part critical, part exploratory as if the author was attempting to make sense of this passing world, paying little heed to what followed afterwards. What he captured was the transitory sense of modern Ireland, a departure from the old symbolic order but to what end? If Moran represented the past, something to return and keep returning to irrespective of the cost, his death represents a break with tradition and the cultural symbolic and a last vindication perhaps to the struggle for independence – both the literal struggle in the nineteen twenties and the struggle of another generation fifty years later.

[101] David Malcolm, *Understanding John McGahern*, p.109.
[102] Eamonn Wall, 'The Living Stream: John McGahern's *Amongst Women* and Irish Writing in the 1990's', in *Studies*, p.305.

CHAPTER FIVE

BRIAN MOORE

BRIAN MOORE (1921 – 1999) was born in Belfast to a middle-class Catholic family and while he spent most of his life in Canada and in America, it was Ireland, particularly the west coast of Ireland, which remained very much a part of his inspiration as a writer. Moore acknowledges this affection when he says: "there is something about this place, some sense of the past thrusting itself forward, something eerie - ghostly - something almost metaphysical, which can change our normal way of seeing things ... The West is a place where I feel, suddenly that anything might happen, perhaps even a miracle."[1] He was educated at St. Malachy's College in north Belfast and at the age of 20 be left home and served abroad as a supply clerk with the British Ministry of War Transport during World War Two. Eamon Maher suggests that 'a loss of faith' was probably one of the main reasons why he left Belfast in 1942:

> In spite of the fervour of the Moore household, young Moore soon discovered that he 'lacked the religious sense.' His problems began with confession. He doubted that it was necessary to announce his sexual peccadilloes to a stranger. So he began to lie in confessional and was surprised afterwards at how little fear he experienced of God's retributions.[2]

In 1948 he went to Canada, working as a journalist for the *Montreal Gazette (*where he met his first wife, Jacqueline Sirois) supplementing his meagre income by writing pulp fiction under the *nom de plume* of Bernard Mara and Michael Bryan. By 1953 he had quit his job as a journalist and had become a Canadian citizen. He began his career as a serious novelist with the publication of *The Lonely Passion of Judith Hearne* in 1955 and *The Feast of Lupercal*, published some three years later. After an acrimonious

---

[1] Liam Heaney, 'Brian Moore: Novelist In Search Of An Irish Identity', in *Contemporary Review*, p.12.
[2] Eamon Maher, *Crosscurrents and Confluences*, p.125.

separation in 1964, he would later move to Malibu, California with his second wife, the Canadian Jean Denney, where he lived until his death on the 12th of January, 1999.

If Moore neatly segues the urban/rural bind of Broderick and McGahern, there are other similarities which he shares with the authors, most notably in his, at times confusing, religious ideology. As Jo O Donoghue writes:

> Much of the interest in Moore's novels over the past thirty years has focused on his attitude to Catholicism… he is frequently considered a 'Catholic' novelist, but he is surely an enigma or even unique in being a 'Catholic' novelist who has lost his faith and who therefore is much more interested… in people who lose or have lost theirs.[3]

However, Moore's interests in faith were not those of, say, Graham Greene. For example, unlike Greene's whiskey-priest, Judith Hearne's loss of faith is brought about by a series of cataclysmic events and her doubts are indistinguishable from her sexual longing and desperate social position. Judith assumes that 'Religion was there: it was not something you thought about, and if, occasionally, you had a small doubt about something… well that was the Devil at work and God's ways were not our way' (*LPJH*, 50). But her faith is shaken, not by intellectual doubt, but by social circumstances. She doubts when she learns that James Madden was 'a doorman, a lackey, a servant. Common, common as mud' (*LPJH*, 81-82) and not the affluent hotel manager she initially believed. This revelation sparks a drinking binge and social disgrace – she flees to the church for solace and begs for a sign: 'why am I alone, why did I yield to the temptation of drink, why, why has it all happened like this… please dear Lord, give me a sign, give me strength' (*LPJH*, 102).

Because one questions faith is not in itself a sign that one has lost their faith. O'Donoghue suggests that 'Judith's attitude towards religion is itself revealed as being based on observance rather than on belief.' This is not entirely true. All believers are subject to phases of doubt. Her plea in the church draws equivalence to the Biblical passage concerning Christ on the Cross: 'And about the ninth hour Jesus cried out with a loud voice, saying, "*Eli, Eli, lama sabachthani?*" that is, "My God, My God, why hast thou forsaken me?"'[4] A second Biblical allegory comes at the close of the novel when Judith attacks the tabernacle in the Church, 'But the door rejected

---

[3] Jo O'Donoghue, *Brian Moore – A Critical Study*, p. 9.

[4] *Matthew* 27:45-46.

her. It would not open. *Blood ran from the nails.* The altar cloth slid sideways along the marble of the altar table. Candlesticks crashed on the step' (*LPJH*, 176 – my italics). 'And behold, the veil of the temple was torn in two from top to bottom; and the earth shook and the rocks were split.'[5]

Judith's route to her own personal Calvary is torturous – but it comes more from losing face than faith. She is a single woman in a country where a good man is a 'prize' (*LPJH*, 63) to be won or lost and a woman is 'up for auction, a country auction, where the auctioneer stands up and says what am I bid?... because its either that or back on the shelf for you' (*LPJH*, 167). Like Broderick's Athlone, Belfast is a repressive place offering little sympathy to a lonely, sexually frustrated woman: 'The order, the neatness, the floodlit cenotaph, a white respectable phallus in sinking Irish bog… the dour Ulster burghers walking proudly among these monuments to their mediocrity' (*LPJH*, 76).

It is not so much the Church but its representatives that fail Judith, for this is a society that pays more attention to the aesthetics of righteousness than the application of Christian charity. Father Quigley's fire and brimstone sermon (*LPJH*, 52-55) is a mere performance, where the weather adds to 'this sombre preliminary lighting' (*LPJH*, 52). The culmination of the sermon is when he 'leans forward, grabbing the edge of the pulpit as though he were going to jump over it' (*LPJH*, 54) and intones dramatically: '"They-don't-have-time-for God."' (*LPJH*, 54) But when Judith seeks him out in desperation for confession, he thinks to himself: 'A general confession no less. And I promised to see Father Feeny for golf at half-one' (*LPJH*, 143). It could be argued that Judith has far more faith than Quigley – it is society then rather than any intellectual probing that shakes it to the core.

As Robert Sullivan states:

> Although religion permeates Moore's books, from his first novel to the recent *The Statement*, he is not concerned (unlike Joyce) in these early novels with intellectual doubt as such, although Bernard Rice approaches this position in *The Lonely Passion of Judith Hearne*. Rather he is anxious to explore the social and, in consequence, psychological repercussions the Church effects on its dependants, especially in their time of need.[6]

---

[5] *Matthew* 27:51.

[6] Robert Sullivan, *A Matter of Faith – The Fiction of Brian Moore*, p.20.

Another similarity with Broderick and McGahern is Moore's debt to French literature, as Maher states: 'He maintained, and with justification, that the French respect and cherish their writers and intellectuals, something that could not be said of many other countries and especially not Ireland.'[7] The pessimistic, helpless worldview he promulgated in novels such as *The Doctor's Wife*, owed much to Camus' absurdist approach. It may also be said that the way in which the author abnegates his omnipotent control in the novel harkens back to the French *nouveau roman* and practitioners such as Butor and Robbe-Grillet. (Having said that, Moore remained very traditional in terms of 'form' unlike the *nouveaux romanciers*.) One could also argue that the character of Judith Hearne owes much to Flaubert's Emma Bovary – both gain the sympathy of the reader by openly revealing their petty egocentricities and foibles in a manner that elicits not reprimand, but compassion.

As O'Donoghue writes:

> In the case of Judith Hearne, her faults, her misconceptions and her delusions are the result of a blighted life that has been created for her by circumstances outside her control – in short, a determined life. By the same technique, Flaubert creates in Emma Bovary a character whose faults are manifest, but with whom the reader none-the-less sympathises.[8]

In terms of a Lacanian reading of *The Lonely Passion of Judith Hearne*, it is perhaps important to point out how Judith Hearne is obsessed with the reality of the symbolic order. Her dilemma has its ontological aspect. For her problem is not just whether Belfast can give her a husband, but whether being can give her a sign, an earnest of transcendence:

> Empty. And above her, the night sky… nothing beyond it but the stars, the planets, with the earth spinning among them. Surely some great design kept it all moving, some Presence made it meaningful (*LPJH*, 104)

'Show me a sign' prays the distracted Judith, but no sign is given to her (*LPJH*, 147). For Lacan, neither the imaginary nor the symbolic can fully comprehend the Real, which remains out there somewhere beyond their reach. Our instinctive needs are shaped by the discourse in which we express our demand for satisfaction. However, discourse's moulding needs not satisfaction but desire which runs on a chain of signifiers. When 'I' express my desire in words, 'I' am always subverted by the unconscious

[7] Eamon Maher, *Crosscurrents and Confluences*, p.126.
[8] Jo O'Donoghue, *Brian Moore – A Critical Study*, p.39.

which presses on with its own sideways game. Lacan proposes that the subject of the Cartesian *cogito* is in fact one and the same as the subject of the unconscious. Psychoanalysis can thus operate with a Cartesian method, advancing from doubt to certainty, with the crucial difference that it does not start from the statement 'I think' but from the affirmation 'it thinks' *(ça pense).*[9] Lacan rewrites Descartes' phrase in various ways, such as: 'I think where I am not, therefore I am where I do not think.'[10] Lacan also uses the *cogito* to distinguish between the subject of the statement and the subject of the enunciation. In designating the enunciation as unconscious, Lacan affirms that the source of speech is not the ego, nor consciousness, but the unconscious; language comes from the Other, and the idea that 'I' am master of my discourse is only an illusion. The very word 'I' *(Je)* is ambiguous; as shifter, it is both a signifier acting as subject of the statement, and an index which designates, but does not signify, the subject of the enunciation.[11] The subject is thus split between these two levels, divided in the very act of articulating the *I* that presents the illusion of unity.[12]

As is the case with Judith, the unconscious desire works on a metaphoric and metonymic substitutions and displacements which elude consciousness, but reveals itself in dreams, jokes and art: 'Traffic lights flashed red, amber, and green in empty futility. Two late-goers passed below on the pavement, the voices loud, unreal in argument' (*LPJH*, 155). Judith Hearne finds the solid empirical world inadequately significant; a world of signs which say nothing, where the Sacred Heart of Jesus is as inarticulate as the traffic lights in the street.

Judith retreats into a world of fantasy and make-believe. As such, Lacan viewed fantasy as a form of psychic projection which concealed a more distressing image. Thus he first conceived of fantasy as a defensive structure designed to protect against the perception of "lack" in the maternal other, that is, of castration. Lacan compares the fantasy scene to a frozen image on a cinema screen – just as the film may be stopped to avoid showing a traumatic scene, so also the fantasy scene 'is a defence which veils castration.'[13]

---

[9] Jacques Lacan, *The Seminar. Book XI. The Four Fundamental Concepts of Psychoanalysis*, pp.35-36.

[10] Jacques Lacan, *Écrits* (1977), p.166.

[11] *Ibid.*, p.298.

[12] Jacques Lacan, *The Seminar. Book XI. The Four Fundamental Concepts of Psychoanalysis*, p.139.

[13] Jacques Lacan, *Le Séminaire. Livre IV. La relation d'objet*, p.120.

Following on Freud's idea of fantasy – a scene which is presented in the imagination which stages an unconscious desire – Lacan questioned the relationship between fantasy and fixation. He also addressed the larger question of memory. He suggested that fantasy need not be diametrically opposed to memory, rather that fantasy might rework memory depending on the pressure of unconscious desire and the defensive strategies of the subject. Thus Lacan stressed that fantasy fundamentally worked to transform memories of real events. This defence is reflected in the fantasy that stages the fulfilment of, or props up, the subject's desire. Desire comes into being in place of satisfaction, as a defence against *jouissance*

In particular, he made it clear that the subject is always represented in fantasy, as in the dream. Freud's list of detachable objects – the breast, penis, faeces – to which Lacan added the voice, the gaze, and the phoneme, all these amount to the object-causes of desire that cannot be truly represented. Desire staged in fantasy is not the subject's own, but the other's desire, the desire of those around me with whom I interact. Indeed, the original question of desire is not directly 'What do I want?', but 'What do others want from me? What do they see in me?' One of Lacan's most oft-repeated formulas is: 'man's desire is the desire of the Other.'[14] This can be understood in many complementary ways, but the most important to remember is that desire is essentially 'desire of the Other's desire', which means both desire to be the object of another's desire, and desire for recognition by another. Lacan takes this idea from Hegel, via Alexandre Kojève, who stated: 'Desire is human only if the one desires, not the body, but the Desire of the other… that is to say, if he wants to be 'desired' or 'loved', or, rather, 'recognised' in his human value…. In other words, all human, anthropogenetic desire … is, finally, a function of the desire for 'recognition.'[15]

Judith Hearne imagines herself in many different guises for James Madden. She views herself as a loving spouse, sitting prettily on his knee asking how his day went. She sees herself as some battered wife whose husband 'struck out with his great fist and sent her reeling, the brute. But contrite afterward, he sank to his knees and begged forgiveness' (*LPJH*, 25). She views herself as Delilah, 'stricken by her deed' (*LPJH*, 72); later she would be, '*A grand dame*, Miss Judith Hearne of Bella vista keeping company with Maud Gone McBride' (*LPJH*, 157) or as a gypsy: 'Her

[14] Jacques Lacan, *The Seminar. Book XI. The Four Fundamental Concepts of Psychoanalysis*, p.235.
[15] Alexandre Kojève, *Introduction to the Reading of Hegel*, p.6.

frame, plain as a cheap clothes-rack, filled now with soft curves' (*LPJH*, 18). Since sexuality is the domain in which we get closest to the intimacy of another human being, totally exposing ourselves to him or her, sexual enjoyment is real for Lacan: something traumatic in its intensity, something impossible in the sense that we cannot ever make sense of it. This is why a sexual relation, in order to function, has to be screened through some fantasy. For Lacan, all drives are sexual drives, and every drive is a death drive since every drive is excessive, repetitive, and ultimately destructive.[16] The drives are closely related to desire; both originate in the field of the subject, as opposed to the genital drive, which (if it exists) finds its form on the side of the Other.[17] However, the drive is not merely another name for desire: they are the partial aspects in which desire is realised.

Finally, *The Lonely Passion of Judith Hearne* ties in with some of the other key tropes in this book. Like Broderick's Willie Ryan, Judith is an outsider who finds herself institutionalized against her will. Like Lily Fallon in *The Fugitives*, she projects her desires and fantasies onto a man who is incapable of reciprocating. Akin to young Mahoney, she questions her faith, a seismic fracture occurs but neither come to a resolution with their doubts – for Judith, it is a spiritual questioning; for Mahoney, more a moral dilemma. Lastly, Judith's battle with the big Other – God who literally watches over her and her Aunt, who acts as her guilty conscience – this battle draws similarities with Moran's daughters in *Amongst Women* – they too struggle to emerge from their father's pervasive image. The novel also expands the boundaries of the investigation to Northern Ireland and the grey post-war years of stagnation before the outbreak of the 'Troubles' in 1969. Indeed, like McGahern's postage stamp community in Leitrim, this too is a society on the verge of extinction, a snapshot of people whose way of life will be blasted away, not so much by the cold winds of modernization but by the bombs and bullets of a vicious civil war.

The Lonely Passion of Judith Hearne

It was through Judith Hearne that Brian Moore gained international recognition. First published by André Deutsch in 1955, *The Lonely*

---

[16] Jacques Lacan, *Écrits* (2006), p.848.

[17] Jacques Lacan, *The Seminar. Book XI. The Four Fundamental Concepts of Psychoanalysis*, p.189.

Passion of Judith Hearne is set in Belfast and concerns a middle aged spinster (and secret drinker) Judith Hearne. The novel opens with the crucial scene where Judith is unpacking her meagre belongings in yet another bed-sitting room. She unpacks immediately the representations of the two major influences in her life: her aunt's photograph and an oleograph of the Sacred Heart. For Robert Sullivan, they represent both 'Judy's abiding involvement with the past and her reliance on the church for companionship', but also 'those two repressive apparatuses of family and Church that hold her desires in check.'[18]

She treks downstairs in search of a hammer, encountering both her new landlady, Mrs Henry Rice, and her son, Bernard. Bernard, an odd, childish individual, 'all bristly blond jowls, tiny puffy hands and long blond curly hair' (*LPJH*, 9), who acts in some ways as a counterpoint to Miss Hearne's essentially selfless nature. He is an opportunist who stares at Miss Hearne, 'rejecting her as all males had before him' (*LPJH*, 9). The next morning, when Judith arrives down to breakfast, she encounters James Patrick Madden, brother of her landlady, 'loudly dressed…a yellow tie with white golf balls on it, a suit of some brown silky stuff on it like shantung' (*LPJH*, 20). In time, Judith will build up an imago around Madden 'big, stern and manly' (*LPJH*, 25) and conjecture wildly about his life in America. When he tells Judith that he 'was in the hotel business right on Time's Square' (*LPJH*, 24) she immediately assumes that he owned the hotel.

It is the first of many instances where they speak at cross-purposes to each other – when she suggests that Bernard is 'a little queer' (*LPJH*, 47), he assumes that she is making reference to his sexuality when she is in fact employing the formal use of word, meaning strange or unorthodox. Later, when he takes Judith to the cinema and discusses his plans for opening a burger joint in Dublin, he believes he is talking to a future business partner when Judith assumes that he is making plans for marriage (*LPJH*, 75). Miscommunication is, perhaps, the greatest tragedy in the novel. After they return to the boarding house that evening, Mrs Henry Rice lets slip Madden's true occupation, caustically remarking: '"Opening the doors of taxi's, that's more in his line"' (*LPJH*, 79). Judith is shocked by this development and to console herself and to quieten the voice of her disapproving aunt on the mantelpiece. She thinks bitterly: 'A doorman, a lackey, a servant. Common, common as mud' (*LPJH*, 82), as she turns to alcohol for solace. As George O'Brien states:

[18] Robert Sullivan, *A Matter of Faith – The Fiction of Brian Moore*, p.15

> Neither of them… can see beyond the fantasies each has developed about the objectives of the relationship. This failure obviously limits the relationship's potential, while at the same time highlighting how similar Madden and Judith are in their social isolation and spiritual emptiness.[19]

With her fantasies in tatters, we begin to piece together the true strands of Judith's wretched existence. Desperately wanting a husband and family of her own, she instead spends the best years of her adult life as companion and nurse to her Aunt D'Arcy, the relative who took care of her when both her parents died. After the death of Aunt D'Arcy, she is left with limited financial resources and is forced to live in a number of run-down boarding houses, all of which she is eventually asked to vacate because of her drinking. She teaches piano and embroidery to an ever-diminishing handful of students, has very few possessions, and fewer social attachments. In fact, her only social involvement is tea with the O'Neill family on Sunday afternoons. Professor Owen and Mrs. Moira O'Neill represent the sort of society that Aunt D'Arcy would approve of. Only later do we find how one-sided even this relationship is. The O'Neills secretly dread her visits – their son, Shaun, says before her arrival: '"Let's say ten minutes before the advent of the Great Bore."' (*LPJH*, 59) The rest of the family scatter and it is left to Moira to entertain Judith, though even she succumbs to dozing by the fireside.

Once Judith learns of Madden's station in life, she turns first, notably, to alcohol and only then to the Church. She continues to pray for a 'sign' but as her prayers go unanswered, she drinks even more and begins to lose her faith in God. She causes a scene in the boarding house and finally confronts Madden, though such an action is anathema to her conventional principles whereby 'The male must pursue' (*LPJH*, 112). He rebuffs her advances, coldly but comprehensively. Her dreams shattered, she goes to confession, to a Father Quigley, but even he cannot bear to listen to Judith for more than a few minutes.

When a series of humiliating incidents culminates in her drunken assault of the tabernacle in the parish church, she is taken to a nursing home to recover. There, under the supervision of nuns, her faith (outwardly) seems to be returning. The novel ends ambiguously, for Judith shows no sign of wanting to return to the outside world as she continues to be watched over by her aunt's picture positioned on the dressing-table by her bedside. Judith appears to be obsessed with the reality of symbolism in

---

[19] George O'Brien, 'The Aesthetics of Exile', in Liam Harte & Michael Parker (eds), *Contemporary Irish Fiction*, p.35.

a way which suggests an authorial preoccupation. At times, the novel forsakes the immediacies of realism for a dialectic between sign and silence, sacrament and significance. Faith and daydreams – of human or divine love – are all that Judith Hearne has, the only hope or motive of her life, besides her 'sinful' indulgence in drink that leaves her 'more lonely, more despised,' and that promises no future but growing 'old in a room, year by year, until they take [her] to a poor-house' (*LPJH*, 175). As these are undermined, her doubt precipitates her 'passion' which subsequently erupts. Need exceeding fear or shame, she challenges the heart of her illusions, performing a sacrilege which, in proving nothing but her need, leaves her in what Moore later calls in *Catholics* 'the hell of no feeling, that null, that void.'[20] With all her passion spent, she becomes knowingly reliant on the personification of a world of familiar objects – imagination's 'miracles' – as her only comfort in an otherwise barren future.

There is desolate pathos here, and grotesqueness, but more than that, a kind of heroic resilience, like Faulkner's Dilsey or Steinbeck's Rose of Sharon, all the more impressive since Judith Hearne lacks their maternal purpose, has no one to share life with, no one to undergo it for – except herself, and the friendly projections she knows are as unreal as they are necessary. The partial heroic note of this conclusion, along with the depth of passion that Judith Hearne has managed to express, allays any charge of treason – of forcing us to contemplate something irreconcilably depressing.

Imagination and Escapism

In his fundamental text, *The Subversion of the Subject and the Dialectic of Desire in the Freudian Unconscious*, Lacan tried to place fantasy in the genesis of the psychic apparatus by locating it within his 'graph of desire.' The major difficulty here is that the object of the drive, the object of physiological need, and the object of narcissistic love/hate maintain within each other a relationship of fundamental and irreducible heterogeneity. Lacan also provides more specific formulas for the fantasy of the hysteric and that of the obsessional neurotic.[21] While the various formulas of fantasy indicate the common features of the fantasies of those who share the same clinical structure, the analyst must also attend to the unique features which characterise each patient's particular fantasmatic scenario.

[20] Brian Moore, *Catholics*, p.71.
[21] Jacques Lacan, *Le Séminaire. Livre VIII. Le Transfert*, p.295.

These unique features express the subject's particular mode of *jouissance,* though in a distorted way. The distortion evident in the fantasy marks it as a compromise formation; the fantasy is thus both that which enables the subject to sustain his desire,[22] and 'that by which the subject sustains *himself* at the level of his vanishing desire.'[23] Lacan holds that beyond all the myriad images which appear in dreams and elsewhere there is always one 'fundamental fantasy' which is unconscious.[24] In the course of psychoanalytic treatment, the analyst reconstructs the analysand's fantasy in all its details. However, the treatment does not stop there; the analysand must go on to 'traverse the fundamental fantasy.'[25] In other words, the treatment must produce some modification of the subject's fundamental mode of defence, some alteration in his mode of *jouissance.*

For Lacan, psychoanalytic treatment must locate the subject's unconscious fundamental fantasy. At the same time the subject's particular mode of enjoyment is exposed, and freed as much as possible from the desire of the Other, in relation to which the fantasy is always a compromise formation. The objective of any treatment is always to produce a change in the subject's defensive processes, to remove obstacles in order to allow the subject access to his or her own enjoyment. Lacan fully recognized the power of the image in fantasy, but he insisted on the fact that its functional value derives from the place that it comes to occupy in the larger symbolic structure. Although Lacan recognises the power of the image in fantasy, he insists that this is due not to any intrinsic quality of the image in itself but to the place which it occupies in a symbolic structure; the fantasy is always 'an image set to work in a signifying structure.'[26] Lacan criticises the Kleinian account of fantasy for not taking this symbolic structure fully into account, and thus remaining at the level of the imaginary; 'any attempt to reduce [fantasy] to the imagination…is a permanent misconception.'[27] In other words, its value derives from the fact that the image in question (a representation of something unconscious) must be able to play its role as a signifier. Most notably, he insisted that fantasy would perform the essential function of 'knotting' the psychical registers of the symbolic, the imaginary, and the real—and thus

[22] Jacques Lacan, *Écrits* (2006) p.780.
[23] Ibid., p.272 (emphasis added).
[24] Jacques Lacan, *Le Séminaire. Livre VIII. Le Transfert*, p.127.
[25] Jacques Lacan, *The Seminar. Book XI. The Four Fundamental Concepts of Psychoanalysis*, p.273.
[26] Jacques Lacan, *Écrits* (2006) p.272.
[27] Ibid., p.272.

constituting what Freud called psychic reality. For Lacan, 'fantasy is not simply a work of imagination as opposed to hard reality, meaning a product of the mind that obfuscates the approach to reality, the ability to perceive things as they really are.'[28]

There is an opposition between reality and imagination where fantasy is not simply on the side of the latter but, rather, it becomes a way in which the subject gains access to reality – a sort of snapshot that guarantees our sense of reality. Thus when our fundamental fantasies are shattered, the subject sustains a loss of reality. Imagination and fantasy are the key concepts in *The Lonely Passion of Judith Hearne.* At first, Madden dreams of setting up a business in the West Indies: '"A little business, something the natives don't have, maybe a curio shop for the tourists. A little capital, you could have yourself a time"' (*LPJH*, 39). Later, that fantasy transplants itself to Dublin: '"What Dublin needs is a good American eating-place, right in the centre of town"' (*LPJH*, 74). His nephew, Bernard, comments cynically on this: '"Ah, I know him the sod, he'll bluster and bluff out with another mad scheme, he'll be off to Connemara to drain the bogs of Ireland for uranium, handing out the big talk…"' (*LPJH*, 111) Bernard, of course, has his own fantasies: '"I'm writing a great poem. A *great* poem and it may take years to finish"' (*LPJH*, 130). Mary, the servant-girl, dreams that Bernard will marry her: '"He's a good date, you can eat all the pastries you like when you're out with him and he's a lovely dancer"' (*LPJH*, 70).

It is Judith's fantasies, however, that dominate. Judith is, to borrow Michael Paul Gallagher's phrase, an 'imaginist.'[29] In the first two chapters she thinks she will be happy in her new residence. Between chapters 2 and 12 she thinks that she will be able to develop a relationship with James Madden. She thinks that the O'Neill family love her as much as she loves them. She feels assured of God's love for her. She has hopes in Father Quigley: 'And at Mass, that day when I saw him first, I knew he would take poor Father Farrelly's place, a real Shepard, and maybe even better than Father Farrelly' (*LPJH*, 141). She believed that her friend, Edie Marrinan, was '[a] healthy girl, full of high spirits, not the sort that needs building up' (*LPJH*, 95). Edie, rather, was a morbid alcoholic and it was she who first introduced Judith to alcohol. She has an unerring belief in the etiquette and deportment instilled in her by her aunt – when she first

---

[28] Jacques Lacan, *The Seminar of Jacques Lacan XII : Crucial Problems for Psychoanalysis*, p.57.
[29] Michael Paul Gallagher, 'Brian Moore's Fiction of Faith', in *Gaélian,* 5, p.94.

accompanies Madden to Mass, her initial thoughts are: 'Out walking with a strange man, what would Aunt D'Arcy have said?' (*LPJH*, 47) After Mass, she informs Madden that she plans to call on the O'Neills although she chides herself for 'the old boasts… the shields against pity, against being forced to say that nobody wants to see you that particular day' (*LPJH*, 57).

At the end, all the things which make her life barely tolerable are gone. Mrs Rice has thrown her out of the boarding house for being drunk and disorderly. Mr Madden has turned her down. Her idealized relationship with the O'Neills comes to a close after she appears drunk in their house, telling Moira O'Neill that she never really liked her and Moira thinks to herself: 'For after all… drunk or not, it must cost her something to say that to me. Because now she can never pretend again' (*LPJH*, 166). She has obliterated most of her savings after checking in to the most expensive hotel in Belfast; on one last spree and a protracted taxi ride that takes her from the home Edie resides in, to the O'Neills, to Father Quigley and finally to the church. Jeanne Flood would argue that Judith '[i]s a victim *because* she is a child.'[30] She goes on to say: 'Judith Hearne, who is so completely victimized by family and religion, is guilty of her inability to achieve an adult place for herself within the family system.'[31]

Certainly, she is barely able to fend for herself – she needs people to tell her what to do. She looks to the oleograph of the Sacred Heart and her aunt's portrait for direction. She also expects James Madden to do all the running in the relationship but it is left to his nephew to offer advice, irrespective of his dubious motives. When all else fails, she goes in search of Father Quigley and when she encounters him, Judith '[f]ell on her knees at his feet, clutching his trouser leg… "Oh Father, Father, help me," she sobbed' (*LPJH*, 171). When she is admitted to a home, her bills are paid for by the O'Neills. Her financial future, precarious as it might be, is dependent on an annuity of one hundred pounds a year and the prospect of marriage, but as her aunt condescendingly remarked:

> [w]ith this depression in industry, eligible young men are hard to find, and the few that there are want a *dot* and if there's no money, then they want a great beauty, a beautiful woman can improve a man's chances, especially if she comes from a good family… and then speaking of great beauties, you'll never have a quarter the looks of your poor mother. No, you take

[30] Jeanne Flood, *Brian Moore*, p.19.
[31] Ibid., p.21.

> after the Hearnes, more's the pity. And they were nothing to write home about. Plain (*LPJH*, 90).

Though Judith took classes in shorthand, she was unwilling to abandon her aunt, consoled in part by her advice: '[t]here was plenty (of money) until the right man came along and even if he didn't' (*LPJH*, 28) Thus, by the time of her aunt's death, Judith is little more than a child pinning her hopes on fantasies and a dwindling capital for her future happiness and security. Unable to deal with the enigma of the Other's desire, Judith demands that the Other make demands on her; demand leads to more demand in a kind of vicious cycle. She is dependent upon her aunt's demands; they give her a sense of purpose. This is why she asks for a sign. What she does not seem to realize is that desire is not so much something you have as something you do not have: it springs from the lack, and no-one can truly say what Judith wants, desire having no unique object.

Fantasy thus becomes a way of defending yourself against the lack in the Other and the incompleteness of the Other is something Judith cannot abide. Certainly, one can view the inadequacy of the Other in terms of desire, but it can also be viewed from the point of view of knowledge and power as well. When Judith is in the church, she looks for answers to her plight: 'Why should life be so hard for me, why am I alone, why did I yield to the temptation of drink, why, why has it all happened like this?' (*LPJH*, 102) She's seeks knowledge ('why'), power ('give me strength') and desire ('you know the things I wanted, the home, children to raise up to honour and reverence You'). In the curious way that God and her aunt acted a surrogate parents for the orphaned Judith, she assumes the mentality of a child – at first, she asserts that these 'parents' are the strongest and most capable of them all.

This is the sort of boasting which would be typical in a child and Judith, as I have suggested, is little more than that: 'So she played. Woman, she saw her womanish glass image' (*LPJH*, 18). But the image does not reflect reality: when she leaves the looking glass and opens the wardrobe, she breaks 'the unity of its imagined face' (*LPJH*, 19). The allusion here to both image and imago is deliberate, I feel – she also dresses underneath her nightgown, a habit picked up at the Convent school she attended. In her first meeting with Mrs Henry Rice, she is boastful of her aunt:

> 'My aunt comes from a very old Belfast family,' she said. 'They've nearly all died out now, but they have a very interesting history, my aunt's people. For instance, they're all buried out in Nun's Bush. That's one of the oldest cemeteries in the country. Full up now. It's closed, you know.' (*LPJH*, 10)

Comparatively, her belief in God is also unerring and absolute: 'Religion was there: it was not something you thought about… her prayers would be answered. God is good' (*LPJH*, 50). In the minds of most children, their parents should be able to take care of everything – it is a wish that the parents not be lacking in any way. Obviously, this is not the case and when Judith begins to doubt, that her 'parents' lack somehow, it has grave ramifications for her. This leads her to seek out people she perceives as higher authorities – Father Quigley and, in part, the O'Neill family – for answers. The crushing realization that each system of beliefs is but one among many leads Judith to an existential crisis: the Other is lacking, there is no God, no ultimate being who can tell me who and what I should be. As Lacan states, 'There is no signifier that can… answer for (account for or take responsibility for) what I am.'[32]

Freud spoke of a 'primal fantasy' or *Urphantasie* as a kind of unconscious origin myth presenting to the subject a representation of his own conception.[33] Freud, in *Moses and Monotheism*, contradicted the Biblical story of Moses with his own retelling of events which claimed that once Moses led his followers into freedom they subsequently killed him in a rebellion. Years after the murder of Moses, the rebels formed a religion which promoted Moses as the Saviour of the Israelites. Freud said that the guilt from the murder of Moses is inherited through the generations and it is this guilt that then drove people to religion to make them feel better.[34] Slavoj Žižek proposed that the fundamental fantasy amounts to much more, that it aims to transform our anxiety into guilt. That is, mankind prefers some definite atonement rather than the transient world of anxiety.[35]

Judith Hearne commits a sacrilege for this reason – much better to offend God than confront a meaningless universe where no punishment follows our sin. Afflicted by her paralysing anxiety regarding the meaningless of the world, Judith creates an unconscious fantasy, a specific debt for contravening God's will:

> 'You!' she screamed. And red light filled her eyes, golden doors merged, fell away in crumbling segments. He came out, terrible breathing fire, His

[32] Jacques Lacan, quoted in Jacques-Alain Miller, *Ornicar? 25*, (1987), p.32.
[33] Jean Laplanche and J. B. Pontalis, *The Language of Psycho-analysis,* p.332.
[34] Richard F. Sterba, 'Freud's "Moses and Monotheism" and the Three Stages of Isrealitish Religion', in *Psychoanal Q,* pp. 125-126.
[35] Slavoj Žižek, *The Puppet and the Dwarf: The Perverse Core of Christianity*, p.128-129.

> face hollow-cheeked, His eyes devouring her. His mother ran up the alter steps, her painted face still sadly smiling, lifted her as she lay broken on the steps. Saint Joseph knelt gravely on her right. (*LPJH*, 176)

Judith's vision of God is in stark contrast to the oleograph on her bedroom wall: 'His eyes kindly yet accusing. He was old and the painted halo around His head was beginning to show little cracks' (*LPJH*, 7). The fundamental fantasy dictates that we are sinners; we are guilty of disrupting the fundamental order and we are duly excluded from it: 'Cast into outer darkness. Loss of faith, loss of God, the greatest sorrow the human soul can feel…' (*LPJH*, 140) An ordered cosmos, complete in itself, holds no place for the subject. Short of 'hell-flames' (*LPJH*, 140) and redemption, we cannot belong to it.

From a Lacanian perspective, the fundamental fantasy produces its own reality by means of proto-representation, where the world of experience is regarded as fantasmatic or in an imaginary totality. In the course of psychoanalytic treatment, the analyst reconstructs the analysand's fantasy in all its details. However, the treatment does not stop there; the analysand must go on to 'traverse the fundamental fantasy.'[36] In other words, the treatment must produce some modification of the subject's fundamental mode of defence, some alteration in his mode of *jouissance* . As Žižek states:

> The fundamental fantasy provides the subject with the minimum of being, it serves as a support for his existence -- in short, its deceptive gesture is 'Look, I suffer, therefore I am, I exist, I participate in the positive order of being.'[37]

Fantasy thus projects the social qua totality by imagining it as totalized or complete from the position of transcendence, from the privileged subject's perspective. Reality emerges from the real precisely when the world of human existence is conceived from the perspective of the Other. In order to think of the world as 'ontologically closed', we think of some viewpoint from which it appears in totality. Reality is always borne from such a totalizing view and as such, reality is a product from what we imagine as an omniscient subjectivity.

It is through the master signifier – the phallus – that we can collectively share our guilt, through a sense of shared accomplishment and

---

[36] Jacques Lacan, *The Seminar. Book XI. The Four Fundamental Concepts of Psychoanalysis*, p.273.
[37] Slavoj Žižek, *The Ticklish Subject,* p.281.

by relinquishing our desires to follow the dictates of the Law. For it is through the master signifier that we enter into and become active participants in the community. We can only overcome our immediate desires and needs to the extent that these are opposed by specific prohibitions. In effect, the master signifier is responsible for the conscious effects of the unconscious fundamental fantasy; it paints a cosmological picture of the world as a whole by creating the space of ideality.

The mystery of the phallic signifier gives birth to a kind of transcendence, heralding the end of our search for a 'solution' to the mystery it poses. Around this signifier, we are convinced that there is a meaning in love. The meaning is out there and in a position that makes sense, not just of some particular phenomenon but, rather, of our lives as a whole. The search for the meaning of love is that the meaning will 'make sense' of all the absurdity in our life.

Judith's search for love is more a search for belonging – she belongs no-where and looks to the O'Neills as a surrogate family, she remembers the O'Neill children as 'babies in your little woolly suits' (*LPJH*, 62). She looks at Shaun O'Neill as 'a boy, a baby boy' (*LPJH*, 66). She tells Moira: '"You'll never know what it meant to me… to come here and sit with a family and feel that I belonged here."' (*LPJH*, 166) They are her idealized family, an ideal which again, does not bear up to reality – the O'Neills cannot stand her. She thinks of James Madden as 'so big and stern and manly' (*LPJH*, 25). She fantasizes about Madden/Mature/Samson ravishing her, 'tearing at my dress, ripping it away, his toga thrown aside, his huge hands feel me, press me close, his body, muscled, hard' (*LPJH*, 105). The reality is again more squalid, when Madden rapes the housemaid, Mary: 'He had found her; in the darkness he tore and shook her like dog meat… he heard himself moaning, heard her muted terrified pleading' (*LPJH*, 87). Judith's search is predicated upon this hermeneutic affect, wherein the very search for a meaning instantiates it. It would all makes sense but Judith cannot seem to find the meaning to her questions. Thus, it is not simply that the master signifier fascinates us – the search also subsequently provides consistency to our lives.

Thus, traversing the *fantasme* has nothing to do with the act of dismissing the fantasies that obscure our perception of the real state of things or the attendant act of achieving a certain distance from our daydreams and superstitions. Fantasy acts as a support when a line is drawn between imagination and reality. In Lacan's view:

> [t]raversing the *fantasme* involves the subject's over-identification with the field of imagination: in it, and through it, the subject breaks the constrains of fantasy and enters the terrifying, violent territory of pre-

synthetic imagination, where *disjecta membra* float around, not yet unified and domesticated by the intervention of a homogenizing fantasmatic frame.[38]

Show Me a Sign

Lacan, in his essay, "The Insistence of the Letter in the Unconscious," criticised Saussure's concept of the sign, where the two elements – signified and signifier – are linked by an arbitrary but indissoluble bond. Saussure argued that there is unity between language, that the concept ultimately leads into a referential theory of language – thus, the elements of language acquire meaning not as the result of some connection between words and things, but only as part of a system of relations. Lacan, in turn, argued that the relationship between signifier and signified is extremely unstable, introducing rather a 'cut' (*coupure*) into the Saussurian sign, with an, 'emphasis on the bar as a formula of separateness rather than reciprocity of signifier and signified.'[39] Saussure's model is as follows:

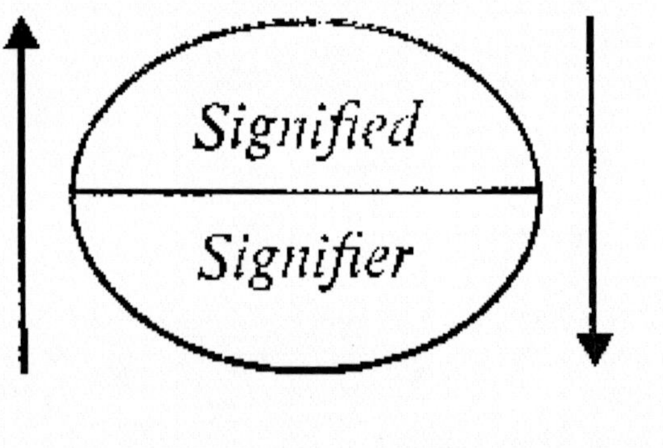

Figure 2 – The Saussurian Sign

In Lacan's model, the position of the signified and signifier is thus inverted, showing the primacy of the signifier which is capitalized, whereas the signifier is reduced to lower-case italics. The arrows and circle are abolished, which represents the absence of a fixed relationship

[38] Jacques Lacan, *The Seminar of Jacques Lacan XII : Crucial Problems for Psychoanalysis*, p.63.
[39] Bice Benvenuto, *The Works of Jacques Lacan*, p. 110.

between signifier and signified. The bar between the two no longer represents a union but the resistance inherent in signification:

$$\frac{S}{s}$$

Figure 3 – Lacanian algorithm

Roman Jakobson argued that there was a fundamental difference between horizontal and vertical language, a difference related to the distinction between *langue* and *parole*. Thus, in the vertical dimension, each sentence is selected from a set of possible elements and could be substituted for another in the set. In the horizontal dimension, the elements are combined in a sequence, which constitutes a *parole*. This distinction applies at all levels – phoneme, morpheme, word and sentence.[40] Lacan ascribes to this theory, in which each signifier is reducible to differential elements, and these, operating in a signifying chain, form the basis of meaning. Lacan makes the link from these phonemes to the letter, which he defines as, 'the essentially localized structure of the signifier.'[41]

For Lacan, 'The subject is what is represented by the signifier, and the signifier can only represent something for another signifier'.[42] According to Benvenuto:

> Lacan stated that the signifier can only operate if it is present in the subject. The signifier anchors itself to the subject, marking its place with a letter, and whether or not the subject knows, reads or denies it, the subject will function like a signified and will always slide under the signifier.

---

[40] Roman Jakobson – see the chapters, 'Two aspects of language and two types of aphasic disturbances,' pp.239-259 and 'Shifters, verbal categories, and the Russian verb', in *Selected Writings, vol. II, Word and Language*, pp.130-147.

[41] Jacques Lacan, 'The insistence of the letter in the unconscious,' in *Modern Criticism and Theory*, pp. 61-2.

[42] Jacques Lacan, quoted. in Benvenuto, *The Works of Jacques Lacan*, p. 118.

> Thus the subject is constituted as secondary in relation to the signifier, while signification has a life of its own.[43]

Thus, Lacan posits the idea that the subject who uses language is born into and constituted by it, and more explicitly is constituted in and through the signifier. Language does not detract from what we believe to be true, rather the truth speaks through and is produced by language. The subject produces truth, whether or not he realises it, which is why the analyst pays close attention to the subject's mistakes or unintended statements. Lacanian psychoanalysis has identified this endless running from one signifier to another as the linguistic forms of metaphor and metonymy.

Lacan defines metonymy as the diachronic relation between one signifier and another in the signifying chain. For Evans:

> Metonymy thus concerns the ways in which signifiers can be combined/linked in a single signifying chain ('horizontal relations'), whereas metaphor concerns the way in which a signifier in one signifying chain may be substituted for a signifier in another chain ('vertical relations'). Together, metaphor and metonymy constitute the way in which signification is produced.[44]

Lacan linked metaphor and metonymy to Freud's concepts of condensation and displacement, both essential modes of functioning of unconscious processes. Though it appears that Lacan regards metaphor in strong, positive terms and metonymy in weak, negative ones, he nonetheless emphasizes that metonymy provides the possibility of metaphor. He refers to the insufficiency of the metaphor and criticizes the tendency of linguists to privilege metaphor over metonymy. Thus metaphor and metonymy allows connections to be made between the overall structure of the analytical dialogue and the structure of the material on which that dialogue may dwell. As Bowie states: '[t]he unconscious, in this view, is no longer structure 'like a language', for it has no existence outside language and no structure other than the one that language affords.'[45] If we look at the way that Lacan uses these concepts in his essay "The Purloined Letter", he states 'Speech remains. You can't help the play of symbols, and that is why you must be very careful in what you say. But the letter, for its part, that goes away.'[46]

---

[43] Bice Benvenuto, *The Works of Jacques Lacan*, p.116.
[44] Dylan Evan's, *An Introductory Dictionary of Lacanian Psychoanalysis*, p.113.
[45] Malcolm Bowie, *Lacan*, p.71.
[46] Jacques Lacan, *The Seminar: Book II*, p. 198.

In *The Lonely Passion of Judith Hearne*, we can find an analogue of Judith as the Queen, with Father Quigley cast in the figure of the Dupin/analyst. She searches for something, 'anything, a bolt of lightning. Strike me down, anything' (*LPJH*, 163). This search for the sign is akin to the dogged pursuit of the letter. Akin to the letter, we have no idea what it represents but we are aware that she has indeed lost something – faith perhaps but it is faith represented by a sign – and the sign moves from one character to another. She has received the sign from God: 'Was it the answer to her prayers, was it the Sacred Heart giving her a sign…?' (*LPJH*, 55) The dilemma in the novel occurs when the sign is taken from her by Madden which constitutes a change in the symbolic chain she belongs to. She is now a part of a symbolic chain that is foreign to her with the signifier, or sign from God, being the driving force behind the signifying chain that motivates the characters into their respective places.

Madden's theft of the sign is described by Judith thus: 'She only wondered if he were in the church, sitting cruelly after destroying her faith' (*LPJH*, 117). Madden exhibits a curious change of character, and one could pinpoint this as another example of the signifier's power as an unconscious influence on its subjects. Madden loses his manly character for one that Lacan would describe as having an *odor di femina*, or feminine character. While 'the male must pursue', Madden retreats. When he is with Judith in her bedroom, she states accusingly: "'You!' […] 'And I thought you were a man. A man who could do his own asking, not a man who would send a rotten fat atheist around to talk for him'" (*LPJH*, 135). To better clarify this theme, one could first structure the idea of repetition by breaking down the two principal repeated scenes; the primal scene of Judith's ignorance wherein the major players are the Judith, Madden, and Mrs Henry Rice and her son, and the second scene of Judith's mental collapse wherein the major players Judith, Moira O'Neill and Father Quigley.

Lacan imagines the two scenes as related by a series of glances: the first glance is ignorant of everything happening, the second feels safe by the ignorance of the first, and the third takes advantage of the seconds' false sense of security. The characters can be interchanged in terms of the glances: Mrs Henry Rice and Father Quigley are ignorant; Judith feels safe because of that ignorance, and Madden and Bernard Rice recognize that sense of security and act upon it to their gain. In "The Purloined Letter", Lacan is interested in the way in which the letter affects each character and moves them from glance to glance within the scene structure, causing them to repeat a scene in which certain actions and similarities can be noticed.

Indeed, he reasons that the actions and thoughts of the characters in each scene are entirely predicated on the movement of the letter as a signifier, and the characters are powerless except to act within the symbolic order that the signifier places them in. It is because of the role of the letter in the unconscious that the analyst must focus not on the meaning or the signification of the analysand's discourse, but purely on its formal properties; the analyst must read the analysand's speech as if it were a text, 'taking it literally' *(prendre à la lettre)*. There is thus a close connection between the letter and writing, a connection which Lacan explores in his seminar of 1972–3.[47] Although both the letter and writing are located in the order of the real, and hence partake of a meaningless quality, Lacan argues that the letter is that which one reads, as opposed to writing, which is not to be read.[48] Writing is also connected with the idea of formalisation and the mathemes; Lacan thus speaks of his algebraic symbols as 'letters'.[49]

Thus, Father Quigley is ignorant of Judith's problems, 'Shepard, he looked at his sheep. What ails her? Father, he did not comprehend what his child was saying' (*LPJH*, 172). Once he receives the gift of the sign, he is moved on to the third spot, where he attempts to act upon Judith's false sense of security: '"I'm sure you're making a special effort to pray hard in these days of rest and repose"' (*LPJH*, 180). He is on much surer territory when the gift of the sign passes on to Father Quigley who now places himself in the third spot or glance. The difference between these two scenes is well illustrated by Jo O'Donoghue:

> Earlier there was no sin, merely scruples; now he has the security of the sin of blasphemy to guide him in his treatment of the woman. She has committed the sin of blasphemy in the church and he will be happy to revert to his traditional role, the role in which he was trained: he will be the confessor, the judge who takes the place of God.[50]

So the gift which was first presented by the Holy Spirit has now gone full circle, back to 'the judge who takes the place of God.' Thus the repetition automatism is directly influenced by the trajectory of the signifier along the signifying chain. It simply slides along the signifying chain detoured

---

[47] Jacques Lacan, *The Seminar. Book XX. On Feminine Sexuality and The Limits of Love*, pp. 29-38.
[48] Ibid., p.29.
[49] Ibid., p.30.
[50] Jo O'Donoghue, *Brian Moore – A Critical Study*, p.23.

from its intended trajectory and as a result affecting the subjects who possess it at any given time. However, what is most interesting in his reading of "The Purloined Letter" is Lacan's assertion that in this story, the sign is indeed that of a woman:

> For the sign is clearly that of woman, because she brings out her very being therein by founding it outside the law, which ever contains her – due to the effect of origins – in a position of signifier, nay, as fetish. In order to be worthy of the power of the sign she need but remain immobile in its shadow, managing thereby, moreover, like the Queen, to stimulate mastery of non-action that the Minister's 'lynx eye' alone was able to see through.[51]

From our reading of this passage, we may assume that Lacan believes that the letter, that is, the actual letter of the story, is the signifier which aligns woman (in this instance, the Queen) with the sign (in the position of signifier), reconfiguring the discussion in a somewhat ambiguous fashion. Lacan also introduces the sexual concept of the fetish, thereby drawing allusion to the woman and the signifier. It would appear then that Lacan has double-sexed the signifier in metonymic fashion. A cursory reading traces the letter in the story in its function as the letter of the signifier; but the woman-signifier-fetish analogy, once introduced, cannot be ignored and thus we are obliged to read it alongside the first reading. As Lacan states:

> Hence the letter exists as a means of power only through the final summons of pure signifier either by prolonging its detour… or by destroying the letter, which would be the only sure way, as Dupin proffers at the outset, to be done with what is destined by nature to signify the cancelling out of what it signifies.[52]

We could also read this passage thus: destroying the woman (sign) is the only sure means to signify the cancelling out of what she signifies. The letter, the signifier, is explicitly female and sexual: 'Just so does the purloined letter, like an immense female body, sprawls across the space of the Minister's office when Dupin enters it.'[53] Woman is now not neatly equated with the signifier, but adopts a position of giving it up, 'offering' it, as Lacan puts it. We notice how Lacan implies the Queen's active role

[51] Jacques Lacan, *Écrits* (2006), p.22.
[52].Jacques Lacan, *Écrits* (2006) p.22.
[53] Ibid., p.26.

in the loss of the signifier/letter, how he does not see it so much in terms of a theft but as a voluntary act of surrender on the part of the woman. The Minister adopts that feminine surrender in his own relation to the letter, 'offering' it, as it were, to Dupin in turn. As Lacan states, the sender, 'receives from the receiver his own message in an inverted form. This is why the "purloined letter", nay, the "letter en *souffrance*" (letter in sufferance), means that a letter always arrives at its destination.'[54] That is to say, the letter has its destination in and through suffering, through violence, as the object of pursuit. Thus we see that in the way that the signifier always returns to the one who deploys it, only in reverse form, and this is the proper place for the signifier we also read: Judith Hearne is 'raped' the thing which she values has been taken, but this is the result of her own concealed invitation for the loss of that value. It comes back to her, in reverse, in its violation. Analysis is analogous to rape insofar as it violates the imaginary integrity of the ego and in *The Lonely Passion of Judith Hearne*, it could be argued that Father Quigley plays the part of the analyst, tearing down Judith's faith in confession, emphasising rather that the individual, the unbeliever, was in permanent conflict with their surroundings: 'the poor blind devil without a friend in this world or the next' (*LPJH*, 180).

Certainly, this is a contentious point but if we look at the trajectory of the sign in this story, we see Judith receiving the sign of faith, the sign removed, forcefully, by James Madden, Bernard Rice and Father Quigley and then returned to her at the close of the novel:

> And You. Were You ever? Is this picture the only You?
>
> It is here and You are gone. I is You. No matter what you are, it still is part of me.
>
> She closed her eyes. Funny about those two. When they're with you, watching over me, a new place becomes home. (*LPJH*, 187)

This is a foundational premise of Lacanian psychoanalysis where the unity of the ego is false, imaginary — and this is why Lacan so viciously attacked ego psychology, which sought to discover and produce this nonexistent unity: 'I is You… it is still a part of me.' In Freudian terms, the desiring subject can be thought of as the ego which defends itself against the kind of satisfaction the id strives for. Desire prefers the pleasure of fantasy to the satisfaction of the drives – desire in the novel is tantamount to defence as the drives pursue a kind of satisfaction that is

---

[54] Ibid., p.30.

abhorred, particularly in Belfast society: '"They've got time for sin... time for naked dancing girls in cinemas... time to do any blessed thing you care to mention"' (*LPJH*, 54). While it inhabits the id's pursuits, the ego nevertheless provides substitute satisfactions. But as Judith Hearne learns to her cost, woman cannot live on desire alone.

Cold Heaven

First published by Jonathan Cape in 1983, *Cold Heaven* begins, in Terence Brown's words, '[i]n an entirely recognizable world, one in which realism seems securely at home.'[55] Indeed, from the opening paragraph, we get a sense of allegory at play – the marriage of Dr. Alex and Marie Davenport has gone sour, she has been having an affair with a colleague of his and is now contemplating how to break the news to him. They are holidaying on the Côte d'Azur and subtly, as they set out on a *pedalo* into the 'solitary waters' of the Baie des Anges, 'Marie slackened her efforts but Alex continued determinedly, steering the pedalo straight out into the Mediterranean' (*CH*, 9). Marie's slackened efforts sum up her attitude to the relationship – 'she now noted his every fault' (*CH*, 9) – but Alex remains oblivious to her indifference and continues on determinedly. He decides to go for a swim but is struck by a speed-boat and is taken, stricken, to the hospital.[56] Once Marie arrives at the hospital, we are given our first hints that all may not be as it seems. We are told that, '[t]oday was the anniversary of Carmel' (*CH*, 18) while an old man sits outside, like death, removing pieces from a checkers board.

When Marie is informed that her husband has died, she returns to her hotel and guilt rather than grief envelopes her: 'He is dead. I have been punished' (*CH*, 25). When she returns the next day, she is informed that the body is missing and when she queries whether a misdiagnosis was possible is informed: "Your husband was dead... there was absolutely no vital signs" (*CH*, 32). Afterwards, as she returns to the hotel she discovers that her husband's passport, wallet and clothes are missing. She contacts the airport and learns that her husband boarded a flight to New York that

---

[55] Terence Brown, 'Show Me A Sign – The Religious Imagery of Brian Moore' from *Irish University Review*, p.43.

[56] Like much in Moore's fiction, this episode is partly biographical – the author was struck by a speedboat shortly before the publication of *Judith Hearne* and lay hospitalised for six weeks – see Patricia Craig, *Brian Moore – A Biography*, pp.119-120.

morning. Thereafter, we are engaged in a game of cat and mouse – Marie follows her husband back to New York but he steadily avoids her pursuit. When she contacts Daniel, the man with whom she is having the affair, he arranges to meet her in the aforementioned Carmel, a coastal town in Southern California. Her husband, perhaps aware of this arrangement, journeys there himself unbeknownst to Marie. When she arrives at the Point Lobos Motor Inn, she first goes for a walk and we are again led to believe that something had happened there a year before but we are given, at this stage, only strange hints of some dread premonition: 'She felt a shiver of fear as though she confronted the lineaments of a dread, yet familiar face' (*CH*, 70). Marie stumbles across a colony of nuns, the Sisters of Mary Immaculate, and there encounters Mother Paul, the head of the community, and another, curious nun, the saint-like Mother St Jude. When she returns to the motor-inn that evening, she learns that her husband has a room rented but he appears oblivious to the circumstances that brought him there – he has been slipping in and out of death. He has become a Lazarus-like figure but his only concern is with avoiding the adverse publicity of his circumstances: "For the rest of my life I wouldn't be known for my work or anything else. I'd just be a god-damn medical freak" (*CH*, 97).

The second part of the book opens with Marie visiting Monsignor Cassidy, 'God's golfer' (*CH*, 133) dressed in 'green madras slacks, purple izod tennis shirt, and white golfing shoes' (*CH*, 123). Here we learn of Marie's predicament. A year before she had visited the Point Lobos Inn along with her lover, Daniel. After he had departed, she went for a walk and was witness to a Marian apparition. She was instructed to 'tell the priests' that 'the rock must be a place of pilgrimage' (*CH*, 126). While she dismisses the apparition on the grounds she doesn't 'believe in an afterlife or religion or any of that' (*CH*, 124) she nonetheless feel that she and her husband are being persecuted for their silence. While the Monsignor remains sceptical, his cousin, Father Ned Niles, takes an interest in the case.

When Marie finally meets Daniel at the motor-inn, he convinces her to transfer Alex to a hospital in San Francisco. Alex continues to lapse in and out of a death-like state and Marie is now convinced that the only way for her to save her husband is to conform with fate (or faith) and surrender herself to God's will. She visits Father Niles and, while she continues to resist her appointed role as witness, he tells her: "Surely you want us to do whatever's necessary so that you'll be spared any more things happening to your friend?" (*CH*, 177). When she visits her husband in the hospital, he decides to abscond once more and she is left to facilitate his return to Point

Lobos. There she appears finally willing to meet her appointed fate. She returns to the colony of nuns and learns that Mother St Jude has been plagued with nightmares similar to her own experience. She agrees to go with her to the place where the apparition first appeared and with them goes Sister Anna, 'a plain uneducated girl who in the old days would enter into an order as a lay sister' (*CH*, 266).

Once more, the apparition appears, but while Marie refuses to acknowledge the message, Sister Anna becomes a witness and Marie finds herself abnegating her vision to the younger nun. When both Father Niles and Monsignor Cassidy arrive to investigate, a pact is formed between herself and Monsignor Cassidy. She will be allowed to escape from her appointed role and the responsibility for the vision will go to Sister Anna. The novel closes with Marie now finally resolved to end her marriage with Alex, returning to the Point Lobos Inn and 'rehearsing what she would say to him' (*CH*, 287).

Michael Paul Gallagher commented that *Cold Heaven* offered a 'surprising capacity in agnostic Irish writing to express reverence in the face of sanctity.'[57] The sense of dealing with something Moore himself cannot understand but, at the same time, that he cannot *disprove*, is brought out in the following quotation from an interview with the author prior to the publication of *Cold Heaven*:

> The book was terribly hard to write. I worried terribly about it, because I don't believe in miracles or miraculous appearances, but I do believe in and am very interested in people who are truly religious, people who are saints.[58]

We have witnessed earlier in this book how the Church controlled society – that is, there is no differentiation between the symbolic order of Catholic society and the rigid rules of a repressive Church. But society had changed in the intervening years – whereas Judith Hearne could boast of her Aunt's family being buried in 'one of oldest cemeteries in the country' (*LPJH*, 10). *Cold Heaven* represents a more transient society where Marie flits between Nice, New York, Carmel, San Francisco and Carmel once more. Her apartment in New York is sublet from one of her husband's colleagues, and New York itself is a:

---

[57] Michael Paul Gallagher, review of *Cold Heaven*, *Irish University Review* (1984) p.133.

[58] Interview with Marie Crowe, 'Marie Crowe talks to Belfast writer Brian Moore,' in *Irish Press*, p.9.

> Unreal city: the city in which she had been born… the sky above its monumental buildings tinctured with a flamingo hue of a dying summer's day as a taxi carried her along the East River Drive, turning off into garbage littered streets, rushing past clicking traffic lights, clattering over ruptured pavement… (*CH*, 42)

We become immediately aware of the analogy with Eliot's *The Waste Land*: 'Unreal City / Under the brown fog of a winter's dawn /a crowd flowed over London Bridge, so many / I had not thought death had undone so many,'[59] or of Baudelaire's 'Les sept vieillards': 'Fourmillante cité, cité pleine de rêves / Où le spectre en plein jour raccroche le passant.'[60] As Jo O'Donoghue states:

> In *Cold Heaven…* Catholicism treads warily in a secular society. *Cold Heaven*, as a well as creating a world of inexplicable apparitions and contemplative ascetics, is the world of sophisticated medicine, of jet travel almost at will, across America and between continents, of motels and care-hire firms.[61]

Catholicism has adapted to this changing world and this is best exemplified in the figure of Monsignor Cassidy. When Father Niles comments to him: "Quite a life you have, Barney. Championship golf course, celebrities, beautiful climate, rich parish, well-run school, good curate. And this refectory is like a resort hotel", the Monsignor agrees but wonders to himself whether Father Niles would have the 'tact needed to deal with people in the fifty percent bracket' (*CH*, 122). Catholicism has thus become something of a fad, a status symbol where a trip to the church is no more different than a trip to the golf course. In *Judith Hearne*, it was a symbolic obligation – society expected you to be present at Mass – whether you believed or not was immaterial. This can be evidence in the following exchange between Jamesie and Ruttledge in John McGahern's *That They May Face the Rising Sun*:

> 'I don't believe,' he mimicked. 'None of us believes and we go. That's no bar.'
>
> 'I'd feel like a hypocrite. Why do *you* go if you don't believe?'

---

[59] T.S. Eliot, *The Waste Land: A Facsimile and Transcript of the Original Drafts Including the Annotations of Ezra Pound*, p.xxii.

[60] Charles Baudelaire, *Selected Poems*, p.89.

[61] Jo O'Donoghue, *Brian Moore – A Critical Study*, p. 172..

> 'To look at the girls. To see the whole performance,' he cried out, and started to shake with laughter. 'We go to see all the other hypocrites…'[62]

The ironic part to *Cold Heaven* is that Marie, the agnostic, is visited by the sort of sign which would have saved Judith Hearne from a break-down. In the world of Judith Hearne, a sign from God would be considered miraculous – in *Cold Heaven*, it is something of a nuisance. As Terence Brown states:

> The realist's world has dissolved in a vision of artistic meaning. Accordingly, the rest of the novel is haunted by the possibility of presence in the signs which in *The Lonely Passion of Judith Hearne* had intimated the full horror of absence: "But now, in this church, she feared the doll's stupid eyes as she feared the naked sky, thunder, and the jumbled rocks and twisted cypress trees. There was a presence here." (*CH*, 78)[63]

There are other, more subtle references to *Judith Hearne* in the novel. The image of the *Pieta* is invoked in both: where Marie cradles Alex to her breast in the opening chapter, 'She lifted him up and cradled him in her arms, his blood trickling onto her breasts' (*CH*, 11). In *Judith Hearne*, it is the scene where Father Quigley attends Judith after her sacrilege in the church: 'And he, His fingers uplifted in blessing, bent over her, His bleeding heart red against His white tunic. Lifted her in His arms and His face was close to hers' (*LPJH*, 177). Both Judith and Marie thrice deny the presence of God; Judith in the company of Mrs O'Neill: "Is there a God at all, I've been asking myself" (*LPJH*, 168), in the presence of Father Quigley: "Father, I can't believe anymore… I just don't feel God is there any more" (*LPJH*, 172) and, finally, in the Church: "I have renounced You, do You hear me, I have abandoned You" (*LPJH*, 175).

As Patrick Hicks explains, Marie, equally, denies the Virgin three times:

> Her first denial is of the ocular ("I saw nothing"), her second is of the audible ("I heard nothing"), and her final denial mixes the two senses together (*CH*, 248-49). As a novel of spiritual semiology, it is noteworthy that Marie denies God at the precise moment when evidence of his existence finally occurs.[64]

---

[62] John McGahern, *That They May Face The Rising Sun*, p.2.

[63] Terence Brown, 'Show Me A Sign', in *Irish University Review* (1986) p. 45.

[64] Patrick Hicks, *Brian Moore And The Meaning Of The Past – An Irish Novelist Reimagines History*, p.121.

Other comparisons have less to do with Biblical inferences and more the relationship between the Church and the laity. When Judith goes to confession, Father Quigley's first response is: "A general confession no less. And I promised to see Father Feeny for golf at half-past one" (*LPJH*, 143). Equally, when Marie goes to Monsignor Cassidy to explain the significance of Carmel, he responds: "Take your time", but to himself: 'Although he hoped this wouldn't take long. He planned to be on the golf-course by two-thirty' (*CH*, 124). Both Monsignor Cassidy and Father Quigley are at a loss on how to deal with such matters of personal and spiritual crisis. For the Monsignor: 'He looked again at Marie Davenport. How was he going to handle this?' (*CH*, 129). For Father Quigley: 'Shepherd, he looked at his sheep. What ails her?' (*LPJH*, 172). It is ironic, perhaps, how one pastor cannot comprehend a singular loss of faith and the other cannot comprehend the expression of God's presence, but this has less to with the Church than with society.

In *The Waking of Willie Ryan* or *Amongst Women*, we witness the ritual of the dead – "In the old days people were killed with those ghastly wakes – drinking and roaring and carrying on at the very foot of the corpse" (*WR*, 188); or, in *Amongst Women*: 'Word had to be sent to Woods to come and lay out the body. Whiskey and sherry and stout had to be bought for the callers, sandwiches made, the priest and the doctor to be notified. Rose insisted on going herself to the undertakers…' (*AM*, 181). The ritual and symbolism of the Church has been jettisoned by a society where death is dealt with in abstractions. People seem as vacuous and superficial as the Church in the novel:

> Marie could not remember Alex ever mentioning a family burial place. Was it in Boston? She realised how little she knew about his life… Marie did not know Alex's mother well but had the impression that Mrs Davenport did not approve of her… She wondered how much his mother would grieve for him. Who would really grieve for Alex? (*CH*, 22)

This closing section will duly look at the some of those changes which have occurred in society, in the long span between Judith Hearne and the hedonistic, jet-setting Marie Davenport. It will examine the way in which the disintegration of a repressive order can, in itself, lead to a sense of absence and drift which can no longer be salved by faith alone. Finally, it will look at the role of women, do they remain passive – in *Cold Heaven* they are simply a vehicle for a dialogue between Church and the divine – or is Marie's attempt to signal herself as a secular, sexual and independent woman come at the cost of her mortal soul, as the novel appears to suggest?

The Dutiful Daughter

The dutiful daughter is one who must submit to the Father's Law. Her submission may take various forms: a submission to the oedipalization of desire, to the patriarchal denigration of her pleasure, to femininity defined as passive, castrated, superficial, and narcissistic; or even a submission through what appears to be resistance to the oedipal law – the so-called masculinity complex. In her introduction to the first translation of Lacan's Seminar XX, *On Feminine Sexuality*, Juliet Mitchell outlines the history of Freud's development of the castration complex as the inaugurator of sex and sexuality. Lacan, she suggests, remains true to Freud's perspective of the, 'fragmented subject of shifting and uncertain sexual identity.'[65] He follows Freud in arguing that '[t]o be human is to be subjected to a law which decentres and divides: sexuality is created in a division, the subject is split; but an ideological world conceals this from the conscious subject who is supposed to feel whole and certain of a sexual identity.'[66] Thus sexual identity clearly refers to one's place as either male or female, and to one's object of sexual choice. The fragile nature of sexual identity is restated a few pages later by Jacqueline Rose, who writes that for Freud, as for Lacan, 'sexual difference is constructed at a price ... that involves subjection to a law which exceeds any natural or biological division'.[67] The phallus, in Rose's reading, becomes a 'concept' which 'stands for that subjection, and for the way in which women are very precisely implicated in its process'.[68]

Through Mitchell and Rose's interpretation of Freud's, and later Lacan's, theory on sex and sexuality we become aware that sexuality, and subjectivity itself, is a fragile accomplishment rather than a given position, but an accomplishment that is necessary for recognition of the self as a subject. Sexual identity operates as a law in Lacan's thesis – we are 'enjoined' to take up a sexed position, lining up according to whether one has or does not have the phallus. Thus 'male' and 'female' are notions emerging out of fantasy.[69]

While some feminist critics would accuse Lacan of phallocentrism – as Elizabeth Grosz states: 'When two sexual symmetries are represented as

---

[65] Juliet Mitchell & Jacqueline Rose (eds.) *Feminine Sexuality – Jacques Lacan and the École Freudienne*, p.26.
[66] Ibid., p.26.
[67] Ibid., p.28.
[68] Ibid., p.26.
[69] Ibid., p.33.

one, phallocentrism occurs'[70] – Rose defends Lacan against the charge. Rather than being an 'unproblematic assertion of male privilege',[71] the phallus is a function of a symbolic order that is androcentric, something which requires that the subject relate itself to a phallus whose status is fraudulent, and a castration complex that is necessary for the inauguration of sexual identity. It follows that, with anatomy shown to be a sham, the claim to male privilege is unfounded because the male, like the woman, is also subjected within the symbolic order. Woman however is placed within the symbolic order as an object. Further, Rose argues that Lacan's statement that 'The woman does not exist', with the 'The' under erasure, should not be interpreted literally. Rather, what Lacan does in this statement is show that woman as 'an absolute category and guarantor of fantasy' does not exist.[72] It is the phallic function that excludes the woman: she is excluded *by* and not *from* the nature of words.

Thus, in Rose's reading of Lacan the woman is necessary for man's ability to acquire his own self-knowledge and truth. But if the notion of 'woman' is a fantasy, and so it would follow that 'man' must be too, for each subject must line up behind a door marked 'male' or 'female', and in choosing which door their biology is not implicated. Lacan refuses the possibility of any pre-discursive reality and so there can be no feminine outside language. The 'feminine', it follows 'is constituted as a division in language, a division which produces the feminine as its negative term. If woman is defined as other it is because the definition produces her as other.[73]

Siobhán Holland, in an excellent study of the ambivalence of patriarchal speech, comments on how Marie finds herself in a 'no-win' situation. When she attempts to register her difference from other visionaries and maintain control over her story, the Church subsequently disregards any miraculous experience it cannot assimilate within its own carefully regulated narrative. While the affair she is conducting with her husband's colleague might seem to mark her out as a subversive, her dissent is discounted and her actions compared to other, once-disbelieving saints. Father Niles reminds Monsignor Cassidy of the 'Saul of Tarsus analogy. The biblical connection: the prophet, unwilling, chosen by God' (*CH*, 165). Even her adulterous affair can be written off; as her behaviour makes

---

[70] Elizabeth Grosz, *Jacques Lacan – A Feminist Introduction*, p.174.
[71] Rose, *Feminine Sexuality*, p.44.
[72] Ibid., p.48.
[73] Ibid., p.54.

her a Magdalene figure whose redemption helps confirms God's patriarchal benevolence. As Holland notes:

> Her best attempts to signal herself as a secular, sexual and independent woman are easily assimilated into a patriarchal narrative. This achieves its effect not only by idealizing the Virgin Mary, but also by celebrating her visionaries in order to elaborate on its models for ideal or salvaged femininity.[74]

The words spoken by the apparition helps to undermine Marie's sense that she is in control of her own voice. The vision tells her: "Marie, I am your mother. I am the Virgin Immaculate… [t]his rock must be a place of pilgrimage… Marie, you will tell the priests…" (*CH*, 126). These words seem to indicate that Marie is merely a vehicle for dialogue between a divine agent and the Church. Nor does Marie seem to have any choice in the matter as she believes her husband's life is at stake: 'He had done nothing wrong. He was the victim of a terrible accident that was all. Or the victim of her refusal to obey' (*CH*, 92). Marie's belief in her own sense of independence is undermined by her fear that some powerful deity has complete control over the ways that she and her vision will be understood. Father Niles attempts to validate Marie's experience through a declaration of belief, arguing that by simply reporting the matter to the Church implies some form of belief:

> 'Tell me, Mrs Davenport,' he said. 'One of the slight discrepancies in your story is that you say you don't believe in any of this and yet you must believe it, in some way. For instance, you seem to believe in it strongly enough to feel that if you don't come forward and tell what happened, something bad might happen to this friend of yours.' (*CH*, 174)

Father Niles attempts to dismiss her role in the matter tells us that Marie merely stands as a means to an end and cannot speak out without her speech being recuperated into the hagiographical tradition she wants to reject. However, Moore seems to suggest that the absolute freedom Marie seeks is denied to all the characters in the novel – they too are contingent upon careful repetition for their authority. Monsignor Cassidy considers this dilemma when he strikes a deal with Father Niles:

---

[74] Siobhán Holland, 'Re-citing the Rosary: Women, Catholicism and Agency in Brian Moore's *Cold Heaven* and John McGahern's *Amongst Women*', in Liam Harte and Michael Parker (eds.) *Contemporary Irish Fiction: Themes, Tropes, Theories*, p.62.

> But if I don't let him do this, then he will be under no obligation to me. He can tell this story to anyone he meets, he can write it up and publish it. He's not a priest anymore, he's a writer; and writers want to make a name for themselves. He could write this up as his investigation, not mine; how he tracked down the story despite the indifference of a certain Monsignor. He could make me look stupid, or worse. Indeed he could. (*CH*, 208)

Father Niles himself knows also that he can only command the attention of his superiors if he speaks within the conventional limits of discourse about Mariology. His authority is always an effect of power garnered from the careful repetition of the Church's discourse on miracles and, like Marie, he is limited by the need to recite these conventions.

According to Lacan, the differences between the two sexes are positioned in the mode of being (for the feminine), and having (for the masculine), the phallus:

> Let us say that these relations will turn around a 'to be' and a 'to have', which, by referring to a signifier, the phallus, have the opposed effect, on the one hand of giving reality to the subject in this signifier, and, on the other, of derealizing the relations to be signified.[75]

Through the phallus, each sex is positioned as a speaking being, giving reality to the subject. Through the phallus, the reality of anatomical sex becomes bound up with the meanings and values that a culture gives to anatomy derealizing the relations to the signified. Yet it could be argued that a man can only be affirmed as phallic through the other who desires (and therefore lacks) what he has. Thus, the processes placing the woman as a subject with respect to the phallus is more challenging and her relation to desire of the Other more tenuous. Her castration complex functions to ensure that she accepts her castrated condition as a *fait acompli* – thus, she resolves her oedipal entanglements by accepting that she does not have the phallus. However, in compensation for her turning from the mother to the father as primary love-object, she acquires a number of strategies and devices for gaining pleasure even if she has to relinquish the active pre-oedipal position. The characteristics of femininity that Freud outlines – seductive, coquettish behaviour, conceit, vanity and jealousy – are a consequence of her acceptance of her lack. The woman often transfers her early relationship with her mother onto her male partner. The need to anticipate from someone else what the woman once wanted to possess makes her dependent in a way that leads both to masochism (with the

[75] Jacques Lacan, *Écrits* (1977), p.289.

castigation she receives relating to her position in coitus) and to narcissism (which is expressed in her greater need to be loved than to love). Presenting another perspective in *On Narcissism: An Introduction*, Freud stated that following puberty, women, 'especially if they grow up with good looks, develop a certain self-contentment,' that exercises 'a great attraction for those who have renounced part of their own narcissism.'[76] Such are the strategies developed to ensure that, even if she doesn't have the phallus, she may become the phallus, the object of desire for another.

There is little doubt that Marie is aware of her beauty as illustrated in the café episode in New York. She is singled out by 'a boy sitting further down the counter, looking her over. She knew his sort. He was fat and cocky, yet unsure, looking for a chance, any chance, to get into conversation' (*CH*, 53). He tells her, 'I thought you were a model, apart from your looks [...] You're certainly pretty enough to be in the movies. You know what I mean?' (*CH*, 54).

Her narcissism is evident in the way she describes her first encounter with Daniel:

> He did not try to impress her with his knowledge or importance. Unlike other doctors he did not seem accustomed to laying down the law. She found him shy, but he could make her laugh. He told quiet jokes, watching her, with a lopsided grin. He made her feel pretty, made her feel she was the person he most wanted to talk to at the party. He danced with her five times that evening. Unlike Alex, he was not a good dancer, but unlike Alex, he had fun dancing. (*CH*, 150)

While it is evident that Daniel has renounced part of his own narcissistic persona, Marie displays her own behavioural tics openly, clearly willing to put up with her husband callous indifference – that she perseveres so long with the relationship hints either at masochism:

> Suddenly she felt not fear, but a familiar resentment at his selfishness, his assumption that his career transcended anything else in their lives, his sending her off to service the car or deal with the superintendent and the plumber, or asking her to pack his suitcase for his trips because 'I'm too busy,' (*CH*, 114)

Or at apathy:

> He was the one who was in love. I didn't really care about finishing graduate school. I didn't know what I wanted to do. When I wrote that

[76] Joseph Sandler, *Freud's "On Narcissism : An Introduction"*, p.289.

> paper on Baudelaire, Professor Haines said: 'Obviously Miss Gillan is a hedonist.' I laughed and thought, 'Well that's no crime.' But after I married Alex, I remembered what Haines had said. Did I marry just to have an easy life? If so, I have paid for it. (*CH*, 107)

Woman retains her position as the object of the other's desire only through artifice or appearance. Illusion, deception, make-up or the veil become the method she relies upon to cover and make visible her essential assets. They are her means of seducing the other, of becoming a love object for him. However, it is only in so far as she is the object of the other's desire that she can be the phallus. All her artifice is directed to this end. It projects her in a series of images which more or less approximate the ideal, prescribed behaviour of femininity. In *Cold Heaven*, we witness the classic Madonna/Whore dichotomy – Marie's sexual impulsiveness offset by the nuns in the field: 'representations of reality rather than reality itself' (CH, 75) and the apparition in the guise of a virginal, saintly girl.

In a sense, Marie never receives the affirmation of her subjectivity that she desires. At best, Daniel and Alex's desire for her affirms her as a sexual being but not as a unique, specific subject. Daniel has loved before – his wife, Elaine, 'a loud stout girl' (*CH*, 150) – while his attraction to Marie appears purely aesthetic. As a character, he gives nothing away about himself and seems callously indifferent to those who will be hurt by the affair. When he quizzes Marie about the matter, he asks whether she feels badly about it. When she replies: "Of course I do. Don't you?" He replies half-heartedly: "I don't know. No I'd rather we got it over with" (*CH*, 148). The fact that his step-daughter has been injured in a horse-riding accident (*CH*, 99) or that Marie's husband is slipping in and out of a death-like coma appears to be of little concern to him. Indeed, it could be argued that Marie has substituted one man obsessed with work with another who is single-mindedly obsessed with his own abstract impulses – in the complex duality of their relationship, they appear as a suitable complementation to one another.

For Lacan, woman is not a subject who acts in relation to the phallus; she is the phallus only in the comedy of copulation, an object of man's passion, love or gratification. The man too, for his part, participates in this play of semblances. He too must confirm having the phallus through the desire of an other. He must appropriate the woman as love-object, make her his own, for only then is the alignment between penis and phallus confirmed. This masquerade or veil is typically 'feminine' in either men or women, Lacan claims, because it operates to deny or cover or lack. He states:

> Paradoxical as this formulation may seem, I am saying that it is in order to be the phallus, that is to say, the signifier of the desire of the Other, that a woman will reject an essential part of her femininity, namely, all her attributes in the masquerade. It is for that which she is not that she wishes to be desired as well as loved.[77]

Thus, it is through the masquerade that a woman's 'not-having' the phallus is transformed into 'being' the phallus. This is an idea which Lacan developed from Joan Riviere's paper "Womanliness as Masquerade", which saw the notion of masquerade as an important contribution to the theory of female sexual development. She argues that both the mother and the father are the little girl's rivals and objects of her sadistic fury. Woman thus strives to be affirmed as a unique, desirable, special subject, an individual distinct from all women; yet romantic love relations involve putting her on a pedestal and/or a reduction to the position of sexual object.

In *Cold Heaven*, what is more clearly affirmed for Marie is not her subjectivity but her ability to be reduced to a desiring object, which she shares with all women in patriarchy. She is a sexual receptacle or object, wanting what men have. Marie is duly perused by both Daniel and the stranger in the coffee shop for purely sexual reasons. She acts as a trophy wife to Alex – another possession. She is harried by Father Niles, but his interest in her is as a receptacle for a divine message – nothing more. In this sense she is interchangeable with any other woman. Indeed, Daniel's surface interest in both his friend's and his step-daughter's condition hint that Marie could find herself replaced by some other, token female body. He does not appear particularly loyal.

In the sexual act, woman finds her demand for affirmation frustrated; she is homogenized to the category of passive object. Yet although sexual relations are the culmination of romantic impulses and the most intimate form of expression, they do not provide any sense of gratification for woman's demand for recognition. The man also finds his expressions of romantic love frustrated. He desires his possession of the phallus to be affirmed through the woman's desire for his penis, which is, in the symbolic sense, detachable from him and capable of being given to her. She desires access to the phallus he owns. It is ironic then that sexual relations problematize the very link between penis and phallus that man tries to affirm. Sexual intercourse becomes both the affirmation of his possession of the phallus and a reminder of the possibility of castration.

---

[77] Jacques Lacan, *Écrits* (1977), pp.289-90.

For a moment at least, he fills the woman's lack and at that moment becomes the site of lack himself. In the process of taking the woman, the man is reminded of her lack. He is thus reminded of the possibility of his own. The man proclaims his love for the woman, but when she takes him as her sexual object his desire is reduced to a sexual performance, and thus the phallus is reduced to the penis – in that sense, he cannot satisfy the woman's desire.

The conquest of her enigma forces him to confront the question of castration. This is why, even if the man distinguishes between two types of women – one, an alter-ego he respects but holds no mystery for him; the other, a phallus, an object of fascination and desire – the latter collapses into the former after a period of close familiarity. His sexual partner becomes more an object of affection than of desire after sustained intimacy. Then his desire transplants itself to another woman and the cycle starts again. From being an object of desire, the woman becomes the other of demand.

Her demands – for attention, love, fidelity and so forth – reduce her from the status of being the phallus, the object of desire, to becoming the other, the subject of demand. The transient nature of human relationships is alluded to more than once in *Cold Heaven* – Alex loses interest in Marie after a period of sustained familiarity and the same applies for Daniel and *his* wife. The fact that he has a step-daughter indicates that this has happened before to his wife – it may continue *ad nauseam*. Once Father Niles gains possession of the divine message from Marie, it is then conferred to a more compatible female – Sister Anna. Marie is subsequently discarded. It may be argued thus that the novel stands more for a crisis of possession than of faith – that a true act of the divine can be lost so arbitrarily in the shuffle speaks more of the irrelevance of modern society than the myriad relationships that dominate the novel.

God Whispers to Us in Our Pleasures

Jo O'Donoghue spoke of *Cold Heaven* as being 'shrouded in mystery':

> What emerge from it as regards the development of Moore's attitude to belief and religion are firstly a new sense of the possibility of genuine goodness and remarkable self-forgetfulness, that has its origins in religious

> belief... there is the implicit admission in the novel that there really is no possibility of understanding spirituality other than by experiencing it.[78]

O'Donohue's suggestion that Moore found some sort of middle ground in his dealings with the Church is an intriguing one. Patricia Craig notes: 'One or two of Brian Moore's relatives considered it brave of him to put himself into Judith Hearne, in the form... of Bernard Rice.'[79] Rice, a fat mother's-boy and would-be poet is given to expressing his anti-religious rants whenever it suits him and while it is true that Rice is the mouth-piece for the author's opinions, that is as far as any attempt at self-portrait goes. I would agree with O'Donoghue that Moore approaches *Cold Heaven* as an honest broker. One could note the acerbic portrayal of the nuns in *Judith Hearne* - 'What was it old John Harvey once said: the Sisters of Mercy have no charity, and the Sisters of Charity have no mercy. And it was true' (*LPJH*, 159) – and the residue of anger which he felt towards the religious orders had yet to be tempered in his early fiction. In an interview with Julia Carlson in 1987, the bitterness Moore felt about his educational upbringing in St Malachy's is immediately apparent:

> I went to St Malachy's, which was the only Catholic boarding school in Belfast at the time. It was a terrible school [...] boys who went to terrible schools like St. Malachy's became priests. They went on to teach and treat their pupils as they themselves had been treated and to have the same set of opinions.[80]

St Malachy's was, in Patrick Hick's words, 'authoritarian, Republican, and the very symbol of success for males in the Moore family.'[81] There is little doubt that Moore's greatest concern with Catholicism was the authoritarian nature of the Church. It left a lasting impression but not an overwhelmingly negative one. As Eamon Maher writes:

> There was no obvious bitterness towards religion in his writing, rather a sense of loss in people like Judith Hearne, who could not find in religion what she had lost in the struggle for self-respect and recognition as a human being.[82]

---

[78] Jo O'Donoghue, *Brian Moore – A Critical Study*, p. 186.
[79] Patricia Craig, *Brian Moore – A Biography*, p.125.
[80] Julia Carlson, *Banned in* Ireland, pp. 111-115.
[81] Patrick Hicks, *Brian Moore and The Meaning of the Past*, p.24.
[82] Eamon Maher, *Crosscurrents and Confluences – Echoes of Religion in Twentieth-Century Fiction*, p.127.

In *Cold Heaven*, Maria has nominal interest in religion and like the author himself, her experience of Catholic boarding school coloured her vision of the religious orders. Yet, she has, 'a biography of Catherine Labouré, a book on the happenings at Beauraing, and a paperback entitled *A Woman Clothed by the Sun*' on her bookshelves. (*CH*, 62) As a young woman, Catherine Labouré became a member of the nursing order founded by Saint Vincent de Paul. Catherine stated that on the night of July 18, 1830 she woke up after hearing the voice of a child calling her to the chapel, where she heard the Virgin Mary say to her: "God wishes to charge you with a mission. You will be contradicted, but do not fear; you will have the grace to do what is necessary. Tell your spiritual director all that passes within you. Times are evil in France and in the world."[83] Beauraing is a small town in the southern, French speaking part of Belgium, and it was here that the Blessed Virgin appeared to a group of children, between late November 1932 and January 1933. *A Woman Clothed by the Sun*, written by John J. Delaney, considers the eight most significant apparitions of Mary: that of the Miraculous Medal at Paris, those at La Salette, Lourdes, Knock, Fatima, Beauraing, Banneux — and also the sixteenth-century appearance of Mary at Guadalupe, with its profound message for Americans.

Had Marie been a true non-believer, such texts would have been of little interest to her. She argues to Monsignor Cassidy that it is only when the strange occurrences begin in Nice that she began to take the matter seriously, but the evidence of these texts in the apartment in New York illustrate a passing interest nonetheless. In a conversation with Andy O'Mahoney on RTÉ radio Moore stated:

> I wanted to point out the elements of the supernatural… that there are things in the world that are not understood by us but we also have the choice to accept those things or reject them. My heroine in Cold Heaven actually rejects [it]… and is allowed, quite seriously, by the Monsignor at the end of it, to make that decision and go away because the Catholic Church has never forced anyone to believe in miracles.[84]

While this is a contentious point in itself, Moore is clearly expressing his topical interest in the subject. Akin to Marie, the whole mysticism of the Church, with its rituals and symbolism, is little more than a curio for the author. Yet, a residue of bitterness remains. When Marie considers the

[83] Alban Butler et al, *Butler's Lives of the Saints*, p.220.

[84] Brian Moore in Conversation with Andy O'Mahoney, *Dialogue*, RTE, 1986.

Colletine nuns, hidden away from the world behind a two-way mirror, she is filled with rage 'against this religion that asked such inhuman sacrifices' (*CH*, 78). When Daniel and Marie are leaving the Irish bar in San Francisco, Marie advises Daniel against giving money to a false nun in the doorway, "They're not real nuns, they're frauds." To which he responds: "What's the difference?" (*CH*, 157). Only by surrendering yourself to the patriarchal discourse of the Church can you find peace, and while Mother St. Jude is ascribed a saintly role, it is only through the total deconstruction of the self that this can occur. As Robert Sullivan writes:

> Although religion permeates Moore's books, from his first books to the most recent, *The Statement*, he is not concerned (unlike Joyce) in these early novels with religious doubt as such… [r]ather, he is anxious to explore the social and, in consequence, psychological repercussions the church effects on its dependants, especially in their time of need.[85]

While I agree with Maher and others that Moore is not deliberately critical of religion, his viewpoint is that of the modern agnostic. The Church draws a certain amount of morbid curiosity, as Sullivan states, it is not so much about belief as the way in which belief is controlled by a closed sect of individuals more interested in golfing jaunts than the spiritual well-being of their flock. His view of the Church has changed of course, and a priest no-longer wields the quasi-mystical power he witnessed in the Belfast of his youth. They, like the Colletine nuns, are locked away behind two-way mirrors, a virtual smoke-screen for what is, in essence, an empty theatrical performance. The question that Moore poses in the novel is a universal one – if indeed we had proof of some miraculous occurrence, who would care? Doubt has crept into society and true belief is waning, a message from God a secondary concern for those more interested in a hedonistic lifestyle. While I agree that the novel is by no means anti-clerical, it offers a deeply ambivalent view on morality and the uncomprehending nature of society. Like the Yeats poem from which the novel gains its title, the novel hints only at the confusion and emptiness of death, a suitable reward perhaps for the heated passions that distract us in life:

> *Ah! when the ghost begins to quicken,*
> *Confusion of the death-bed over, is it sent*

[85] Robert Sullivan, *A Matter of Faith – The Fiction of Brian Moore*, p.20.

Out naked on the roads, as the books say, and stricken
By the injustice of the skies for punishment?[86]

[86] W.B.Yeats, "Cold Heaven", in *The Collected Poems of W.B. Yeats*, p.125.

CONCLUSION

'Man', according to W.H. Auden, 'is a history-making creature who can neither repeat his past nor leave it behind.'[1] I chose to focus on a time span in Irish history that began just before the heady days of the nineteen-sixties and culminated in '[t]he terrible waste of energy and resources and enthusiasm' of what Conor Brady termed 'The Geldoff generation.'[2] In the intervening years the symbolic order has altered slightly. The Church's authority in Ireland has been in terminal decline and the patriarchal order has become increasingly discredited – Keith Grint suggests that the picture is one of 'increasingly embattled senior men confronted by young women undeterred by history or tradition.'[3] The reality, of course, is more complex but in comparison to the rights and privileges of Irish women in the early nineteen-sixties, the tacit hegemony of the Irish male is no longer taken for granted.

However, for Michel Foucault, history is not the direct result of human actions. On the contrary, it is a succession of epistemological structures that dictate what the subject and the object of history are that determine it. The sum of the epistemological structures that influence each particular age is called *episteme* – the Greek word for science. The *episteme* is an unconscious and anonymous system of rules whose primary function is to regulate knowledge. In other words, an *episteme* is the corpus of norms that dictate what knowledge is and how this has to be developed and addressed.[4] The passage from one episteme to another is not a fluid one. Contrary to some theories, history does not follow either a linear progress or a teleological path. The occurrence of events is not determined by an internal logic. The world does not tend towards perfection or an ultimate goal. Basically, there is no continuity to history.

Traditional historiography and philosophy '[a]ssume that words keep their meaning, that desire still points in a single direction, that ideas retain

[1] W.H. Auden, *The Dyer's Hand*, p.137.
[2] Conor Brady, 'The lost potential of Geldoff's generation', in Irish *Times*, 17 July 1985.
[3] Keith Grint, *The Sociology of Work*, p. 223.
[4] Michel Foucault, *Archaeology of Knowledge*, pp. 211-212.

their logic; and this ignores the fact that the world of speech and desire has known invasions, struggles, plundering, disguises, ploys'.[5] Thus, the subject ceases to be the agent of history, always tending towards certain, specific goals as intended by Western tradition and civilization. The death of God, announced by Nietzsche in *Thus Spake Zarathustra*, is the end of such teleological concept of history. For Foucault, this creates an empty space. This emptiness is the condition of possibility of a new way of thinking and theorizing. It is the end to the rule of continuity and of traditional humanism.

The embrace of unchecked capitalism in the nineteen sixties left Ireland open to the swirling tides of the international markets. One could easily draw a comparison between mid-seventies Ireland and the current global recession which has plunged the country into an economic maelstrom, but today we appear even more ill-equipped to deal with the repercussions – one may argue that Ireland has grown comfortable in unabashed hedonism and without any of the old, familiar mainstays of society – the Church, the family, trusted political institutions and employment, emigration as a release valve, etc. – we appear utterly at a loss to deal with circumstances which are hardly novel for Ireland.

When we read Broderick, McGahern or Moore, we are immediately struck by one glaring absolute – people put up with their lot, however begrudgingly, or they simply left the country. As Shelia states in *Amongst Women*: "If we don't do well in the exam, if we don't get anything here… you may see us in London soon enough" (*AM*, 85). In *The Dark*, young Mahoney tells his father: "I can go to England and pay you back from there", to which his father caustically replies: "Anyone can go to England… if you've a fiver in your pocket and the boat fare you can go to England, that's all that's wanting" (*TD*, 85). Both Marie Fogarty in *The Fugitives* and James Madden in *The Lonely Passion of Judith Hearne* find themselves having to emigrate. It was the 'priest and the doctor and not the guerrilla fighters who had emerged as the bigwigs in the country Moran had fought for' (*AM*, 88). Society was relatively inflexible – if you had inherited wealth such as the Ryans in *The Waking of Willie Ryan* you had some choice but for most of the protagonists in these novels there were few options save hard graft and a possible white collar career or the emigrant boat and whatever fortune or misfortune that brought you.

So Irish society has become more fluid – the opening up of third-level education, the increasing industrialization of the country, the plethora of

[5] Paul Rabinow (ed.), *The Foucault Reader*, p. 76.

opportunities in the healthcare, IT or construction sectors – such opportunities meant that the options facing young people in Ireland were more diverse and the spectre of emigration rarely arose during the boom years of the late nineties and the decade after save as a personal choice or whim. Expectations rose and the stale, hegemonic society of the nineteen-sixties seemed to be part of another world, another time. When the property market crashed, the crisis was blown wholly out of proportion and an unprecedented level of panic and self-recrimination set in:

> Not only, moreover, is the crisis a global one, but it is worse in Ireland than in most other countries. Because of the scale of our dependency on a property bubble, we are hit harder and because of the appalling mess that has been made of the public finances we have fewer options for stimulating the economy. So if we're looking for reasons to be cheerful, they're not likely to be found in any short-term prospect of a recovery.[6]

Lacan thought that psychosis began with the era of the ego, which in turn began in the seventeenth century. Although the ego's era begins before the advent of capital, it was nonetheless accelerated by the arrival of the latter. Lacan duly implied that the ego would act as if there were no limits, pushing off into outer space on the strength of its imperative to expand. His theory suggests that the ego seeks to make the world in its own image by reducing the cultural orders into a solitary mirror of sameness – this is achieved by producing a proliferation of goods which become the hallmark of the modern life. Lacan is dismissive of Hegel's optimism on 'progress as history unfolds' or the 'appeal to any tomorrow.'[7] Building on the Hegelian master-slave dialectic, Lacan states, '[t]he problem is knowing whether the Master-Slave conflict will find its resolution in the service of the machine…'[8] This outlook draws similarities with that of the German philosopher Theodor Adorno who argued that there was no such thing as a universal history - '[f]rom the savage to humanitarianism'- but only one 'leading from the slingshot to the megaton bomb.'[9] It is none too surprising that Lacan found in Hegel's Master-Salve dialectic a radical description of the human subject's aggressiveness. In this conflict, the

[6] Fintan O'Toole, 'Can we Remake Ireland's Future?', in *The Irish Times*, 3 January 2009.

[7] Jacques Lacan, 'The neurotics individual myth,' in Laurence Spurling *Sigmund Freud: Critical Assessments, vol. II, The Theory and Practice of Psychoanalysis*, p. 80.

[8] Jacques Lacan, *Écrits* (1977), p.27.

[9] Theodor Adorno, *Dialectic of Enlightenment*, p.320.

struggle revolves around pure prestige or face – the slave's goal was to become master by cancelling him out; the master only remained thus in reference to a slave who must, by definition, be defeated. Lacan equated Hegel's master with the Other – the locus from which the subject speaks and desires throughout his life.

Coexisting with language, yet desiring from within, the *je* – the object of the Other's discourse – mistakenly thinks it can represent its own totality by designating itself in a statement. This is assumption of the master/slave model – the speaking subject is oppressed from within by identity fixations of the *moi.* The latter is paradoxically a rival of its own Other but obliged to wait for recognition from the world outside. Thus man is inclined to a whole range of aggressive behaviour – from envy and jealousy to truly aggressive acts, even the mortal negation of the self or other. In my estimation, the timeframe of this book could be considered the beginning of the 'era of the ego.' The advent of industrialization in the sixties meant that there was now technology which was capable of fulfilling the desires embodied in the foundational fantasy. On a global scale, those fantasies which we once could only dream of began to suddenly materialize. By the nineteen-sixties the technology arrived in Ireland which made them come true – corrupting our temporal parameters in the process. Thus, when the world is turned into a world of objects the power of the fantasy is reinforced. On this matter, Eugene O'Brien's comments on the primacy of desire are prescient:

> One need only remember the fall of the Berlin wall… despite the radical uncertainty of moving to a capitalist system, the desire for possessions, for a better life… was the motive force for directing traffic across the ruins of that forbidding wall. Indeed commodity fetishism, the engine which drives capitalist economies, is the practical embodiment of desire – I need a new phone, a bigger PC with more Ram and a Pentium 4/5/6 processor.[10]

Martin Heidegger located the origin of the metaphysical mind-set in Platonic philosophy. He situates metaphysics as a privileging of space over temporality and argued that this privileging resulted in the repression of the historical process. He saw technology as a force which threatened to make this repression absolute. It does so because technology confines

---

[10] Eugene O'Brien, '"Kicking Bishop Brennan up the Arse…": Catholicism, Deconstruction and Postmodernity in Contemporary Irish Culture', in John Littleton and Eamon Maher (eds.), *Irish and Catholic? Towards an Understanding of Identity*, p.47.

human experience with certain rigid grids that closes off the processes of connection with the world other than those based on the relation between the human as subject and the world as object. We could note, for example, how the rise of urbanization in Ireland has led to the creation of this new aggressive, go-getting society. As Lacan states:

> Such a note of aggressivity as one of the intentional co-ordinates of the human ego, especially relative to the category of space, allows us to conceive of its role in modern neurosis and in the 'discontents' of civilization.[11]

He appears to be saying here that aggression increases in the spatial restrictions of an urban environment. He also makes passing reference in this paper to 'the living space in which human competition is becoming ever keener.'[12] Aggressiveness motivates the drive to dominate and Lacan's theory on aggressiveness indicates the connection between the spatial dimensions of the ego and the spatial environment in which it exists. In *Amongst Women*, the contrast between the isolated Moran farmhouse and Shelia's new home in suburban Dublin is striking:

> It was a low, detached bungalow in a new estate of a couple of hundred bungalows, exactly the same, the front gardens still raw with concrete. Already in some of the back gardens lines of nappies fluttered. Inside, the house had carpets and neat inexpensive furniture. Shelia showed off each room – stating the price of each piece of furniture – with touching pride. (*AM*, 151)

In *Cold Heaven*, Marie is accosted by a stranger in a café who follows her outside and offers to buy her a drink: "Ah come on. Give me a break. I'm a nice guy… just one drink, okay?" When Marie continues to walk away, ignoring him, he responds: '"Thanks for your courtesy." His voice was now sarcastic. "Thanks a lot. Cunt"' (*CH*, 55). An urban environment also lends to a sense of isolation. With the disintegration of the 'community', those 'awake and watchful' streetscapes of Broderick's Athlone (*TF*, 9) people have found themselves increasingly alienated and figures like Judith Hearne or Mrs Prell in *Cold Heaven* become more and more commonplace:

[11] Jacques Lacan, 'Aggressivity in psychoanalysis', p.25.
[12] Ibid., p.27.

> Mrs Prell's door was ajar, and as Marie drew near to it, Mrs Prell staged her familiar stratagem of coming out dressed for the street, as if she were going down the corner for some errand; poor lonely Mrs Prell, who waited behind her door until she heard passing footsteps, then came out to talk about the weather, her grandchildren, the crime-rate… with the relentless discursiveness of the true solitary for whom such encounters are the high point of a silent day. (*CH*, 56)

The structure of the society in which we live has altered greatly and, in consequence, so have the behaviour, the norms and obligations of the people who inhabit this island. The symbolic order of the nineteen sixties is vastly different from the one in existence today and this fact is one of the central tenets to this book. If we look at history as a series of epochs we may pose the question – why did the symbolic order in Ireland change, what caused that change and what are the repercussions of that change? I think these are key questions and essential to our understanding of modern Irish literature and society. To begin with, it must be established once more that the symbolic order is a fluid organism. Yes, the theory remains inflexible: while the order is fixed and stratified its constituents are forever shifting and developing. It is not a superstructure determined by biology or genetics. Each individual is unique in this sense, '[h]is history… unified by the law, by his symbolic universe, which is not the same for everyone.'[13] In the opening chapter I made reference to a number of changes which occurred over the course of the timeframe of this book – the declining influence of the Church, the role of women in society, the father-son or -daughter relationship and the decline in the primacy of the family. Let us look at each of these issues again briefly.

The Church

Writing in the Catholic periodical *The Furrow* in 1959, Father John Kelly, an Irish Jesuit priest, aired the opinion that:

> Too many people in Ireland today are trying to make do with a peasant religion when they are no longer peasants anymore; we are a growing and developing middle-class nation, acquiring a middle-class culture, and we must have a religion fit for our needs.[14]

---

[13] Jacques Lacan, *The Seminar. Book I. Freud's Papers on Techniques*, p.197.

[14] Quoted in Louise Fuller, *Irish Catholicism Since 1950: The Undoing of a Culture*, p.61.

Father Kelly's advocacy of a more intellectual grasp of our faith bucked the trend of what was, in essence, an ultra-conservative institution. Episcopal authority in Ireland, once virtually monolithic, was beginning to show signs of wear and tear. By 1967 the Irish Catholic magazine was drawing attention to the fact that television was beginning to displace the rosary as a focal point for family gatherings in the evening. Concurrently, there was a steep decline in the membership of the Legion of Mary and Our Lady's Sodality throughout the sixties and seventies.[15] The process of change was not yet being viewed as the process of decline – but suddenly, previously unmentionable subjects such as ecumenism and divorce were being openly discussed. The 1970's' feminists saw the social values of Catholicism as a major obstacle inhibiting equal opportunities in Ireland, however personally devout they may be. I alluded to the fractious debates on contraception and divorce already in the introduction – the key issue here is that Episcopal authority no longer quelled debate on such matters, such as we saw with the Mother and Child scheme in 1951. While it was illegal to purchase contraceptives until 1991, the State began to look increasing ridiculous as it set itself against the liberalizing trends that had been sweeping the globe since the late 1960s'. Young people were no longer willing to simply follow dictates and ask no questions and the Bishops could only mouth the decree, 'no change' in response to the rising clamour for individual choice and freedom.

The result was that people began to walk away from the Church. At first, those numbers were small and as late as 1990 it could be claimed that 85 per cent of the Irish adult population attended Mass on a weekly basis. By 1997 even the most optimistic survey showed this had fallen to 65 per cent.[16] I explained in the first chapter the reason for this rapid collapse but the reality is that the seeds of dissent had already been sown as far back as the 1950s. The Church, with its rituals and symbolism, is prevalent in the writing of all three authors in this book. As one of the props to the symbolic order of the period 1955 – 1990, the hierarchy draws similarities with my reference to the family – both were patriarchal, fixed and stratified while their authority was drawn and subsequently copper-fastened by the government. In the constitution of 1937, woman is firmly

[15] James S. Donnelly Jr., 'The Troubled Contemporary Irish Catholic Church', in Brendan Bradshaw and Dáire Keogh (eds), *Christianity in Ireland: Revisiting the Story*, p.274.

[16] Ibid., p.285.

tied to the hearth and home[17] while the Church was allocated a 'special position' in the State.[18] While the latter article was removed in a referendum in 1973, the former remains steadfastly in place. A Catholic priest has a central role in three of the texts (Father Mannix (*WR*), Father Quigley (*LPJH*) Father Niles and Monsignor Cassidy (*CH*)), and a walk-on part in the rest (Father Gerald (*TD*), 'unnamed' (*AM*) 'The Canon' (*TF*)). The portraits are none too flattering and while Father Mannix and Monsignor Cassidy are somewhat redeemed by their subsequent behaviour at the close of each novel, the rest display a number of unwholesome traits – Father Niles, God's 'Recording Angel' (*CH*, 269), is so wrapped up in self-publicity he's 'not a priest anymore' (*CH*, 208). Father Gerald, who enters the bed of his young charge and quizzes him on his sexual behaviour, is also a dubious character. Father Quigley who falls asleep listening to one of his parishioners in the throes of a spiritual and mental crisis is once more at a remove from his congregation.

Religion then is one of the keys to our understanding of these texts and in this book I have argued that the Church provides a service to society – it is not a spiritual service, but it does help to perpetuate the patriarchal firmament of the community and offer leadership of sorts. Aside from Judith Hearne, nobody seems to pay much heed to the priest but he is a useful weather-vane to the mores of society and acts as a bulwark of sorts against the onslaught of all sorts of possible depravity. He is useful then in dispatching Willie Ryan to a mental home or covering up potential scandals such as is the case with Father Gerald or Monsignor Cassidy. The Canon in *The Fugitives* rails against 'murder, sin and devilment of the worst description sweeping the country' (*TF*, 44) and Father Quigley covers every possible indiscretion imaginable, from 'naked dancing girls in the cinema (!)' to reading 'trashy books and indecent magazines' (*LPJH*, 54). Only the unnamed priest in McGahern's *Amongst Women* emerges as somewhat devout clergyman but there are less than 5 lines devoted to him and he exits from proceedings as quickly as he arrives.

---

[17] Article 41.2.1: 'In particular, the State recognises that by her life within the home, woman gives to the State a support without which the common good cannot be achieved.'

Article 41.2.2: 'The State shall, therefore, endeavour to ensure that mothers shall not be obliged by economic necessity to engage in labour to the neglect of their duties in the home.'

[18] Article 44.1.2: 'The State recognises the special position of the Holy Catholic Apostolic and Roman Church as the guardian of the Faith professed by the great majority of the citizens.'

Catholicism has generally seen sexual desire in a negative light and this became the hallmark for Irish society from the foundation of the state to the early nineties. Until the nineteen sixties, this was unquestionable fact. From the sixties onwards however, *something* was happening to Irish society. My argument is: (a) the opening up of the economy heralded in what could be termed the 'era of the ego'– a new importance placed on commodities and materiality: (b) The symbolic order, which is fluid, was changing with the times – in Ireland, there was a greater resistance to that change but it occurred nonetheless: (c) Education – the advent of free second level education had a marked effect upon society and helped open up a monolithic class structure which could almost be almost be termed feudal: (d) The Church began to look antiquated and out of touch – every act of resistance deemed a further step backwards: (e) The rise of Irish feminism which sought to undermine both the inherent discrimination faced by women in society and the stereotype of the placid, Irish housewife content with her lot: (f) The media – the introduction of television and the effective end of literary censorship in the mid-sixties.

Many of these issues tied in with each other such as when Archbishop McQuaid summoned Charles Haughey, then Minister for Justice, to his palace in order to show him a copy of Edna O'Brien's *The Country Girls*. McQuaid noted approvingly Haughey's disgust: 'Like so many decent Catholic men with growing families,' McQuaid recorded, 'he was just beaten by the outlook and descriptions.'[19] As O'Brien stated in an interview with Julia Carlson:

> I had offended several fashions. I offended the Catholic Church. I betrayed Irish womanhood. They even used the phrase – I was a 'smear on Irish womanhood.' I betrayed my own community by writing about their world. I showed two Irish girls full of yearning and desires. Wicked![20]

When asked what kind of image of women she thought people wished to see in Ireland, she responded: "The pedestal image: devoid of sexual desires, maternal, devout, attractive..."[21] O'Brien was castigated for daring to write about female sexuality but set against the liberalizing trends of Vatican II, the judgement looked somewhat tired and predictable. Four years later, when John McGahern's *The Dark* was banned (as detailed in chapter four), the outcry was sufficient to lead to a relaxation in the laws.

---

[19] John Cooney, *John Charles McQuaid: Ruler of Catholic Ireland*, p.348.
[20] Julia Carlson, *Banned in Ireland: Censorship and the Irish Writer*, p.76 .
[21] Ibid., p.76.

The more the Church set themselves against the modernizing trends in this new era, the more isolated from reality they became. And yet the unyielding superstructure of Church remained intact for the next thirty years – the time-span of this book. Rather than asking: 'Why did the hegemony of the Church collapse in Ireland?' a more pertinent question would be: 'How did it last so long?' The answer to that question again ties in with the scope of this investigation – opposition remained marginalized. When I made reference to the clerical portraits in the six novels at hand, I pointed out that the clergy emerged in a rather unflattering light. The writer served his purpose too – he was saying what practically everybody else was thinking but too afraid to commit to print. Such is the nature of the parochial Irish system. Feminists too remained marginalized – like O'Brien, they were branded anti-Catholic and accused of betraying Irish womanhood and while they had retained a curio value the reality is that the old myths were still the most comfortable ones to wear for the majority of the Irish population. As one incensed (and, remarkably, female) reader wrote to the *Irish Independent* in 1971:

> Looking at the women's page (of the *Irish Independent*) you would hardly suspect Ireland is a Catholic country. For months you have been brainwashing married women to have careers outside the home and pressing for a change in laws relating to contraceptives with, once, even a suggestion that we "take a look" at abortion. I believe it is all part of a plan to prepare the ground for "permissive" legislation, directly contrary to the teaching of the Catholic Church.[22]

When Mary Robinson, at the time a Law Lecturer in Trinity Collage Dublin, attempted to introduce a bill repealing the prohibition on sale of contraceptives into the Senate, she failed to muster the perquisite support of six Senators to even debate the matter. Simply put, while Parliament existed as a sort of men-only club, albeit with a few token female representatives from time to time, the opinions and concerns of Irish women would remain on the side-lines for the next twenty years.

However, in retrospect, the repeated successes of the Church in the contraception debates of the early seventies, the acrimonious abortion referendum of 1983 and the even more bitter divorce referendum of 1986 were, in essence, Pyrrhic victories. They succeeded only in alienating vast swathes of the population and their pious denunciations on promiscuity

---

[22] Quoted in Anne Stopper, *Monday At Gaj's: The Story of the Irish Women's Liberation Movement*, p.174.

merely served to set them up for a greater fall when revelations emerged about Bishop Eamonn Casey fathering a child with an American divorcee. It would seem that Irish people will tolerate much in their appointed leaders (both spiritual and political) but they will not suffer such blatant hypocrisy. The first instinct of the Church when revelations about sexual abuse emerged was typical: they simply chose to try and sweep it under the carpet. But the reservoir of repression and deceit at the sick heart of Ireland had been festering for too long and papering over the cracks had been a policy that worked only when people were willing to accept blindly the dictates of the Bishops. By the early nineteen-nineties that was no longer the case and, like the Berlin Wall, once the first section collapsed, the rest followed with astonishing rapidity. Simply put, the Church was swept away by the scale of the disaster. By the late 1990s' there was no social capital to be gained from declaring yourself a devout Catholic. Young people, who had come out in record numbers to welcome the Pope to Ireland in 1979, departed in droves and ordinations to the priesthood subsequently collapsed. My belief is that the Church offered status of sorts to the people and in such a class-conscious society, pious, often degrading supplications to the faith were the norm. We saw this in *The Waking of Willie Ryan*, in *Cold Heaven*, in *The Lonely Passion of Judith Hearne* and in *The Dark*. It was a club whose members were treated differently and the status of having a priest in the family or of making magisterial donations to the Church or of having priests as family acquaintances cannot be under-estimated. This can be best reflected in the following passage from *The Waking of Willie Ryan*:

> 'Did you give him (Father Mannix) any money at the door?' Mary leaned forward, hands on hips, and searched her husband's flushed face.
>
> 'Did I what?' blustered Michael. 'Is it me give that fellow money! Isn't it enough that we have to contribute to every sale-of-work, bazaar, and jumble sale in the whole country without giving him any more?'
>
> 'The Church is all changed.' Mary pressed her fingers against her temples. 'They have no use for anybody now except the working class that they can ride roughshod over. It's a different proposition with us, and they know it.' (*WR*, 51)

What is apparent then is that a bargain of sorts was struck between most priests and the mercantile classes – each side served their own purposes. The priest could be called on to perform the onerous tasks in society for a price, to perform the rituals that perpetuated the *status quo* in return for monetary benefits such as Monsignor Cassidy's Volvo station-wagon or paid-up membership to the local golf course. This arrangement helped perpetuate the symbolic order for a further thirty years, from the nineteen-sixties to the early nineties but each side was obliged to keep up a façade of sorts. Propriety was key and any such transgressions were pounced upon and heroes of desire like Willie Ryan or Judith Hearne were promptly ejected and sent, literally, for immediate treatment. It was a cosy relationship but with the deluge of scandals in the nineties the Church could no longer perform in this role. They were utterly discredited and the mercantile classes found that they could operate well enough without them anyhow, turning their attention to the vulgar accruement of commodities instead. By the late nineties Tom Inglis could state:

> Irish Catholics are not only becoming protestant – that is, devising their own spiritual and moral path to salvation – they are also becoming more secular. The decline of influence of the institutional Church in the religious field has been matched by a decline in influence in other social fields, particularly in politics, education, health, social welfare and the media. In terms of individual behaviour, being religious or acquiring religious capital is no longer necessary to the acquisitions of other forms of capital. Irish Catholics can attain status, honour and respect, and they can attain political, economic and social power, without having to have Catholic religious capital or to have their forms of capital symbolically legitimized by the Church.[23]

The conscious or unconscious act of repression is evident in all six novels – sexual repression, the repression of desire. Thus we have the twisted desires of Ward in *The Fugitives* and Mahoney Sr. in *The Dark* – community as the watchman of society ready to pounce on any blatant expression of desire, 'coiled up, immobile, with hooded eyes…' (*TF*, 9) in *The Fugitives*. All these vices are evident in *The Waking of Willie Ryan*, in *The Lonely Passion of Judith Hearne* and in *Amongst Women*:

> Mrs Reynolds paused to watch Rose make her way round by the bridge to the post office and muttered venomously, 'There's no fool like an old fool', as if confronting the worst part of her own nature… in the full face of the ridicule she went to the post office evening after evening, ridicule she willed not to see or notice. (*AM*, 25)

I chose Lacan because of the particular nature of Irish society: a psychological reading of this society was the best approach to parse out the various nuances in the text where the emphasis was not so much on what was being said as what was left unsaid. In summation, Lacan

[23] Tom Inglis, *Moral Monopoly: The Rise and Fall of the Catholic Church in Ireland*, p. 206.

conceived the symbolic order as the locus of particular set of social, legal and linguistic conventions underlying society. The "big Other" does not exist as a substance but is nonetheless effective as it is continuously posited so that the organization of complex social forms becomes possible. For this fictional realm of structural differences to emerge as a coherent entity, *jouissance* as the inert substance of enjoyment must be sacrificed. From a Lacanian perspective, *jouissance* is forbidden to the one who speaks. The possibility of the 'free movement' within the sphere of culture and meaning is opened up by this repression, yet that which has been repressed paradoxically functions as the pivot on which a social entity is suspended. Indeed, society is constituted in the continuous act of repression and gains its ontological consistency only through this negativity. Why then such repeated references to the Church? As an example, one show look at the story of Genesis and how it functions as the archetype of a community structured around the repression of a forbidden substance of enjoyment. The story of Adam and Eve serves as an illustration as to how the purely internal impossibility of enjoyment subsequently becomes focalized in a taboo grounding a (albeit, tiny) social group.

The Role of Women in Irish Society

Aside from *The Dark*, women play an integral part in each of these six novels. Broderick, perhaps, has the least sympathetic outlook and his female protagonists are often portrayed as unscrupulous gold-diggers, nymphomaniacs or embittered scandalmongers. Whether his closet homosexuality (compounded by his staunch orthodoxy) or deep attachment to his mother had a part to play in his caustic portraits is speculative. From time to time he could create proud, somewhat intractable female characters who find themselves discarding their feminine poises in order to shape up to their vacillating men-folk but more often than not the novelist lapsed back into stereotype.[24] McGahern created a number of saintly, self-sacrificing housewives ostensibly based on his own mother Susan McGahern (Elizabeth Reegan in *The Barracks*, Kate Moran in *The Leavetaking*, Rose Brady in *Amongst Women*, etc.) and, occasionally, he also pencilled in the daughters of the household (*The Dark*, *The Leavetaking*, etc.). In *Amongst Women* we are introduced to

[24] See Peter D. Guy, 'The Lives of John Broderick', in *Studies* (Autumn 2008) p.254.

Moran's daughters and while they are credibly drawn, they never stop *being* Moran's daughters – weathervanes to his personality, dancing attendance on his whims and fancies. At times, McGahern could be deeply misogynistic in his female portraits such as the case with Josephine in *The Pornographer*. Moore is often celebrated for his portrayal of female characters, particularly in his 1953 debut *The Lonely Passion of Judith Hearne*, and his 1976 Booker shortlisted novel *The Doctor's Wife*. But his sixth novel *I am Mary Dunne* (1968) is the first in which the narrative is an uninterrupted internal monologue by a woman. A feminist novel written before the wave of feminist novels began; it set out the predicament of a sophisticated young woman who realizes that she is defined, even in her own mind, by men. Moore once wrote, 'There isn't a man alive who has the faintest idea of what a woman is, how she thinks and feels....are we ever going to get through the Iron Curtain of male generalizations about women?'[25]

Lacan's description of the Symbolic places women and men in different positions within the Symbolic order in relation to the Phallus. Men more readily misperceive themselves as having the Phallus – being closer to it – while women see themselves as further from that centre. Because of the distance from the Phallus, the poststructuralist theoretical feminists argue that women are closer to the margins of the Symbolic order. They are not as firmly anchored or fixed in place as men are and thus, they are closer to the Imaginary, to images and fantasies, and further from the idea of absolute fixed and stable meaning than men are. Because women are less fixed in the Symbolic than men, women and their language are more fluid, more flowing and more unstable than men. It is worth noting here that when a critic like Helen Cixous talks about 'women' and 'woman', sometimes she means literally the physical beings with vaginas and breasts and sometimes she means it as a linguistic structural position. Woman is a signifier in the chain of signifiers within the Symbolic, just as man is – both have stable meaning because both are locked in place, anchored, by the Phallus as centre of the Symbolic order.

I have already made reference to the marginalization of women in Irish society at this time, how they were repressed by institutionalized patriarchy in the Church, by their agents in government and advocates in the social sphere. In the opening chapter, I suggested that was, in part, a reaction to colonialism. Uncritically adopting the gender division imposed

---

[25] Quoted in Robert Fulford, 'Brian Moore: A writer who never failed to surprise his readers', in *The Globe and Mail*, 12th January 1999 – obituaries.

by colonialism, Irish decolonization attempted to deny its representation as an essentially feminine race by reconfiguring the division along wholly unequal lines. The Church, as I have stated, also played its part and when 'Mother Ireland' was officially fused with 'Mother Church' in the Constitution of 1937, the Irishwoman's body was identified as a vessel for the production of children within marriage. She had no other clearly demarcated role. Judith Hearne's draws a bitter analogy between the marriage market and a country auction: '"[a]nd he starts at a high price, saying what he'd like best. No offers. Then second best. No offers. Third? No offers. What am I bid, Moira? And somebody comes along, laughable, and you take him."' (*LPJH*, 166) In *The Waking of Willie Ryan*, Mary marries Mick Ryan, '[s]o she'd get his money from the farm to set up properly. Everybody knows that, and more than everybody' (*WR*, 42). In *Cold Heaven*, Marie berates herself for marrying Alex, '[j]ust to have an easy life...' (*CH*, 107) Rose Brady in *Amongst Women* is forced to make much of the running in her courtship but once Moran deigns to embrace the inevitable, however unwillingly, he is then forced to comply with the tradition where the male must pursue. For Rose, she is no longer, 'exposed and vulnerable... from a given and confident position she would now be able to move outwards' (*AM*, 30).

A woman's identity was thus defined by her success in finding a suitable husband, in her procreative ability[26], in her devotion to the Church and family. That the conditions and standing of women at home and in public life have ameliorated in the intervening years is indisputable but the extent and impact of that change remains contentious. Let me quote in full a passage from Pat O'Connor's *Emerging Voices* which neatly sums up this debate:

> Any discussion of changes in the position of women in Irish society over the past thirty years tends to elicit two views: that it has changed

[26] For example, in director Jim Sheridan's movie *The Field* (1991), there is a rather humorous exchange between 'The Bull' McCabe and the local matchmaker, where the two thrash out the prospects of a match between McCabe's son Tadgh and a local girl. When McCabe queries whether, 'She will produce an heir?' the matchmaker replies: 'She comes from good stock.' Elsewhere, in John McGahern's *That They May Face The Rising Sun*, John Quinn, in spite of raping his bride in full view of the wedding congregation, is still described as 'only doing his best... he's contributing to the race. Like the rest of them he's only trying to find his way to the boggy hollow' (p.37). The view of women as little more than barnyard animals is a depiction that arises in numerous Irish novels and movies of this period and afterwards.

> completely, and that it has not changed at all. It is easy to find evidence for both statements. Those endorsing the first view draw attention to the fact that, for example, since the 1970's, different wage scales for men and women have been abolished; the 'marriage bar', obliging women to retire on marriage from a variety of jobs in the public service has been lifted, inequalities based on gender have been substantially eliminated from the social welfare system; legal entitlements to maternity leave, without the possibility of dismissal has been established; divorce has been introduced and so forth… On the other hand, it can be argued that many elements in the lives of Irish women have not changed. Irish women are still under-represented in the political system, at the higher echelons of the economic system and in the institutional Church system… their average wage is lower than men's; they are huddled into a small range of paid occupation, predominately service ones; and they typically carry the main responsibility for domestic and child care activities… issues surrounding sexuality, especially abortion, are highly emotive, and the ideology of the family is still firmly embedded in the Irish Constitution.[27]

From the 1960s, the worldwide movement querying the position of women began to make itself felt in Ireland. Certain female structures of authority existed at that time, even it was in such limited areas as the convent, the Association of Business and Professional Women and the Countrywoman's Association. Change followed quickly in the 1970's and many of the advances referred to by O'Connor were implemented and not before time. However, attitudes remained unreconstructed and the reply of Fianna Fáil TD Tim O'Connor to a WPA questionnaire[28] on woman's issue could be considered typical: 'In my own county the women are doing a great job of work in keeping their homes going and bringing up their families. This I think is just what Almighty God intended them to do.'[29]

While inroads were being made into bringing some form of equality into the public and private sector, the next great battle for women was over control of their own bodies – as I mentioned before, the divisive campaigns concerned contraception, abortion and divorce. This opened up a spilt in the movement, particularly an urban/rural divide. For many women it was simply a matter of tackling Catholic social power head on. This was an unpalatable option for many in the Catholic heartlands where the Church retained considerable influence and often resorted to underhand

---

[27] Pat O'Connor, *Emerging Voices – Women in Contemporary Irish Society*, p.1.
[28] The Women's Political Association or WPA was headed by Mary Robinson to advocate change in such blatantly discriminatory legislation as the marriage ban.
[29] Mary Holland, in *Magill*, Vol. 1, no.2, November 1977, p.37.

tactics.[30] When the authority of the Church collapsed in the early nineties, the Catholic opponents to such issues foundered without coherent leadership. Legislation on the sale of contraceptives, on Divorce and the decriminalization of homosexuality were duly and swiftly implemented.

The outlook of each author conditioned the behaviour of their female protagonists – McGahern's view on women could now be considered hopelessly antiquated. However, there is little doubt that the changing Symbolic Order impacted on his fiction: Moran's daughters do display certain degrees of self-sufficiency and independence, even perhaps a feminist outlook. Shelia becomes engaged, 'without benefit of Moran's approval' (*AM*, 150). She leaves the hayfield where the family are working to make love to her husband (*AM*, 165). When Moran shouts at her children she 'never again brought her children to the house except for very brief visits' (*AM*, 170). Mona has 'many admirers… content to move within the authority of her beauty without any serious demands; and if they did they were let go at once' (*AM*, 168). Maggie returns home with her children when her husband finds himself out of work. She discovers to her horror 'that he had drunk everything that he had earned while she was away… she put the children into day-care and went back to nursing full time. From then on she would always have her own money' (*AM*, 169).

Broderick, on the other hand, failed to mature his female portraits and for the most part they remained, even into his later fiction, scheming, mendacious figures of mock-authority, asexual crones or naïve young women who are used and disabused at will. But there is a sense of resilience in his female characters also – in *The Fugitives*, Lily Fallon is the only character who displays any initiative while Mary Ryan in *The Waking of Willie Ryan* is portrayed as a ruthlessly effective operator who manipulates her son and husband at will. Moore was an author who showed true insight into the female psyche and his characters probably best represent the shifting nature of woman's position in society – from Judith Hearne, the alcoholic spinster in a desperate search for a man, to Marie Davenport, who fights the Church at their own game and emerges victorious: 'that known and imperfect existence that she had fought to regain against ineluctable forces, inexplicable odds. The priests were gone. It was over' (*CH*, 286-87).

---

[30] There were many examples of extraordinary crude manipulations by the clergy at local and national levels during both the Abortion & Divorce Referendums – such incidents were reported in several sections of the national press with a significant sense of outrage. See John Fulton, *The Tragedy of Belief: Division, Politics and Religion in Ireland*, pp. 166-67.

Father-Son-Sister-Daughter-Mother

The confusing tangle of intra-family relationships is one of the key themes in these six novels. Paddy's attraction to his sister in *The Fugitives* is partly sexual: '[b]efore she realised what he was doing he had seized her in his arms and kissed her on the lips,' and afterwards, 'She did not understand… the meaning of the scene Paddy had just made; but something instinctive stirred in her mind, a hidden intuition like the tormenting memory of a half-remembered dream that would explain everything if she could recall it' (*TF*, 55-56). In *The Waking of Willie Ryan*, Willie confesses to an incestuous relationship with his brother (*WR*, 112) while his nephew effectively marries his mother (well, a woman made in her likeness). In *The Dark*, Mahoney Sr. uses his son for sexual gratification. In *Amongst Women*, a large part of the fascination which Moran holds for Rose and his daughters is sexual. Before his marriage to Rose, Moran shares his bed with his youngest son, Michael. Tellingly, McGahern writes: 'Tomorrow night Rose would lie in the boy's place' (*AM*, 39). His daughters' have an oedipal attraction for him also. He is their 'first man'. In *The Lonely Passion of Judith Hearne*, there is an oblique, somewhat incestuous reference to Madden and his daughter, Shelia. When he assaults the housemaid, Mary, in Bernard's room he thinks both of Mary's nakedness and images of Shelia, 'taking her pants down behind my back' (*LPJH*, 43). He flails her buttocks and thinks of a similar punishment handed out to his daughter – the images are uniformly sexual.

Lacan's use as transformation from *jouissance* to desire does not involve, as castration does for Freud, a paternal injunction that prohibits and represses incestuous or oedipal fantasy. It is rather that this oedipal fantasy is a creation of the effect of symbolic castration. And this is where Lacan brings an interesting twist to Freudian theory. For Lacan the fantasy of incest is not the cause of primary repression but rather is produced after the formation of the unconscious. The signifiers of the desire of the Other that constitute the so-called 'chain reaction' at work in the unconscious represent the desire of the mother for 'something,' (or someone) other than the real child. It is with the help of these signifiers that the child will fabricate a fantasy of what could bring fulfilment to the mother. It is as if we are thinking – at the level of the unconscious – not with our own words but with the words of the Other. This is why Lacan can say that the unconscious is the discourse of the Other and that the desire of the subject is the desire of the Other. The Other sex is always woman, for both male and female subjects.

As Lacan states: 'Man here acts as the relay whereby the woman becomes this Other for himself as she is this Other for him.'[31] It is in this sense that an incestuous fantasy becomes a secondary formation; although this oedipal wish will lead back to the very place that enabled desire to be born: the *jouissance* of the Other. What has become inaccessible thanks to castration returns as the most desirable of all forbidden or impossible objects. In *Totem and Taboo* Freud argued that the prohibition against incest provided the foundation for all subsequent human laws. That is, the most fundamental desire of all human subjects and its prohibition represents the governing principal of all societies. As with the law, the prohibition operates only within the realm of culture but the law is founded upon that which it seeks to exclude, that is the desire to break and transgress. According to psychoanalysis, there is simply no way a subject can avoid this tension between the law and the desire to transgress it. Thus, we are not simply guilty if we break the law and commit incest, but rather we are always-already guilty of the desire to commit incest.

It is the father who transmits the law to the child – the law of incest prohibition – and subordinates the child's desire to the law. This is the symbolic father and he is the fundamental element in the symbolic order. However, there is also the primal father who is perceived to be outside the law. This is the imaginary father, an imago of all the imaginary constructs that the subject builds up in fantasy around the father. He can be construed as either an ideal father or as a figure of absolute power who aggregates to himself the women and wealth of the primal horde by expelling his sons and rivals. Psychosis and perversion both involve, in different ways, a reduction of the symbolic father to the imaginary father. Succinctly, this is the 'the father who has fucked the kid up.'[32]

In this matter, I have made passing reference to the Ireland of this period (1955-1990) as being a sick society – the number of instances of sexual abuse by a parent, guardian or spouse is excessive – it is evident in the writing of these three authors that the community was aware of the problem but largely chose to ignore it, to wash their hands of the matter. When Madden rapes the housemaid, Mary, in *The Lonely Passion of Judith Hearne* he thinks to himself: '[n]o, no, I'm all right, just normal, any normal man would take it if it was offered like that. And she won't tell. She knows what's good for her. She won't tell' (*LPJH*, 88). However, when Mrs Henry Rice is informed, her response is typical: '"I don't want

[31] Jacques Lacan, *Écrits* (1966) p.732.
[32] Jacques Lacan, *Écrits* (1977) p.308

to hear it. For the love of God, keep quiet the pair of you, you'll have us all ruined, so you will"' (*LPJH*, 136). Her solution is to give: '[t]hat girl her notice this afternoon,' before commenting acerbically on: '[t]hat slip of a girl that I treated as well as if she was in her own house. Nice gratitude, I tell you' (*LPJH*, 152-53).

The extent of the abuse that occurred during this period only emerged in the 1990s' when the floodgates opened and the Church was rocked by a series of scandals – the horrific exposures of the rapes of children perpetuated by Father Sean Fortune and Father Brendan Smyth and the continuing catalogue of assaults on boys by priests in positions of authority were publicized by developments in media coverage. Programmes such as Mary Raftery's *States of Fear* on RTÉ (1999) revealed the extent of inactivity and cover-ups over abuse scandals in Catholic institutions. The publication of the Ferns Report in 2005 conveyed not only appalling records of sexual exploitations by clerics but a chronic inability among their superiors to handle the social responsibilities they had inherited with their position. Such exposure would have been unthinkable during any point in the period that I am covering. However, the Church cannot act as scapegoat for all the sins of this period and a number of other cases of family neglect and/or abuse emerged, most notably the Joseph McColgan trial in 1995, the Kilkenny incest case and the death of Kelly Fitzgerald in 1993.[33] The preservation and unity of the family was sacrosanct and despite repeated investigation into these and other cases, the desire to keep the family together held precedent over all other concerns.

The Primacy of the Family

The primacy of the family is enshrined in the Irish constitution. Article 41.1.1 recognises the family as, 'the natural primary and fundamental unit group of Society, and as a moral institution possessing inalienable and imprescriptible rights, antecedent and superior to all positive law,' thus

[33] The McColgan case concerned a Sligo farmer who had systematically raped and tortured his four children over a twenty year period. The Kilkenny incest case concerned a father who had raped and tortured his daughter for sixteen years and sired a child by her. Kelly Fitzgerald was systematically abused by her father from the age of five, deprived of food and adequate clothing, demonised by her parents, isolated from her siblings, beaten daily and made to sleep outside the back door with the dogs, attired only in a nightie. At the age of eleven she weighed under three-and-a-half stone. She died three years later from malnutrition and neglect.

guaranteeing its protection by the State. For generations, the Oedipal complex has been both the catalyst and the stabilizer in the struggle for recognition. But family relations are nonetheless periodically vulnerable to both structural and subjective breakdowns. As Lacan states:

> Some systems of kinship are more viable than others. Some lead to impasses which are properly speaking arithmetic and which presuppose that from time to time crises occur within that society, bringing with them ruptures and new beginnings.[34]

These observations on family life provide a framework for understanding Lacan's characterizations of the contemporary decline of Oedipus. From the *fin-de-siècle* to the onset of postmodernism in the late 60's, the ongoing decline of the classical bourgeois family scene structured around the absolute authority of the father resulted in a radical change to the historic setting of psychoanalysis. In Lacan's opinion, Freud himself was only able to articulate the Oedipal myth because the father's function in the West had just begun to enter into decline. One question is why this development did not result in the great emancipation that many expected. Slavoj Žižek puts the question in the following way:

> Why does the decline of paternal authority and fixed social and gender roles generate new anxieties, instead of opening up a Brave New World of individuals engaged in the creative "care of the self" and enjoying the perpetual process of shifting and shaping their multiple fluid identities?[35]

When we look at it this way, the master signifiers take on a new significance. Lacan would have seen them as a formula around which fantasies could coalesce. But as the figure of authority, the master, declines in our culture, so too does the significance of these avowed authorizations and injunctions. The declining primacy of the family occurs most explicitly in John McGahern's *Amongst Women.* Moran attempts to control his family as if a General marshalling his 'troops.' However, his eldest son emigrates to England and refuses all supplications that he return. His other son, Michael, returns but only on his own terms. Moran ruefully walks the fields and in reflectively muses: 'Instead of using the fields, he sometimes felt as if the fields had used him. Soon they would be using someone else in his place. It was unlikely to be either of his sons'

---

[34] Jacques Lacan, *Seminar II*, p. 30.
[35] Slavoj Žižek, *The Parallax View*, p.232.

(*AM*, 130). In *The Dark*, Mahoney Sr. dreams of selling the land and going to live with his son, who is contemplating becoming a priest: 'I could open the door for those calling and find out what they wanted and not have them annoying you about everything. I could fool around the garden… we could bring the old tarred boat and go fishing in the summer' (*TD*, 35). But the father's dream is the son's nightmare. Young Mahoney thinks only of escape and fleeing the land and his tyrannical father. In *The Fugitives* the family home is a battleground where two querulous old women wage an ongoing battle of attrition. Both biological parents are dead. In *The Waking of Willie Ryan*, we encounter the Oedipal struggle between Chris and his mother – his father is irresolute alcoholic and Chris has made up his mind to abandon the family business and his parent's vulgar homestead: 'I don't care for business much, and I spend most of my time out here running this place. I like the land' (*WR*, 24). In *The Lonely Passion of Judith Hearne*, we encounter another Oedipal relationship between mother and son, but one that facilitates both parties. Bernard Rice, a 'monstrous baby swelled to man size' (*LPJH*, 9), is a parasitical creature who '[n]ever did a day's work in his life' (*LPJH*, 47) while is mother is a pathetic figure who stalked the halls of the University, '[w]aiting to give him a feed, a sandwich or a thermos of hot soup' (*LPJH*, 62). There is no family unit whatsoever in *Cold Heaven*. Marie's father shunts her off to boarding school when her mother dies: '[i]t was convenient for him to enrol her as a boarder. She knew that then. She had not forgiven him then. She had not forgiven him since,' (*CH*, 24) and she has no connection whatsoever with her in-laws.

There have been many major upheavals in the thirty years covered by this book, but the fragmentation of the family unit had, perhaps, the greatest impact on the Symbolic order. Akin to the hierarchy of the Church, the structure was monolithic and predetermined. People knew their place in the same way that the Rosary in the Moran household was conducted from the most senior family member (Moran) through to the youngest. What was said and done in the family stayed in the family and this ethos led to many of the terrible and protracted cases of abuse I mentioned earlier. However, the structure offered its own rewards and many people are now looking back at the early sixties with nostalgia and longing. It was a simpler time and the explosion of material Ireland, with our addiction to commodities and status-symbols, has not been welcomed by all. For such a society brings with it its own difficulties – the rise in suicide (especially amongst young people), the surge in murder rates and general crime figures, the rise in teenage pregnancies and drug and alcohol abuse, the increased pressure of the modern world and the slow erosion of family values and stability and so forth. I chose the three writers in this study because one (Broderick) dismissed change out of hand, one (McGahern) lived with change but only on his own terms and another one (Moore) embraced change openly and at times with a wilful disregard for conventions. They offered a startling contrast between the small towns (Broderick) and little villages (McGahern) of sixties Ireland and the great metropolises of modern America.(Moore) We can read much from the development of their characters, from poor Judith Hearne in her fruitless quest for a man to Marie Davenport, who blithely exchanges lovers at will. It is through these writers that the first stirring of rebellion was heard. But they also addressed certain taboos with compassion and their rage at the system which repressed human desire and sexuality is palpable indeed. They disliked the curbing of individual rights and the covering up of blatant abuses, which, in McGahern's case, denied people an occupation and forced them to emigrate.

Today Ireland is a curiously ahistorical nation. We have had, it seems, our period of self-flagellation and *mea culpa's* in the nineties. The emphasis now is on forward thinking. Writers like John Broderick and Brian Moore have disappeared almost completely from the bookshelves while John McGahern is perhaps better known now for his elegiac *That They May Face The Rising Sun* than his earlier novels of oppression and institutionalized abuse. I chose these authors because a retrospective appears timely given our current economic and social situation. We are at a crossroads and Irish society, which has fully embraced modernization and global uniformity, appears somewhat at sea. In my opinion, we need writers like Broderick McGahern and Moore to reinforce our sense of identity. We have come a long way in the past forty years, the cost has been, at times, prohibitively high but it is a struggle worth recounting and if there are lessons to be learned for the future where else are we to find them but in our past?

Bibliography

John McGahern

Primary Sources

The Barracks, London: Panther, 1966.

The Dark, London: Panther, 1969.

The Leavetaking, London: Faber & Faber, 1974.

The Pornographer, London: Faber & Faber, 1979.

Amongst Women, London: Faber & Faber, 1998.

The Collected Stories, London: Faber & Faber, 1992.

That They May Face The Rising Sun, London: Faber & Faber, 2003.

Memoir, London: Faber & Faber, 2005.

Other Writing by John McGahern

'The Image: Prologue to a Reading at the Rockefeller University' in *The Honest Ulsterman,* vol. 8, December, p.10. 1968 with revisions in *Canadian Journal of Irish Studies,* vol. 17, July 1991, p.12.

'An tOileánach/The Islandman' in *Canadian Journal of Irish Studies*, vol. 13, June 1987, pp.1-15

'The Solitary Reader' in *Canadian Journal of Irish Studies,* vol. 17, July 1991, pp.19-23.

'The Church and its Spire' in *Soho Square 6*, London: Bloomsbury, pp.17-27.

'Reading & Writing' in *Irish Writers and their Creative Process* (Jacqueline Genet and Wynne Hellegouarc'h ed.) Gerrards Cross: Colin Smythe, 1996, pp.103-109.

Interviews & Profiles

Battersby, Eileen, 'Blundering through the Dark' *Irish Times*, 27 November 1993.

Carlson, Julia, *Banned in Ireland: Censorship and the Irish Writer*, London: Routledge, pp.53-67.

Carty, Ciaran, 'Out of the Dark' *Sunday Tribune*, 6 September 1987.

—. 'Sex Ignorance and the Irish', *Sunday Tribune*, 29 September 1991.

Deevy, Patricia, 'A Light in the Darkness', *Sunday Independent*, 30 December 2001.

Downy, Mary, 'Unbearable Darkness of Being', *Sunday Independent*, 6 May 1990.

Hamilton, Andrew, 'McGahern claims he was dismissed because of The Dark', *Irish Times,* 11 February 1966.

Herbert, Cathy, 'Window on the World', *Magill*, October 1987, pp. 56-62.

Jackson, Joe, 'Tales from the Dark side', *Hot Press*, 14 November 1991, pp.18-20.

Kennedy, Joe, 'McGahern: "Art is a luxury" An Interview with the Author of *The Dark'*, *Evening Herald*, 11 November 1970.

Luby, Tom, 'In From The Dark', *Irish Times*, 14th June 1979.

Lynch, Audrey L. 'An Interview with John McGahern', *Books Ireland*, no.88, 1984, p.213.

Maher, Eamon, 'Catholicism and National Identity in the Works of John McGahern', *Studies*, 90 – Spring 2001, pp. 70-83.

—. 'An Interview with John McGahern', Appendix to *From the Local to the Universal*, Dublin: The Liffey Press, 2003, pp.143-161.

McGarry, Patsy, 'McGahern Emerges from the Dark' Irish Press, 7 May 1991.

Murphy, Mike, 'John McGahern', in Clíodhna Ní Anluain, (ed.), *Reading the Future: Irish Writers in Conversation with Mike Murphy*, Dublin: The Lilliput Press, 2000 – pp.136-155.

Sampson, Denis, 'A Conversation with John McGahern', *The Canadian Journal of Irish Studies*, vol. 17.1, July 1991, pp.13-18.

Walsh, John, 'Illuminating the Dark Side of the Irish', *Sunday Times*, 29 April 1990.

Whyte, James, 'An Interview with John McGahern', Appendix to *History, Myth and Ritual in the Fiction of John McGahern: Strategies of Transcendence*, Lewistown, Queenstown, Lampeter: The Edwin Mellen Press, 2002, pp.227-235.

Criticism – Books

Goarzin, Anne, *John McGahern: Reflets d'Irlande*, Rennes: Presses Universitaires de Rennes, 2002.

Maher, Eamon, *John McGahern: From the Local to the Universal*, Dublin: The Liffey Press, 2003.

Malcolm, David, *Understanding John McGahern*, Columbia, South Carolina: University of South Carolina Press, 2007.

Rogers, Lori, *Feminine Nation: Performance, Gender and Resistance in the Works of John McGahern and Neil Jordan*, Lanham, New York: University Press of America, 1998.

Sampson, Denis, *Outstaring Nature's Eye: The Fiction of John McGahern*, Washington, D.C., The Catholic University of America Press, 1993.

Whyte, James, *History, Myth and Ritual in the Fiction of John McGahern: Strategies of Transcendence*, Lewiston, Queenstown, Lampeter: The Edwin Mellen Press, 2002.

Individual Articles and Selected Reviews

Bataillard, Pascal, 'John McGahern's Subdued Modernity', in *Études Britannique Contemporaines* 6, January 1995, pp.85-100.

Brown, Terence, 'Redeeming the Time: The Novels of John McGahern and John Banville', in James Acheson (ed.), *The British and Irish Novel Since 1960* New York: St. Martin Press, 1991, pp.159-173.

Cahalan, James M. 'The Conscience of the Midlands: John McGahern', in *The Irish Novel: A Critical History*, Dublin: Gill & Macmillan, 1988, pp. 271-275.

Coad, David, 'One God, One Disciple: The Case of John McGahern', in *Études Britannique Contemporaines* 6, January 1995, pp.57-62.

Cronin, John, '"The Dark" is Not Light Enough', in Studies, no.58, Winter 1969, pp.427-432.

—. 'Art and the Failure of Love: The Fiction of John McGahern', in *Studies*, no.77, Summer 1988, p.201-217.

—. 'John McGahern's Amongst Women: Retrenchment and Renewal', in *Irish University Review*, vol. 22.1, Spring/Summer 1992, pp.168-176.

—. 'John McGahern: A New Image?', in Jacqueline Genet and Wynne Hellegouarc'h (ed.), *Irish Writers and their Creative Process* Gerrards Cross: Colin Smythe, 1996, pp.110-117.

Crowley, Cornelius, 'Leavetaking and Homecoming in the Writing of John McGahern', in *Études Britannique Contemporaines* 6, January 1995, pp.63-76.

Devine, Paul, 'Style and Structure in John McGahern's *The Dark*', in *Critique: Studies in Modern Fiction*, vol.21.1, Spring 1979, pp.48-58.

Foley, Michael, 'The Novels of John McGahern', in *The Honest Ulsterman 5*, September 1968, pp.34-37.

Gitzen, Julian, 'Wheels Along the Shannon: The Fiction of John McGahern', in *The Journal of Irish Literature*, vol.20:3, September 1991, pp.36-49.

Goarzin, Anne, 'Movement de l'image dans les romans de John McGahern', in *La Licorne* 49, 1999, pp.13-27.

Grennan, Eamon, 'John McGahern: Vision and Revisionism', in *Colby Quarterly*, no. 31.1, March 1995, pp.30-39.

Guy, Peter, 'In The Name of the Father: Lacan's *nom-du père* and the Modern Irish Novel', in Eamon Maher *et al*, (eds), *Modernity and Postmodernity in a Franco-Irish Context* Frankfurt am Main, Peter Lang, 2008, pp. 65-77.

Holland, Siobhán, 'Tact and Tactics: A Case for Matrifocality in John McGahern's Amongst Women', in Alan Marshall and Neil Sammells, (ed.), *Irish Encounters: Poetry, Politics and Prose since 1880* Bath: Sullis Press, 1998, pp.115-126.

—. 'Re-citing the Rosary: Women, Catholicism and Agency in Brian Moore's *Cold Heaven* and John McGahern's *Amongst Women'*, in Liam Harte and Michael Parker, (ed.), *Contemporary Irish Fiction: Themes, Tropes, Theories* London: Macmillan, 2000, pp.56-78.

—. 'Marvellous Fathers in the Fiction of John McGahern', in *The Yearbook of English Studies*, no. 35, 2005, pp. 186-198.

Hunt-Mahoney, Christina, 'John McGahern', in *Contemporary Irish Literature: Transforming Tradition*, New York: St. Martins Press, 1998, pp. 225-229.

Imhof, Rüdiger, 'John McGahern', in *The Modern Irish Novel: Irish Novelists After 1945*, Dublin: Wolfhound, 2002, pp. 213-236.

Kennedy, Eileen, 'The Novels of John McGahern: The Road Away Becomes the Road Back', in James D. Brophy & Raymond J. Porter, (ed.), *Contemporary Irish Writing* Boston: Twanye, 1983, pp.115-126.

Kiberd, Declan, 'John McGahern's *Amongst Women*', in Maria Tymoczko and Colin Ireland, (eds), *Language and Tradition in Ireland: Continuities and Displacements* Amherst and Boston: University of Massachusetts Press, 2003, pp. 195-213.

Liddy, Brian, 'State and Church: Darkness in the Fiction of John McGahern', in *New Hibernia Review*, vol. 3.2, Summer 1999, pp. 106-121.

Maher, Eamon, 'John McGahern: A Writer in Tune with his Time', in *Crosscurrents and Confluences: Echoes of Religion in Twentieth-Century Fiction*, Dublin: Veritas, 2000, pp.139-154.

—. 'Disintegration and Despair in the Early Fiction of John McGahern', in *Studies*, vol. 90, Spring 2001, pp.84-91.

—. 'A Glimpse of Irish Catholicism in McGahern's *Amongst Women*', in *Doctrine and Life*, vol. 51.6, July/August 2001, pp. 346-355.

—. 'Catholicism in the Writing of John McGahern', in Michael Böss and Eamon Maher, (eds), *Engaging Modernity: Readings of Irish Politics, Culture and Literature at the Turn of the Century*, Dublin, Veritas, 2003, pp.9-28.

Molloy, F.C., 'The Novels of John McGahern' in *Critique: Studies in Modern Fiction* vol. 19.1, Spring 1977, pp. 5-27.
O'Connell, Sean, 'Door into the Light: John McGahern's Ireland', in *Massachusetts Review*, no. 25, Summer 1984, pp. 225-268.
Prior, Lesley, 'Male Power and Female Acquiescence? Exploring Gender Roles Within the Irish Catholic Church with Reference to John McGahern's *Amongst Women'*, in *Irish Journal of Feminist Studies*, vol. 5.1&2, 2003, pp.55-62.
Quinn, Antoinette, 'A Prayer for my Daughter: Patriarchy in *Amongst Women*', in *The Canadian Journal of Irish Studies*, vol. 17.1, July 1991, pp.79-90.
Schwartz, Karlheinz, 'John McGahern's Point of View', in *Éire-Ireland* vol. 19.3, Autumn 1984, pp. 92-110.
Toolan, Michael J. 'John McGahern: The Historian and The Pornographer', in *The Canadian Journal of Irish Studies*, vol. 7.2, December 1981, pp.39-55.
Wall, Eamon, 'The Living Stream: John McGahern's *Amongst Women* and Irish Writing in the 1990s', in *Studies*, vol. 88, Autumn 1999, pp. 305-314.

John Broderick

Primary Sources

The Pilgrimage, Dublin: Lilliput, 2004.
The Fugitives, London: Pan, 1976.
Don Juaneen, London: Pan, 1979.
The Waking of Willie Ryan, London: Panther, 1969.
An Apology for Roses, London: Pan, 1974.
The Pride of Summer, London: Pan, 1977.
London Irish, London: Barrie & Jenkins, 1979.
The Trial of Father Dillingham, London: Abacus, 1983.
A Prayer for Fair Weather, London, Marion Boyars, 1984.
The Rose Tree, London, Marion Boyars, 1985.
The Flood, Dublin, Wolfhound, 1990.
The Irish Magdalen, London, Marion Boyars, 1991.

Articles

'The Future of the Irish Novel', *The Irish Times*, 8 January 1970. Features a discussion between Broderick, Terence de Vere White, Kevin Casey and Richard Power.
'New novels', *Hibernia*, 9 January 1972.

'City of the plain: Some aspects of Athlone', *The Irish Times,* 3 March 1978.

'The Old Master', *The Irish Times*, 11 April 1980.

'A Curate's Egg at Easter', *The Irish Times*, 14 April 1979.

'Letter from Rome', *The Irish Times,* 19 April 1980.

Interviews

Anon, 'If I'd stayed, the drink would have killed me', *Sunday Independent*, 19th September 1987.

Bryson, Sean, 'A lonely leave-taking: why writer Broderick is leaving the town he loves so well', *The Sunday Press*, 27th January 1980.

Carlson, Julia, 'John Broderick', in *Banned in Ireland: Censorship and the Irish Writer*, London: Routledge, 1990.

Murphy, Michael, 'At Bay in Bath', *The Irish Times*, 3 September 1985.

Spray, Campbell, 'I did it all', *The Irish Press*, 16 August 1979

Walsh, Caroline, 'The Saturday Interview. Caroline Walsh talks to the novelist John Broderick', *The Irish Times*, 29 May 1976.

Biographical and Critical Treatments

Boland, Eavan, 'The Lost World: John Broderick', *The Irish Times*, 23rd March 1973.

Ducke, Joe, 'Not so green' in *Criterion* (UCG) 1972, pp. 53.

Gallagher, Michael Paul, 'The Novels of John Broderick', in Patrick Rafroidi & Maurice Harmon (eds), *The Irish Novel in our Time*, Lille: Publications de L'Université de Lille, 1976, pp. 235-243.

Guy, Peter, 'The Lives of John Broderick', in *Studies*, vol. 97, Autumn 2008, pp. 251-263.

—. 'Review of *Stimulus of Sin*', in *The Irish Book Review*, vol.2.4, Autumn 2007, p.46.

Higgins, Aidan, article on Broderick's work in *Hibernia*, April 1967, p.12

Jordan, John, 'The Broderick Path', in *Hibernia*, 30 January 1976.

Kingston, Madeline, *Something in the Head: The Life and Work of John Broderick,* Dublin: Lilliput, 2004.

—. *Stimulus of Sin: Selected Writing of John Broderick,* Dublin: Lilliput, 2007.

Maher, Eamon, 'Sex and Religion in a Midlands Town', in *Doctrine and Life*, February 1998, pp. 73-81.

—. 'John Broderick: Irish Novelist in the European Tradition', in *Crosscurrents and Confluences: Echoes of Religion in 20th century Fiction*, Dublin: Veritas, 2000, pp. 110-124.

McLaughlin, Brighid, 'The Lonely Torment of John Broderick', in *Sunday Life / The Sunday Independent*, March 29th, 1998, pp.1-6.
McMahon, Sean, 'Town and country', in *Eire-Ireland*, vol. VI. Spring 1971, pp. 120-131.
Murray, Patrick, 'Athlone's John Broderick', in *Eire-Ireland*, vol. XXVIL, Winter 1992, pp. 20-39.
O'Brien, Gearoid (ed.) *Seminar Proceedings of the 2001 & 2002 John Broderick Weekend*, Athlone: John Broderick Committee.

Reviews of Broderick's Novels

Casey, Kevin, 'A Dying Fall', review of *The Irish Magdalen*, *The Irish Times*, 6 April 1991.
Daniels, John, 'A Man hunting and running', review of Don Juaneen', *The Guardian,* 7 June 1963.
Donnelly, Peter, 'Little to be learned of the Irish or of London, review of *London Irish*', in *The Irish Independent*, 25 August 1979.
Jordan, John, 'Misanthropy in the Midlands', review of *The Pride of Summer*', in *The Irish Independent*, 10 July 1976.
Kiely, Benedict, 'A Black hymn to Mammon, review of *An Apology for Roses*', in *Hibernia,* 2 February 1973.
Leonard, Hugh, 'Overkill of the money-grubbers', review of *An Apology for Roses*', in *The Irish Independent*, 27 January 1973.
Lucy, Sean, 'Review of The Waking of Willie Ryan', in *The Irish Independent*, 9 October 1965.
McMahon, Sean, 'Coming in from the cold – review of *The Flood*', in *The Irish Independent*, 12 September 1987.
O'Toole, Fintan, 'Parable for racists – review of *The Flood*', in *The Sunday Tribune*, 1 November 1987.

BRIAN MOORE

Primary Sources

The Lonely Passion of Judith Hearne, London: Grafton, 1987.
The Feast of Lupercal, London: Flamingo, 1994.
The Luck of Ginger Coffey, London: Flamingo, 1994.
An Answer from Limbo, London: Flamingo, 1992.
The Emperor of Ice-Cream, London: Flamingo, 1994.
I am Mary Dunne, London: Jonathan Cape, 1968.
Fergus, London: Vintage, 1992.
The Revolution Script, Harmondsworth: Penguin, 1973.
Catholics, London: Jonathan Cape, 1972.

The Great Victorian Collection, New York: Farrar, Strauss & Giroux, 1975.
The Doctor's Wife, London: Flamingo, 1994.
The Mangan Inheritance, London: Flamingo, 1995.
The Temptation of Eileen Hughes, London: Flamingo, 1995.
Cold Heaven, London: Triad/Panther, 1985.
Black Robe, London: Flamingo, 1995.
The Colour of Blood, London: Flamingo, 1994.
Lies of Silence, New York: Doubleday, 1990.
No Other Life, London: Flamingo, 1994.
The Statement, New York: Dutton, 1996.
The Magician's Wife, London: Bloomsbury, 1997.

Other Writings

'The Writer as Exile', in *The Canadian Journal of Irish Studies* vol.2, December 1976, pp.5-16

Interviews

Carlson, Julia, 'Brian Moore', in *Banned in Ireland: Censorship & The Irish Writer*, London: Routledge, 1987, pp. 109-121
Carty, Ciarán, 'Ciarán Carty Talks to Brian Moore', in *Sunday Independent*, 2 June 1985.
Crowe, Marie, 'Marie Crowe Talks to Belfast Writer Brian Moore' in *Irish Press*, 21 June 1983.
Foster, John Wilson, 'Question and Answer with Brian Moore', in *Irish Literary Supplement* 4, Fall 1985, pp.44-45.
Gallagher, Michael Paul, 'Brian Moore Talks to Michael Paul Gallagher', in *Hibernia*, 10 October 1969.
Jones, Dan, 'Brian Moore: A Profile', in *The New Review*, 2 November 1975, pp.47-50.
McAuley, Liam, 'Brian Moore: An Exile's Late Arrival', in *Irish Times*, 26 September 1987.
O'Mahoney, Andy, 'Dialogue' RTE Radio, 20 February 1986.

Individual Studies

Craig, Patricia, *Brian Moore: A Biography*, London: Bloomsbury, 2002.
Dahlie, Hallvard, *Brian Moore*, Boston, Mass: Twayne Publishers, 1981.
Flood, Jeanne M, *Brian Moore*, Lewisburg, Pennsylvania: Bucknell University Press, 1974.

Gearon, Liam, *Landscapes of Encounter: The Portrayal of Catholicism in the Novels of Brian Moore*, Calgary: University of Calgary Press, 2002.

Hicks, Patrick, *Brian Moore and the Meaning of the Past: An Irish Novelist Reimagines History*, Lewiston, Queenstown, Lampeter: Edwin Mellen, 2007.

O'Donoghue, Jo, *Brian Moore: A Critical Study*, Montreal: McGill-Queen's University Press, 1991.

Sampson, Denis, *Brian Moore: The Chameleon Novelist*, Dublin: Marino, 1998.

Individual Articles and Selected Reviews

Brown, Terence, 'Show Me a Sign: The Religious Imagination of Brian Moore', in *Irish University Review*, vol. 18.1, 1988, pp.37-99.

Cosgrove, Brian, 'Brian Moore and the price of freedom in a Secular World', in *Irish University Review*, vol. 18.1, 1988, pp.59-73.

Cronin, John, 'Ulster's Alarming Novels', in *Éire-Ireland* 4, Winter 1969, pp.27-34.

—. 'The Resilient Realism of Brian Moore', in *Irish University Review*, vol. 18.1, 1988, pp.24-36.

Deane, Seamus, 'Brian Moore in Disneyland', in *Irish University Review*, vol. 18.1, 1988, pp.74-82.

Foster, John Wilson, 'Crisis and Ritual in Brian Moore's Belfast Novels', in *Éire-Ireland* 3, Autumn 1968, pp.66-74.

Foster, John Wilson, *Forces and Themes in Ulster Fiction*, Dublin: Gill and Macmillan, 1974, pp.122-130.

French, Philip, 'The Novels of Brian Moore', in *London Magazine* 5, February 1966, pp.86-91.

Fulford, Robert, 'Brian Moore: A Writer Who Never Failed to Surprise his Readers', in *Globe and Mail*, 12th January 1999.

Gallagher, Michael Paul, 'The Novels of Brian Moore', in *Studies*, vol. 60, Summer 1971, pp.89-95.

—. 'Review of *Cold Heaven*', in *Irish University Review* 15, Spring 1984, pp.131-134.

—. 'Religion as Favourite Metaphor', in *Irish University Review*, vol. 18.1, 1988, pp.50-58.

Hayley, Barbara, 'Outward and Visible Signs: Dressing and Stripping in the Novels of Brian Moore', in *Irish University Review*, vol. 18.1, 1988, pp.96-105.

Henry, Dewitt, 'The Novels of Brian Moore: A Retrospective', in *Ploughshares* 2, 1974, pp.7-24.

Hicks, Patrick, 'Brian Moore' in Mary Reichardt (ed.), *Encyclopaedia of Catholic Literature*, Westport: Greenwood Press, 2004, pp.472-480.

Hirschberg, Stuart, 'Growing up Abject as Theme in Brian Moore's Novels', in *Canadian Journal of Irish Studies 1*, November 1975, pp.11-16.

Holland, Siobhán, 'Re-citing the Rosary: Women, Catholicism and Agency in Brian Moore's *Cold Heaven* and John McGahern's *Amongst Women*', in Liam Harte and Michael Parker (eds), *Contemporary Irish Fiction: Themes, Tropes, Theories*, London: Macmillan, 2000, pp.56-78.

Maher, Eamon, 'Religion Without Faith in the Belfast Novels of Brian Moore', in *Crosscurrents and Confluences: Echoes of Religion in Twentieth Century Fiction*, Dublin: Veritas, 2000, pp.124-139.

Mahon, Derek, 'A World of Signs', in *The Irish Times*, 11th June 1988.

McIllroy, Brian, 'Displacement in the Fiction of Brian Moore', in *English Studies in Canada*, vol.15.2, June 1989, pp. 214-234.

McSweeny, Kerry, 'Brian Moore: Past and Present', in *Critical Quarterly* 18 Summer 1976, pp.53-66.

O'Connell, Shaun, 'Brian Moore's Ireland: A World Well Loss', in *Massachusetts Review*, vol. 29.3, Autumn 1988, pp.539-555.

Prosky, Murry, 'The Crisis of Identity in the Novels of Brian Moore', in *Éire-Ireland,* Fall 1971, pp.106-118.

Rafroidi, Patrick, 'The Great Brian Moore Collection', in Maurice Harmon and Patrick Rafroidi (eds.), *The Irish Novel in our Time*, Lille: Publications de l'Université de Lille, 1976, pp.221-236.

Scanlan, John A. 'The Artist-in-Exile: Brian Moore's North American Novels', in *Éire-Ireland* 12, Summer 1977, p. 14-33.

Simmons, James, 'Brian Moore and the Failure of Realism', in *The Honest Ulsterman*, March/April 1970, pp.8-14.

Toolan, Michael J. 'Psyche and Belief: Brian Moore's Contending Angels', in *Éire-Ireland* 15, Autumn 1980, pp. 97-111.

JACQUES LACAN

Primary Sources

Écrits, Paris, Seuil, 1966.

Écrits – A Selection (Alan Sheridan trans.) London: Tavistock Publications, 1977.

Écrits – The First Complete Edition in English (Bruce Fink trans.) New York: Norton, 2006.

*The Seminar. Book I. Freud's Paper on Technique, 1953-54 (*John Forrester trans.) New York: Norton, 1988.

*The Seminar. Book II. The Ego in Freud's Theory and in the Technique of Psychoanalysis, 1954-55 (*Sylvan Tomaselli trans.) New York: Norton, 1988.

*The Seminar. Book III. The Psychoses, 1955-56 (*Russell Grigg trans.) London, Routledge, 1993.

Le Séminaire. Livre IV. La relation d'objet, 1956-57, edited by Jacques-Alain Miller, Paris: Seuil, 1994.

*The Seminar. Book VII. The Ethics of Psychoanalysis 1959-60 (*Denis Porter trans.) London: Routledge, 1992.

The Seminar. Book XI. The Four Fundamental Concepts of Psychoanalysis, 1964. (Alan Sheridan trans.) London: Hogarth Press and Institute of Psycho-Analysis, 1977.

The Seminar. Book XX. On Feminine Sexuality and The Limits of Love. Encore 1972-73 (Bruce Fink trans.) Norton: New York, 1999.

Television: A Challenge to the Psychoanalytic Establishment, New York: W.W. Norton, 1990.

My Teaching (David Macey trans.) New York: Verso, 2009.

Critical Approaches

Althusser, Louis, *Writings on Psychoanalysis: Freud and Lacan* (Jeffrey Mehlman trans.), New York: Columbia University Press, 1996.

Benvenuto, Bice and Roger Kennedy, *The Works of Jacques Lacan: An Introduction*, London: Free Association Books, 1986.

Boheemen-Saaf, Christine van, *Joyce, Derrida, Lacan and the Trauma of History*, Cambridge: Cambridge University Press, 1999.

Bowie, Malcolm, *Freud, Proust and Lacan: Theory as Fiction*: Cambridge: Cambridge University Press, 1987.

—. *Lacan*, Cambridge, Mass: Harvard University Press, 1991.

Bracher, Marc, *Lacan, Discourse and Social Change: A Psychoanalytical Cultural Criticism*, Ithaca, Cornell University Press, 1993.

Brivic, Sheldon, *The Veil of Signs: Joyce, Lacan and Perception*, Urbana: University of Illinois Press, 1991.

Chaitin, Gilbert D, *Rhetoric and Culture in Lacan*, Cambridge: Cambridge University Press, 1996.

Davis, Robert Con (ed.), *The Fictional Father: Lacanian Reading of the Text*, Amherst: University of Massachusetts Press, 1981.

Ellmann, Maud (ed.), *Psychoanalytical Literary Criticism*, London: Longman, 1994.

Evans, Dylan, *An Introductory Dictionary of Lacanian Psychoanalysis*, New York: Routledge, 1996.

Felman, Shoshana (ed.), *Literature and Psychoanalysis: The Question of Reading: Otherwise*, Baltimore, John Hopkins University press, 1982.

Fink, Bruce, *The Lacanian Subject: Between Lacan and Jouissance,* Princeton: Princeton University Press, 1995.

—. *A Clinical Introduction to Lacanian Psychoanalysis: Theory and Technique*, Cambridge, Mass: Harvard university press, 1997.

—. *Lacan to the Letter – Reading Écrits Closely*, Minneapolis: University of Minnesota Press, 2004.

Flax, Jane, *Thinking Fragments: Psychoanalysis, Feminism and Postmodernism in the Contemporary West*, Berkeley, Ca.: University of California Press, 1990

Michel Foucault, *Archaeology of Knowledge* (Alan Sheridan trans.), London: Routledge, 2002.

Gallop, Jane, *Reading Lacan*, Ithaca: Cornell University Press, 1985.

Georgin, Robert, *Lacan,* Lausanne: L'Age d'Homme-Cistre, 1977

Grigg, Russell, *Lacan, language and Philosophy*, New York: State University of New York Press, 2009.

Grosz, Elizabeth, *Jacques Lacan: A Feminist Introduction*, New York: Routledge, 1990.

Hogan, Patrick and Lalita Pandit (ed.) *Criticism and Lacan: Essays on Language, Structure and the Unconscious*, Athens: University of Georgia Press, 1990.

Homer, Sean, *Jacques Lacan*, London: Routledge, 2004.

Jameson, Frederic, *The Political Unconscious: Narrative as a Socially Symbolic Act,* London: Methuen, 1981.

Kojève, Alexandre, Raymond Queneau, Allan Bloom and James H. Nichols (eds.) *Introduction to the Reading of Hegel*, Ithaca, New York: Cornell University Press, 1980

Leader, Darian, *Introducing Lacan* London: Faber & Faber, 2005

Lee, Jonathan Scott, *Jacques Lacan*, Amherst, University of Massachusetts Press, 1990.

Leonard, Garry M., *Reading Dubliners Again: A Lacanian Perspective*, Syracuse: Syracuse University Press, 1993.

Lyons, F.S.L., *Ireland since the Famine*, London: Fontana, 1973.

Macey, David, *Lacan in Context*, London: Verso, 1988.

Mitchell, Juliet and Jacqueline Rose, *Feminine Sexuality. Jacques Lacan and the École Freudienne*, London: Macmillan. 1982

Pluth, Ed, *Signifiers and Acts: Freedom in Lacan's Theory of the Subject*, New York: State University of New York Press, 2008.

Rabaté, Jean-Michel, *Psychoanalysis and the Subject of Literature*, Houndmills, Basingstoke, Hampshire: Palgrave, 2001.

Rabaté, Jean-Michel (ed.) *The Cambridge Companion to Lacan*, Cambridge: Cambridge University press, 2003.

Paul Rainbow, *A Foucault Reader*, New York: Pantheon, 1984.

Rose, Jacqueline, *Sexuality in the Field of Vision*, London: Verso, 1996.

Samuels, Robert, *Between Philosophy and Psychoanalysis: Lacan's Reconstruction of Freud*, New York: Routledge, 1993.

Shepherdson, Charles, *Lacan and the Limits of Language*, New York: Fordham University Press, 2008.

Sterba, Richard, "Freud's 'Moses and Monotheism' and the Three Stages of Isrealitish Religion", in *Psychoanal Q.*, no. 16, 1947.

Wilden, Anthony (ed.) *The Language of the Self: The Function of Language in Psychoanalysis*, Baltimore: John Hopkins University press, 1968.

Wright, Elizabeth, *Lacan and Postfeminism*, New York: Totem Books, 2000.

Zizek, Slavoj, *The Ticklish Subject*: the absent centre of political ontology, London: Verso, 1999.

Žižek, Slavoj, *The Puppet and the Dwarf: The Perverse Core of Christianity*, Net Library, 2003.

OTHER CRITICAL REFERENCES

Adorno, Theodor, *Dialectic of Enlightenment (*Max Horkheimer trans.) London: Verso, 1997

Arensberg, Conrad and Solon T. Kimball (eds.) *Family and Community in Ireland*. Cambridge, Mass.: Harvard University Press 1968

Baker, Houston A., Manthia Diawara and Ruth H. Lindeborg (ed.) *Black British Cultural Studies: A Reader*, Chicago: University of Chicago Press, 1996.

Bakhtin, M.M., *The Dialogic Imagination: Four Essays* (Caryl Emerson & Michael Holquist trans.), Austin: University of Austin Press, 1981.

Bhabha, Homi K., *The Location of Culture*, London: Routledge, 2006.

Binswager, Ludwig, *Being-in-the-World: Selected Papers of Ludwig Binswanger: Translated and with a Critical Introduction to His Existential Psychoanalysis (*Jacob Newman trans.) New York, Basic Books, 1963.

Bloom, Harold, *The Western Canon: The Books and School of the Ages*, New York: Harcourt Brace, 1994.

Bolger, Dermot (ed.), *Letters from New Island*, Dublin: New Island, 1991.

Bradshaw, Brendan and Daire Keogh (eds.) *Christianity in Ireland: Revisiting the Story*, Dublin: Columba Press, 2002
Breen, Richard et al, *Understanding Contemporary Ireland – State, Class and Development in the Republic of Ireland,* Dublin: Gill and Macmillan, 1990.
Buckland, Patrick, *The factory of grievances: devolved government in Northern Ireland*, Dublin: Gill & Macmillan, 1979.
Butler, Judith, *Excitable Speech: A Politics of Performance* London: Routledge, 1997.
Cahalan, James, *Double Visions: Men and Women in Modern and Contemporary Irish Fiction*, New York, Syracuse University Press, 1999
Caswell, Robert, 'The Irish Novel: Exile, Resignation or Acceptance' in *Wascana Review* vol.2, no. 1, 1967.
Connolly, Peter, *Literature and the Changing Ireland,* Gerrards Cross: Colin Smythe, 1982.
Coolahan, John, *Irish Education: Its History and Structure,* Dublin: Institute of Public Administration, 1981
Cooney, John, *John Charles McQuaid – Ruler of Catholic Ireland,* Dublin: O'Brien, 1999.
Corcoran, Neil, *After Yeats and Joyce: Reading Modern Irish Literature*, Oxford: Oxford University Press, 1997
Coulter, Carol, *The Hidden Tradition: Feminism, Women and Nationalism in Ireland,* Cork: Cork University Press, 1993.
Darby, John, *Northern Ireland: The Background to the Conflict*, Belfast, Appletree Press, 1983.
Deane, Seamus (ed.) *The Field Day Anthology of Irish Writing* vol. III, Derry and London: Field Day and Faber, 1991.
Fanon, Frantz, *The Wretched of the Earth*, London: Penguin, 1967
Fuller, Louise, *Irish Catholicism since 1950: The Undoing of a Culture*, Dublin: Gill & Macmillan. 2002
Fuller, Louise, John Littleton and Eamon Maher (ed.) *Irish and Catholic: Towards an Understanding of Identity*, Dublin: The Columba Press, 2006.
Gibbons, Luke, *Transformations in Irish Culture,* Cork: Cork University Press, 1996.
Grint, Keith, *The Sociology of Work*, Cambridge: Polity, 2005.
Harkness, David, *Northern Ireland Since 1920*, Dublin: Helicon, 1983.
Inglis, Tom, *Moral Monopoly: The Rise and Fall of the Catholic Church in Modern Ireland*, Dublin: University College Dublin Press, 1998.

Jameson, Frederic, *The Political Unconscious: Narrative as a Socially Symbolic Act,* Ithaca, N.Y.: Cornell University Press. 1981.
Jung, C.G., *Four Archetypes: Mother, Rebirth, Spirit, Trickster,* London: Ark Paperbacks, 1986.
Carl Jung, Carl Kerényi and R.F.C. Hull, *Essays on the Science of Mythology: the Myths of the Divine Child and the Divine Maiden,* New York: Harpers Row, 1963.
Kavanagh, Peter, *Patrick Kavanagh, Man and Poet,* Newbridge, Kildare: Goldsmith Press, 1987.
Kennedy, Kieran & Brian Dowling, *Economic Growth in Ireland: The Experience Since 1947,* Dublin: Gill & Macmillan, 1975.
Kenny, Mary, *Goodbye to Catholic Ireland – How the Irish Lost the Civilization They Created*, New York: Templegate, 2000.
Keogh, Dermot, *Twentieth Century Ireland – Nation and State,* Dublin: Gill and Macmillan, 1994.
Kerrigan, Gene and Pat Brennan, *This Great Little Nation,* Dublin: Gill and Macmillan, 1999.
Kiberd, Declan, *Inventing Ireland – The Literature of the Modern Nation,* London: Vintage, 1996.
Lee, J.J. *Ireland 1945 – 1970*, Dublin: Gill & Macmillan, 1979.
—. *Ireland 1912 – 1985,* Cambridge: Cambridge University Press, 1990
Lloyd, David, *Anomalous States: Irish Writing and the Post-Colonial Moment,* Dublin: Lilliput, 1993.
Lubbers, Klaus 'Irish Fiction: A Mirror for Specifics', in *Éire-Ireland*, vol. 20. no 2 Summer, 1985.
McCarthy, Eunice, 'Women and Work in Ireland' in Margaret Mac Curtain and Donncha Ó Corráin (eds.), *Women in Irish Society – The Historical Dimension*, Dublin: Arlen House, 1978.
McCarthy, Mary, *On The Contrary*, New York: Octagon Books, 1976.
McNamara, Brinsley, *The Various Lives of Maurice Igoe,* Dublin: Maunsel, 1929.
MacSharry, Ray and Padraic A. White (eds), *The Making of the Celtic Tiger – The Inside Story of Ireland's Boom Economy,* Mercier: Cork, 2000.
Mauriac, Francois, *The Stumbling Block*,New York: The Philosophical Library, 1953.
Meehan, James, *The Irish Economy Since 1922,* Liverpool: Liverpool University Press, 1970.
Messanger, John C. *Inis Beag: Island of Ireland*, Evanston, Il., Holt McDougal, 1969.

Moore, Chris *Betrayal of Trust: The Father Brendan Smyth Affair and the Catholic Church,* Dublin: Marino, 1995

Newman, Robert. D. (ed.), *Joyce's Ulysses: The Larger Perspective,* Newark: The University of Delaware Press, 1987.

O'Brien, Darcy, 'In Ireland After A Portrait' in Thomas F. Stanley and Bernard Benstock (eds), *Approaches to Joyce's "Portrait": Ten Essays,* Pittsburgh: University of Pittsburgh Press, 1976.

O'Brien, Kate, 'Imaginative Prose by the Irish, 1820 – 1970', in Joseph Ronsley (ed.) *Myth and Reality in Irish Literature*, Waterloo, Ontario: Wilfrid Laurier, 1977.

O'Brien, George, 'The Elephant of Irish Fiction', in *Irish Review*, no.30 (Spring/Summer), 2003.

O'Connor, Pat, *Emerging Voices: Women in Contemporary Irish Society*, Dublin: Institute of Public Administration, 1998

O'hEithir, Brendan, *The Begrudger's Guide to Irish Politics,* Dublin: Poolbeg, 1986.

O'Faoláin, Sean, 'Fifty Years of Irish Writing', in *Studies* (Dublin), vol. 51, 1962, pp. 102-103

Rafroidi, Patrick and Terence Brown (eds.) *The Irish Short Story,* Gerrards Cross: Colin Smythe, 1979.

Ryan, Ray, *Writing in the Irish Republic: Literature, Culture, Politics 1949-1999,* New York: St. Martins Press, 2000

Scheper-Hughes, Nancy, *Saints, Scholars, and Schizophrenics – Mental Illness in Rural Ireland*, Berkeley, Ca: University of California Press, 2001

Smyth, Gerry, *The Novel and the Nation – Studies in the New Irish Fiction,* London: Pluto, 1997.

Storey, Mark (ed.) *Poetry and Ireland since 1800: A Source Book*, London: Routledge, 1988.

Stopper, Anne, *Mondays at Gaj's: The Story of the Irish Women's Liberation Movement,* Dublin: Liffey Press, 2006.

Touher, Patrick, *Fear of the Collar: Artane Industrial School,* Dublin: O'Brien, 1991.

Welch, Robert, *Changing States – Transformations in Modern Irish Writings,* London: Routledge, 1993.

Whyte, J.H., *Church & State in Modern Ireland* Dublin: Gill & Macmillan, 1980

Wilson, Thomas M. and Hastings Donnan (eds.), *The Anthropology of Ireland*, Oxford: Berg, 2006

INDEX